On Humanity's Intensive Introspection

Other works of interest from St. Augustine's Press

Joseph Cropsey, *Polity and Economy: With Further Thoughts on the Principles of Adam Smith*

St. Augustine, *On Order [De Ordine]*

Karel Wojtyła [Pope John Paul II], *Man in the Field of Responsibility*

Charles P. Nemeth, *Aquinas on Crime*

Philippe Bénéton, *The Kingdom Suffereth Violence: The Machiavelli / Erasmus / More Correspondence and Other Unpublished Documents*

Gerhart Niemeyer, *The Loss and Recovery of Truth: Selected Writings*

Gerhart Niemeyer, *Between Nothingness and Paradise*

Leo Strauss, *Xenophon's Socrates*

Leo Strauss, *Xenophon's Socratic Discourse*

Pawel Armada and Arkadiusz Górnisiewicz, eds., *Modernity and What Has Been Lost: Considerations on the Legacy of Leo Strauss*

Francis J. Beckwith, Robert P. George, & Susan McWilliams, eds., *A Second Look at First Things: A Case for Conservative Politics*

Roger Scruton, *The Meaning of Conservatism*

Paul M. Weyrich and William S. Lind, *The Next Conservatism*

John C. Calhoun, *A Disquisition on Government*

Ralph C. Hancock, *Calvin and the Foundations of Modern Politics*

Robert Hugh Benson, *Lord of the World*

Peter Augustine Lawler, *Homeless and at Home in America: Evidence for the Dignity of the Human Soul in Our Time and Place*

Rémi Brague, *Eccentric Culture: A Theory of Western Civilization*

Jacques Maritain, *Natural Law: Reflections on Theory and Practice*

James V. Schall, *The Regensburg Lecture*

James V. Schall, *The Modern Age*

Marc D. Guerra, ed., *Jerusalem, Athens, and Rome: Essays in Honor of James V. Schall, S.J.*

Leszek Kolakowski, *My Correct Views on Everything*

René Girard, *A Theater of Envy: William Shakespeare*

C.S. Lewis and Dom Giovanni Calabria, *The Latin Letters of C.S. Lewis*

On Humanity's Intensive Introspection

Joseph Cropsey

St. Augustine's Press
South Bend, Indiana

Manufactured in the United States of America

1 2 3 4 5 6 17 16 15 14 13 12

Library of Congress Cataloging in Publication Data
Cropsey, Joseph.
On humanity's intensive introspection / by Joseph Cropsey
p. cm.
ISBN 978-1-58731-611-1 (clothbound: alk. paper)
1. Political science – Philosophy. I. Title.
JA71.C74 2012
320.01 – dc23 2011037696

∞ The paper used in this publication meets the minimum requirements of the American National Standard for Information Sciences – Permanence of Paper for Printed Materials, ANSI Z39.48-1984.

St. Augustine's Press
www.staugustine.net

I dedicate this volume to my children

Seth and Rachel,

and to the memory of my wife,

Lilian.

Table of Contents

Acknowledgments

I would like to thank

Mary P. Nichols and Dwight D. Allman

for their valued editorial assistance and

Michael P. and Catherine H. Zuckert

for their friendly help in getting this

book to press.

Many of the essays included in this collection were previously published:

"Liberalism, Nature and Convention," *Independent Journal of Philosophy* 4 (1983): 21–27.

"Liberalism, Self-Abnegation and Self-Assertion" was originally published in *The Prospects of Liberalism*, ed. Timothy Fuller in Colorado College Studies, 20 (1984): 32–41. Permission to reprint granted by Timothy Fuller for Colorado College Studies.

"Providential Care for Democracy" was commissioned by the Tocqueville Forum for presentation at Wake Forest University in 1985.

"On the Mutual Compatibility of Democracy and Marxian Socialism," *Social Philosophy and Policy* 3:2 (Spring 1986): 3–18, is reprinted here with the permission of Cambridge University Press.

"Activity, Philosophy and the Open Society," *Order, Freedom, and the Polity*, ed. George W. Carey (University Press of America, 1986), 149–60, reprinted with permission of Rowman & Littlefield.

"On the Dramatic End of Plato's Socrates," *Interpretation* 14 (1986): 155–75, is reprinted here with permission.

"Religion, the Constitution, and the Enlightenment," *Understanding the United States Constitution, 1787–1987*, ed. Timothy Fuller, in Colorado College Studies, 24 (1988): 25–35, is reprinted with permission granted by Timothy Fuller for Colorado College Studies.

"On Pleasure and the Human Good: Plato's *Philebus*," was delivered at the Carl Friedrich von Siemens Foundation in Munich on March 24, 1987, and published in *Interpretation* 16 (1990): 166–92. Permission to reprint granted by Heinrich Meier, Director of the Foundation, and Hilail Gildin, editor of *Interpretation.*

"The Whole as Setting for Man: On Plato's *Timaeus*," was originally published in *Interpretation* 17 (1990): 165–91, and is reprinted here with permission.

"On Ancients and Moderns," was delivered at the Carl Friedrich von Siemens Foundation in Munich on May 8, 1990, and published in German translation, "Über die Alten und die Modernen," in *Zur Diagnose der Moderne*, ed. Heinrich Meier (Piper, München, 1990), pp. 211–246. The essay was originally published in English in *Interpretation*18 (1990): 31–51, and is reprinted here with permission from both Heinrich Meier, Director of the Foundation and Hilail Gildin, editor of *Interpretation*.

"The End of History in the Open-ended Age? The Life Expectancy of Self-evident Truth," was originally published in *History and the Idea of Progress*, eds. A. M. Melzer, J. Weinberger, M.R. Zinman (Cornell University Press, 1995), 97–116, and is reprinted here with permission from Cornell University Press.

"Nature, God, and the Enlightenment: What is at Work in the Whole" was delivered at the Carl Friedrich von Siemens Foundation in Munich on July 3, 2000. Permission to reprint was granted by Heinrich Meier, Director of the Foundation.

Introduction

I wish to make explicit something that vibrates in my production of the contents of this volume, namely, the essence of humanity's habitation of the whole. Most inconclusively stated, we exist in life under the conditions summarily called NATURE and we die – perhaps – in a transition to the supernatural. I need hardly say that I am not about to commit the presumption of seeking to dispose of either projection, but I do wish to consider briefly our dwelling within nature.

We recognize the locution, "Conquest of Nature." We have only to recognize the threat to our existence implicit in the unlimited ability to cause the explosion of nuclear matter as we practice the conquest of Nature; and as we devote ourselves to the multiplicity of pieties rampant among us, we might shudder over the contemplation of transcendent salvation.

So much for our confidence that mankind's inquiry into the question as to the existence of humanity in the whole is alive. The present volume does not presume to dispose of the issue as alive within nature and transcendent of it.

The profundity of the question of humanity's being or existence in the whole is as much intensified by the need to identify the whole as to complete mankind's introspection. This present collection of my hitherto uncollected items attempts to bring together responsibly some of the awesome wisdom of Plato as directed to the wisdom of Parmenides. The difference between Being and Existence, the difference between the eternal that is impervious to affect and that which is moved from without (and within?) is pressed upon Socrates who makes Beauty and Justice things that he will "see" when he will SEE when he, i.e., his soul, ascends to the dwelling of god, that is to say, travels to the location of the empirical IDEAS.

1
Liberalism, Nature, and Convention

Modernity is constituted to some degree by liberalism, and liberalism is composed in part of three ingredients that stand in a relation to one another that illuminates liberalism and thus modernity. The three ingredients are relativism, constitutional guarantees, and personal freedom. I have selected these for consideration not only because of their evident prominence in liberal life but also because of the important place that they occupy in the political construction of Thomas Hobbes. The formal argument with which this paper begins is that relativism, constitutional guarantees and personal freedom stand, in Hobbes's thought, in a consistent relation to sovereignty; and they stand, in the liberal world, in a very different relation to a correlate of sovereignty which I shall call legalism or authoritative conventionalism. The corresponding substantive argument is that the difference between the relation as it exists in Hobbes's thought and the relation as it exists in liberal life points to an "evolution" of liberalism that might perhaps be a decay but that has in any case noteworthy implications for the meaning and viability of liberalism.

Since the liberalism of Hobbes, while occasionally recognized, is not self-evident, the sense in which it is being understood and applied to the argument is indicated as follows, always by reference to *Leviathan*:

"*Relativism*" In chapter 6, Hobbes writes that "whatsoever is the object of any man's appetite or desire, that is it which he for his part calleth 'good'; and the object of his hate and aversion, 'evil'; and of his contempt, 'vile' and 'inconsiderable'. For these words of good, evil, and contemptible are ever used with relation to the person that useth them, there being nothing simply and absolutely so, nor any common rule of good and evil to be taken from the nature of the objects themselves . . ." In chapter 15, he writes that "'good' and 'evil' are names that signify our appetites and aversions, which in different tempers, customs and doctrines of men are different . . ."

"*Constitutional guarantees*" In a short passage near the end of chapter 14, (see also chapter 21) Hobbes pronounces against self-incrimination except with assurance of pardon, and against the use of a man's testimony against his father or wife. In the same place, he argues against the admissibility of evidence obtained by torture. Near the end of chapter 16, he writes that "when a cause is heard, not to condemn is to absolve; but on the contrary, to say that not absolving is condemning is not true." Or, as we would say, the presumption at law is of innocence. In chapter 21, Hobbes shows the ground of a subject's right to sue the sovereign at law. In chapter 27, he argues that "when a penalty is either annexed to the crime in the law itself or hath been usually inflicted in the like cases, there the delinquent is excused from a greater penalty." This is a clear expression of the rule against unusual punishment, meaning thereby no more than a punishment in excess of the one usually attached to the offense. Also in chapter 27, he shows that "no law, made after a fact done, can make it a crime," which expresses our rule against legislation *ex post facto*.

"*Personal freedom*" In chapter 21, Hobbes lays it down that "in all kinds of actions by the laws praetermitted, men have the liberty of doing what their own reasons shall suggest for the most profitable to themselves." And further in the same place, "The liberty of a subject lieth therefore only in those things, which in regulating their actions, the sovereign hath praetermitted, such as is the liberty to buy and sell and otherwise contract with one another; to choose their own abode, their own diet, their own trade of life; and institute their children as they themselves think fit, and the like." We recognize in this the assertion of the subject's freedom of contract and his right to do whatever is not forbidden by the law, a perfect reversal of the ancient political formula that the citizen is free to do only what the law expressly permits. Later in the same chapter, Hobbes reaffirms this principle with the words, "In cases where the Sovereign has prescribed no rule, there the subject hath the liberty to do or forbear according to his own discretion," that is to say, to pursue his happiness with the utmost of liberty, and in a multiplicity of directions of which it is useful to single out the economic: "As if it were injustice to sell dearer than we buy, or to give more to a man than he merits. The value of all things contracted for is measured by the appetite of the contractors, and therefore the just value is that which they be contented to give" (Chapter 15).

The meaning of this liberal charter can be expressed by observing the whence and the whither of it: on what it rests and to what conclusion it tends. It proceeds from the perception of nature as a moral blank, prescribing no obligations, restraints or duties except conditionally – to seek peace if possible, to make war as necessary. What is not conditional is the desire for life and for the power after power that conduces to the preservation of life. On grounds too well known to need recitation, the moral vacuity of nature is expressed alternatively by Hobbes in terms of the natural rights of men and even of the inalienability of the first of those natural rights, namely, under all circumstances "to defend a man's own body" (Chapter 21).

As for the immediate tendency of this liberal doctrine, it may be indicated by the single word sovereignty. What is given to man in the beginning is a gravitation toward life that, in the original anarchy, is assisted no better by peace than by war, or equally badly by both. Hobbes shows how the preservation of life can be united to peace and how war can be expelled, in the main, from municipal life if men admit sovereignty to the regulation of their affairs. The implication of sovereignty is not unfreedom but the absolutization of convention as the reasonable consequence of the moral evacuation of nature. If, primarily or naturally, good means each man's appetite, then artifice must enter effectually and construct a moral world lest there be no moral world at all. But since that construction is strictly limited in its aim to the natural or primary end of preservation, it may not legitimately prescribe obligations that reach to edification or beyond. On these grounds, the "constitutional guarantees" and bill of "personal freedom" – involving inalienable rights and the protected pursuit of happiness – are linked to "relativism," and are all bound to absolutized convention, or sovereignty, the political manifestation of man's flight from nature to art.

Hobbes can thus be thought to have shown that the political concomitant of and support for liberalism is perfect sovereignty; or that liberalism is what mediates benignly between nature seen as a moral wasteland and strict convention regarded as the necessary foundation of satisfactory life. Whichever formulation is preferred, there can be no doubt that the concrete liberalism of our time does not see itself as bound to a doctrine of irresistible sovereignty. Subscribing to the moral relativism of Hobbes, and to the constitutionalism and "individualism" generated within his doctrine, liberalism rejects what he regarded as the practical inference from, or at least the necessary accompaniment of, those elements, namely, strict sovereignty. Manifest is the liberal disposition to regard moral relativism, the constitutional guarantees, and personal freedom ("individualism") as exactly antithetical to sovereignty – conventionalism rather than as its concomitants.

Through the comparison of the Hobbesian and the prevalent mode of liberalism, a fact about conventionalism emerges that is the obverse of a fact about liberalism: conventionalism, or the reduction of the ultimate norms of conduct to convention, is ambiguous, pointing to convention as on the one hand politically objective and authoritative and, alternatively, also as subjective and idiosyncratic ("merely conventional"). Conventionalism, in brief, though resting on the unequivocal premise of the moral vacuity of nature, is capable of becoming instrumental to mutually opposed practical ends – to life *qua* preservation and to life as "active personality." This elaboration of a fact about conventionalism draws attention to the reverse fact about liberalism: liberalism may find its end in individuality reconciled with community or in individuality reconciled at best only with itself. In the latter mode, liberalism reverts to the relativist premise of conventionalism – ". . . these words of good, evil, and contemptible are ever used with relation to the person that useth them . . ." – but declines to draw the conclusion of sovereignty, which is the politicized form of conventionalism. Thus we encounter the familiar fact that present-day liberalism is the project for society in which the guiding principle is the absolutization of the morally idiosyncratic personality whose rule is the rejection of convention. In this mode and to this extent, liberalism is unpolitical, aiming at or lending itself to the project for the withering away of the state.

Between the political absolutization of relativism in the conventionalist sovereignty and the private absolutization of relativism in idiosyncratic personality there exists the intermediate entity, law. It appears, at first glance, that the insistent legalism of Hobbes and the equally insistent legalism of, say, the American Civil Liberties Union reveal a ground on which the Hobbesian and reformed liberalism can be reconciled. But what, more exactly, is the legalism of Hobbes? The rule of law in Hobbes's system is synonymous with the irresistibility of the sovereign, from whom the law emanates. That irresistibility cannot be fully explained by the sovereign's overwhelming power; rather it rests upon Hobbes's singular reconciliation of sovereignty with individual freedom: by a well known argument, Hobbes assimilates the will of each subject to the will of the sovereign. Of course the digestion of the particular wills in that of the sovereign is *a priori* and thus universal, unmindful of the occasions that will arise. Thus each subject learns only *a posteriori* what on a given occasion his will is or was. This outcome, which is Hobbes's version of legitimate government with and by the consent of the governed, is intelligible only as the concomitant of a legal contract of such cogency and power as to suffocate the natural sense that a retrospective will is not only a legal but a simple fiction. At the core of Hobbes's legalism is the priority of mind over will, or of reason over volition: an agreement to own as his the willing of another takes precedence over any subsequent particular willing, because such willing would have to support itself with a claim to an independence that it had knowingly renounced, thus with a claim that is essentially irrational ("absurd").

The legalism of later liberal thought seems to differ from that of Hobbes in every substantial particular. Each law is binding only because and so far as it expresses the active and considerate, surely not the merely acquiescent, and decidedly not the preempted will of each and all. It must be acknowledged, though, that as long as the obvious practical obstacles in the path of converting this notion into a political arrangement are resolved through majoritarianism, there has been no significant progress beyond Hobbes, for, in consenting to the rule of the majority, one has agreed in advance to learn his will after the majority has declared its own. That he has contributed his might to the aggregate of the voices is a fact with ceremonial or spiritual meaning, neither of which is to be depreciated, but it seems to leave intact the passivity of the will and thus the bondage of its owner to the sovereign, albeit to the sovereign as mass. As recent but not only recent events have shown, the rule of majorities does not satisfy all liberal aspirations. The law must be capable of confronting, frustrating, and circumventing majorities, which is as much as to say that the activity of the will of most, and in principle even of the will of all, is not a decisive token that right or justice is at work, and has made itself known once and for all. It is not true that the voice of the people is the voice of God. It might be necessary, in the interest of right, that the law undergo "interpretation," or that the inmost secrets of the government be purloined and published by citizens whom the law cannot bind to any obligation higher than that of their will. It is obvious that legalism and its opposite coexist in reformed liberalism, and can do so because the freedom of the will is the primary good from which law and law abidingness are derivative and to which they are subordinate and must each conform as occasions require. Herein is a clue to the meaning of the departure of the reformed from the protoliberalism of Hobbes, for Hobbes considered insignificant the words "freedom of the will." There is an intimation not only of the fact but of the grounds of the fact that the legalism of reformed liberalism is not meant, and would be unable, to serve as the replacement of Hobbesian sovereignty.

The examination of the majoritarian alternative to Hobbesian liberalism helps to expose the difficulties that beset the project for politicizing, *i.e.* adapting to political life, the activity of the subjective will. As we have seen, so far as reformed liberalism embodies the notion that the citizen is free only so far as he is autonomous – so far as the law is his self-imposed enactment – he will be only formally free (and thus only formally bound) under laws to which he has assented only formally, *i.e.* consenting to a majoritarian regime. If democracy is the preeminently majoritarian form of government, reformed liberalism cannot be unqualifiedly committed to democracy. Stated more generally, the form of government as such cannot legitimate the law, or induce an unqualified obligation to obedience, in the view of the reformed liberalism, because there is no regime in which the obligation to obedience would not be compromised by an *a priori* or merely formal commitment of the subject's will. If he does not retain his freedom on every occasion in the face of the law, he has renounced his freedom in principle. It should be made clear that the tension in reformed liberalism between its legalism and its reservation against law does not have its origin in an appeal either to nature or to nature's god as being more authoritative than the human law and as sanctioning compliance with the latter only conditionally but not in principle. Rather to the contrary, the historic basis for the liberal appeal beyond formal commitment to law seems to be the flight from nature rather than any recourse to it – a flight that has been inspired by visions of the perfection of a human, not a divine will. As the facts of this "flight" become clear, it becomes ever more manifest that the transition from the proto- to the reformed liberalism expresses a fundamental fact about modernity itself. The transformation of liberalism is the working out of a deeply-ingrained stress in the modern understanding and self-understanding, a stress that is energized by the modern project for mastering nature while comprehending everything including man within nature – a project that came to be seen as problematic for the hope of man's himself remaining unmastered by nature. It is, I believe, impossible to be clear about liberalism or modernity without understanding modernity's perplexity about nature. On the one hand, the modern time seems like the age that aspired to make the whole world intelligible by bringing everything, including or preeminently man, within the rational order of cause and effect: no (human) empire within the large empire of nature. That this aspiration must reflect on the status of any human or nonhuman being that pretends to stand outside nature or to transcend it is obvious. But not only the divine is threatened. The threat to humanity that accompanies the promise of man's grasp – intellectual and technical – on nature is investigated precisely by that same author who announced that there is no *imperium in imperio*: Spinoza completes his *Ethics* with a part on freedom after a part on bondage. As one might say, this great modern, in a book on ethics, reveals that the central problem of that discipline is not virtue but freedom; or rather, that there is no virtue if there has been no provision against nature's enslaving embrace. Spinoza achieves his end by assimilating life to activity, in a profound correction of Hobbes. Nature does indeed teach life and its preservation as the authoritative law, but life means activity, while Hobbes thought that life meant passivity – "passion" – desire and fear and hatred. Spinoza transforms life into the consciousness and contemplation of our position within the infinite chain of causes and effects rather than acquiescence in that position. In the event, Hobbes's motion is passivity and acquiescence while Spinoza's quiescence is activity – a rediscovery of familiar insights at the shrines of modernity.

Did the problem of man's relation to nature receive its modern formulation from Spinoza? Perhaps; but the roots of the problem reach to the thinker who is conventionally seen as standing at the head of the modern tradition, Machiavelli. This writer achieved fame by holding out a certain promise to mankind, a prescription for regaining control over its fate. If all events occur either through nature or by chance, that is, either intelligibly or mysteriously, then the greater the scope of our knowledge, the larger the realm of nature proves to be, until, should there ever be a completion of knowledge, the realm of fortune would be evacuated and that of nature would attain its absolute amplitude. It would appear that Machiavelli is designing the project for the maximizing of human freedom or power, and a sign that this is his intention is the obvious "terrestrialization" of the whole of human life that emerges through his work. This is confirmed in another, seemingly different, thrust present in his thought that becomes visible in what is perhaps the most famous passage in all his writing – the opening paragraph of chapter 15 of *The Prince*.

There he makes a remark that is occasionally understood as a denunciation of utopias, but that is in fact a criticism of the men, especially princes, who live as if they inhabited utopia. They wish to live as if their fellow men were good, formed to goodness by the laws that govern them. Commentators are likely to think first of Plato's *Republic* as the scheme that Machiavelli had in mind; but considering the generality of his description, and his remarks elsewhere on the effeminating tendency of Christian education, and his use of the plural number in speaking of the imagined regimes, there is no reason to exclude the kingdom of God and allow to remain only the kingdom of philosophy within the scope of his animadversion. The inflexible profession and practice of goodness is suicidal because it is obnoxious to the variation in times which, as the end of the paragraph in question demonstrates, constitutes our necessity. We are secular beings, immersed in times or in the world.

We are indeed subject to a necessity that appears to deprive us of our freedom; but Machiavelli proposes an expedient, if one that lends itself to misunderstanding and tends to inspire revulsion: one must learn to be able not to be good. It is obvious that Machiavelli did not conceive the world to be in need of a teacher of badness, for he reports the presence of the latter everywhere. One must say that Machiavelli found himself surrounded by badness combined with stupidity, and he saw room for improvement through the shedding of his light. In unsettled times, and it is of the nature of times to be unsettled, force and fraud are *virtù*. (Hobbes, who on this rare occasion seems to exhibit optimism, goes no further than to declare force and fraud cardinal virtues only in times of war; but then, if his addressee were not the subject but the sovereign – who remains in the condition of nature *vis-à-vis* his subject – Hobbes's optimism and his originality would suffer simultaneously by juxtaposition with Machiavelli, from whom he would be indistinguishable.) In any case, learning how to be bad, which means among other things doing it unobtrusively and as little as possible, entails the other famous advice that Machiavelli gives: to assume the nature of a beast when necessary and of a man when necessary and moreover to assume the nature of the fox and of the lion on demand. Without fanfare, Machiavelli teaches the need, and one must suppose therewith the possibility, of bringing nature, withal human nature, in this way into subordination to the will. This is the conquest of time or times. Machiavelli's discovery makes it possible to say that modernity opened with a project for bringing human nature under the control of man's will in the interest of badness rightly understood, *i.e.*, virtue, and all because the human condition is transitoriness, the *saeculum*.

It has been said many times that the modern age is characterized by the great humanistic project, made concrete in natural science, for mastering nature, forcing it to give up its secrets and to obey its conqueror. This image is durable and useful while one thinks only of the relief of man's poverty, illness, and of his ignorance of natural causes. But Spinoza thought also of human freedom and perfection. It goes without saying that neither he nor Rousseau, Kant or Hegel contemplated renouncing the natural science of Newton or Bacon. To put their interest very simply, they had to find means to flee nature without fleeing the science of nature; for if man is left simply within the order of natural mechanism, he is left in a state of servitude that is excruciating, demoralizing, and at last intolerable. But this is an agony that contains within itself the seed of its own amelioration: the source of the problem is man's discovery, or even better his invention of the morally blank mechanistic nature that, to his dismay, turned upon him and proved to contain him; but inevitably it will occur to some man that knowledge about nature is its own consolation, for knowing, as distinct from and independent of the idea of the thing known, is exhilarating, humanizing, and saving. Man is saved by the goodness of knowing or of contemplation, at least as emphatically in the conditions of modernity as in antiquity. It is possible for man, which to begin with means philosophic man, to be within nature and also, by contemplating his inclusion with the detachment possible only for the reflexive mind, to detach himself and objectify nature, himself, and his relation to nature. We have returned to Spinoza.

Two points deserve notice. If there is a contemplation of man and nature and of the relation between them, that contemplation is neither natural science nor philosophy of science. Natural science has nature as its object, and it regards man purely as within nature – as a heavy object, so to speak. Philosophy of science has come to mean either methodology or sociology of knowledge, and does not serve the stated purpose of contemplation, nor therefore emancipation, nor does it seek to do so. What can pretend to emancipate man is philosophy itself, once it has assigned to itself that very task. I believe it is fair to say that modern thought, in a direct line from Spinoza, even from Machiavelli, through Rousseau, Kant, Hegel and Nietzsche, has seen itself and constituted itself as the project for securing human freedom against or outside nature though acts of mind or "spirit" or will. Philosophy has a practical, conscious, emancipating intention and has had for hundreds of years.

Second: one is bound to wonder whether freedom is purely a state of consciousness, and by what acts of mind, will or spirit alone the human being could be emancipated from nature. Can the mere contemplation of the prisoner's bars free him? Certainly not, in the absence of an accompanying, indeed prior, belief that bars do not imprison. And why do they not? Because the only bondage is that of the mind; *i.e.*, the humanity of a man is in his mind and its activity. Prison might induce a man to think about freedom, and to think about the bars, but it will not cease to be confinement until his thought has made himself its object, and finally has made itself its object: thought reflecting on thought discovers freedom. That it does so in confinement is accidental: a man might arrive at the same knowledge by contemplating his freedom as by contemplating his bondage. Perhaps this points to the two different ways by which ancient and modern thought arrived at their insight that freedom is of the mind. But this speculation conceals more than it reveals, and in any case cannot be pursued now.

But what does this rumination suggest for Spinoza's project? That in binding us so ineluctably into the natural order of causation, sealing our bonds with the doctrine of the single substance, he bound our knowledge also into that chain or realm, thus confirming the need for detachment or escape and also making that detachment, if not impossible, then implausible. In terms of the previous image, he makes obscure the source of the thought that the only bondage is that of the mind, and that thus the contemplation of the prison walls *is* freedom. Hume, with his mind apparently on other problems than ours, shook the structure that linked cause and effect with knowledge of cause and effect, or that linked nature and knowledge of nature. Whatever else this accomplished, it gave Kant the occasion for manufacturing, in the best modern tradition, a whole world that is alternative to the world of nature. After all, if science is the construction of a framework imposed upon an object that either has no framework or has one we cannot discover absolutely, then why not extend the construction outside the walls of nature itself – in the interest, as the saying goes, of human convenience?

The belief in the energy and productivity of the will proceeded on its way from Machiavelli to Nietzsche as if under the influence of an accelerating force. From Rousseau Kant inherited the moral and political demand for the autonomy of the will, and Kant vastly increased his patrimony. The details are well known and need not concern us, but we cannot overlook the striking encouragement given by Kant to what I have spoken of as modernity's flight from nature. Hobbes had his reasons for referring to the condition of "mere" nature, but those were superficial in comparison with Kant's, for Kant saw no alternative to the positing of the very realm of freedom where the authority of natural causation is abrogated and where the merely empirical understanding is transcended: beyond nature, where the will comes into its own.

That Hegel represented history, *i.e.*, the whole human experience in essence, as the concrete expression of "spirit's" combat with nature, and that spirit is the will consciously making itself toward freedom, is clear in his words. That for Hegel, as little as for Rousseau or Kant, the reflections on the unbound will were meant to encourage idiosyncratic extravagations is obvious. Thus each of them was compelled to make a politics of good will, which always proved to be based on the rational principle of universality, hence sociality. Letting Hegel speak for them all, the will has reflexively or self-consciously willed its own freedom when it has created itself as the will that is freed from every limitation of mere self, mere passivity or mere nature, and is thus free to will the willworthy – which might as well be spoken of as the general good willed by the general will active in each. Everyone is free to decide whether this consummation is more aptly termed the acme of Freedom or of Reason, though Hegel of course saw it as both.

The doctrine of freedom as the assertion of the will against the bonds of its externality reached a climax with Nietzsche, for whom the will to power, the quintessence of life, becomes the willing of the eternal return of the same as the ultimate defiance and ultimate conquest of the nauseous regularity of nature and the craven declivity of man. Philosophers might hitherto have found the world tedious, painful and stupid, and have forborne to spurn at it only because contemplating it was a clearer mark of superiority. For Nietzsche that was altogether insufficient because passive, Spinoza to the contrary notwithstanding. One conquers not by accepting but by willing, *i.e.*, demanding, and not once but infinitely, that which torments you. The human high-heartedness taught by Machiavelli became febrile with Nietzsche. It need not be said that Nietzsche's hyperthermic voluntarism was not in the interest of advanced liberalism, or political particularism.

The foregoing sketch is intended to support the assertion made earlier that reformed liberalism's appeal beyond the law is not addressed either to nature or to nature's god, but to what offers itself as opposed to, superior to or more humanly relevant than either, namely the will – the active essence – of man. But surely this argument or demonstration appears problematic, for it makes the reformed liberalism the heir of the modern tradition that reaches a climax in the thought of Nietzsche, who did not befriend and was not adopted by present-day liberalism.

I believe that the general truth in which this problem is dissolved is that the will has come generally to be seen as confined by convention as much as by nature, and perhaps not more by the legalistically sanctioned sovereignty elaborated by Hobbes than by the majoritarian or other legalism attached to government informed by the latest liberalism. The modern battle against nature, in the interest of full freedom in the will, proves to have been won not only against nature but also against convention. By the elaboration of its unsurrenderable premise concerning nature's moral vacuity, modernity, or more concretely the liberal manifestation of modernity, has ejected both nature and convention from their positions as givers of norms. What is left is the alternative of the abyss as against human creativity or willing, humanity having its own energy as its norm. Along the way, it happens that legalism, gathered in the net of convention, has not been able to supply to the "reformed liberalism" what was furnished to Hobbes's liberalism by sovereignty.

More broadly stated, both nature and convention, including law, appear to have been weakened in the modern consciousness and inevitably also in the modern liberal consciousness. Astonishingly, this has happened as a result of a centuries-long struggle on the part of "modernity," *i.e.*, of the leading modern writers, to find and strengthen the ground of morality under conditions in which morally neutral nature is an overwhelming fact. Convinced that morality could be distinguished from virtue because morality is inseparable from freedom, they ended by making it their main business to plead the case for morality against nature – because nature had not only ceased to guide but had itself become a condition of constraint. Thus the conscientious efforts of "modernity" to restore its own moral ground through the apotheosis of the will have resulted in the much-noticed drift of the twentieth century toward an aporia of morality. The great authors have succeeded in freeing but they have not succeeded in socializing the will: Hegel's project, so far as it is represented practically or "concretely" in philosophy of history, must be accounted not an error but a failure, for liberal mankind does not see its freedom perfected in law and state. A curious and sad divagation from this tendency exists in those countries, mainly Marxist, where the many have indeed been digested in a one, but with the most brutal disregard for any sentimental "self-consciousness of the will making itself to will the willworthy." If this departure from the tendency is not an exception to but a reversal of the tendency, then the future of liberalism can be read only too plainly. The liberalizing movement of several hundred years would have been seen to carry in itself the seed of its own destruction in its disposition to cure itself with the living virus of its besetting disorder: to the moral vacuum of nature add the moral zero of the will. Meanwhile, liberalism's successor, claiming to succeed it because its contradictions must tear it apart, would inherit its estate because thought had produced a certain climate of opinion and state of morality, and not because of a dialectic of classes. One cannot escape dejection in speculating on the possibility that the element of sovereignty, found in Hobbesian and only to be sought for in the reformed liberalism, has emerged in a violent manifestation not in liberalism but in its impatient predator, which has no illusions about the moralization of the will or, for that matter, about its emancipation.

I have sought to describe the situation of liberalism, of the political expression of human freedom in our age, as a fact, or as a consequence, of one very powerful current of modern thought, namely, that which has found it necessary to go "outside" of nature in order to vouchsafe to mankind a prospect of freedom and morality. Regarding this descriptive enterprise, two things should be said. First, a sense that man's wellbeing requires his attachment to or orientation upon a realm beyond nature is so far from being "peculiarly modern" that modernity may plausibly be described as commencing (with Machiavelli) in a protest against the transcendencies of Scripture and Plato. The Bible is a way of life, and the Ideas are a way of thought; and both proceed from the premise that the phenomenal world cannot be the whole and hence the only world. Let us abstain from the general question whether the phenomenal world is the natural world for Plato, and adopt for our present purpose the formula that it seemed so to such as Machiavelli and Spinoza. If it did not seem so what would they have meant by their strictures about regimes that were not and are not, and kingdoms within kingdoms – impossible, unreal, unnatural? Through this observation, I mean to suggest that the modern flight from nature – apart from the form that it took or the aims it encompassed – is not an aberration of the spirit but is either a universal necessity or an inalienable part of our inheritance, entailed upon us by our pagan and scriptural testators. Should the "flight from nature" be a requirement of human existence, the next task of philosophy would be to discover the egress, not yet found by modernity, that leads neither to the abyss nor to despotism. Perhaps a clue lies in the fact that the early departures from nature were not in the interest of "will."

The second point is a reminder of the existence of that robust strand of modernity that had no commerce with any metaphysical flights from nature, that short but tough line of which the fibers are Hobbes, Locke and Adam Smith. Hobbes and Locke go no further than to present civil existence as a leaving behind of the condition of "mere" nature. They understand nature to be "transcended," but in the restricted sense that the natural end and the natural desires of men are fostered by means that nature itself is unable to furnish but that are made available by the conventions that originate and sustain civil government. Nature surely requires the instruments of human intervention in order to give effect to the laws of nature, which are themselves artifacts produced by reason, but the state of civil society, far from being or aiming at the supersession of man's natural motives – the passions of desire and aversion – is the perfected instrument for their satisfaction. Nature is more successfully effective in the state of civil society, where preservation is protected, than in the state of nature itself. Moreover, the state of nature is not simply superseded but is always incipient in the state of civil society, wherein war can break out at any moment among subjects or between subjects and ruler. In brief, there is no thought of a realm outside nature, and if there were, the state of civil society would not be it and would not be the environment of its existence. This and much more becomes clear in the work of Adam Smith, who calls the social system that he advocated the "system of natural liberty." He can mean only that freedom is precisely the unobstructed if not unguided response to the promptings of nature. The guidance corresponds in the main to that conveyed by Hobbes when he speaks of a man's liberty remaining undiminished even when he is constrained by hedges and ditches to make his journey by road rather than across country. In Smith's liberalism, it is not hedges – which are planted by man – but, in a decisive change of direction, an invisible hand, apparently an organ of nature itself, that guides, hence directs, and thus assists man's responses to nature, reducing by some significant but immeasurable amount the responsibility of human law. The faint anticipation of the principle of natural selection is evident.

How well and on what terms this conception of a cunning of nature, and especially of a freedom within nature, was reconciled to their larger schemes by Kant and Hegel, the spokesmen for the location of freedom outside of nature, cannot be related here. For the present purpose, it suffices to take note of a fact: modernity has responded to its discovery or construction of a morally neutral nature in diverse ways. Having begun by declaring the unity of the whole in a comprehensive nature, modernity with part of its mind saw man's freedom and morality as compromised if there is no extra-natural haven – not an enclave within nature but a ground, in the will, on which humanity can live as if freed from the gravitational pull of natural impulse or natural causation. The ornaments of this development are Kant and Hegel, but especially the former. Then with another part of its mind, modernity learned that freedom is, and exists exactly within, nature; and that the enemy of freedom is presumptuous human intervention in the course of nature, with which nothing can interfere with impunity and from which assuredly there is no escape.

How can this confusion of thoughts be brought into any order? Perhaps as follows. Ascending again to Hobbes, one sees how his relativism, and liberalism in general, eventuated in the strong conventionalism of his doctrine of sovereignty. When we noticed the absence of such sovereignty in the liberalism of our time, we were moved to wonder whether law itself had the status of an authoritative conventionalism that might replace the sovereignty justified by Hobbes. We saw that a vast modern project in the interest of a will exempted from the necessity of nature, while designed to vouchsafe freedom and morality to man in an environment of dumb nature, had the unintended effect of rendering the will stiff-necked before the law. Now we note that there is a simpler current in modernity, that running from Hobbes to Smith, that finds the ground of freedom well within nature, and discerns a threat to natural freedom in the legal conventions that claim to direct the course of man in nature according to a human wisdom higher than that of nature itself. As it appears, there descend from Hobbes two lines of liberal development, one spoken for by Kant and one by Smith. Both renounce the principle of sovereignty, and each has its own means of discouraging the installation of an absolute legal surrogate for that principle that can be, or historically has been, found acceptable by liberalism as it has moved through the twentieth century. Whether liberal society can confront the threats that endanger it, while operating under such a handicap, is of course a grave and disturbing question having implications for the fate of all mankind.

2
Liberalism, Self-Abnegation, and Self-Assertion

Those who set out to investigate liberalism can choose among a number of tasks: to say what it is, to reconstruct its history, to define its influence, to judge it, and doubtless many more. In this paper, I will try to express what might be called the human meaning of liberalism and its political significance, covering a ground similar to that explored by Nietzsche but approaching the task through the evolution of doctrines rather than in the medium of "psychology." My starting point will be four important ingredients of the liberalism of our time that are present also in the political thought of the seventeenth century. Across that gap of time, those ingredients have been transformed and supplemented as the liberal whole that they help to comprise has taken a new shape. In the course of this process, the aims and dispositions of men appear to have been altered. That alteration is what I shall mean by the human meaning of liberalism.

I have maintained elsewhere, ("Liberalism, Nature and Convention," reprinted in this collection) to a degree of detail unnecessary for the present purpose, that relativism, constitutional guarantees and personal freedom are conspicuous in the liberalism of our time and were conspicuous also in the political formulations of Thomas Hobbes, specifically in the *Leviathan*. Those formulations, arrived at through the assertion of a decisive human equality, constitute in fact a charter of protoliberalism. Thus there is an unmistakable if not unbroken line between a classic or pristine liberalism, loosely coeval with the birth of modern political philosophy, and the liberalism we can recognize as our own.

In that original liberalism, it was laid down by Hobbes that "whatsoever is the object of any man's appetite or desire, that is it which he for his part calleth 'good': and the object of his hate and aversion, 'evil'; and of his contempt, 'vile' and 'inconsiderable.' For these words of good, evil, and contemptible are ever used with relation to the person that useth them, there being nothing simply and absolutely so, nor any common rule of good and evil to be taken from the nature of the objects themselves . . ." (*Lev*. ch. 6) Also, "'good' and 'evil' are names that signify our appetites and aversions, which in different tempers, customs and doctrines of men are different . . ." (*Lev*. ch. 15) It might easily be thought, especially from the vantage point of our own liberalism, that Hobbes's intention in setting forth the idiosyncratic basis of the moral distinctions was to enlarge the freedom of each to do as he pleases. That it was not so is disclosed most succinctly in *De Cive* (XII.1) where he writes, "But one and the first (doctrine) which disposeth them to sedition, is this, *that the knowledge of good and evil belongs to each single man*" (original emphasis). Of course Hobbes means that precisely because good and evil are not to be found clinging naturally to objects, the rule of good and evil must be created and imposed politically and, as an emanation from sovereignty, must be understood to be absolutely authoritative, for moral subjectivism is the harbinger of sedition. This turn of thought may usefully be noticed at the outset of our discussion for by its divergence from our own spontaneous liberal understanding, it signals the evolution to which I referred above, specifically in the direction of arbitrary subjectivity.

Besides arguing the relativism that rejects the natural distinctions of good and evil, Hobbes advances a number of legal or judicial propositions that can be found in our own and in other liberal constitutional systems: exclusion of self-incrimination without assurance of pardon, exclusion of evidence elicited through torture, presumption of innocence, proscription of unusual punishment, rejection of legislation *ex post facto* (*Lev.* chaps. 14, 16, 21, 27) and others. For the better understanding not of Hobbes but of liberalism, one might wonder whether the constitutional guarantees of which the foregoing are examples, so far as they lay down criteria for the laws, do not appeal to and thus presuppose certain supra-legal norms of right and in so doing, and to that extent, retract the denial of the natural distinction of good and evil. Hobbes, and the liberal understanding, appear to possess means for judging laws. As the context makes clear, the criterion of good that transcends and prescribes to the laws is the preservation of life, a good that is known to man overwhelmingly and immediately but that is itself without a moral content. As Hobbes would have it, the difference between a good law and a bad one is not the difference between a just law and an unjust one but rather between a law that does and one that does not defer to and give expression to man's illimitable impulse to preserve himself. The steady attrition of the importance of self-preservation between the classical and the present-day liberalism will emerge as a further sign of the evolution of liberalism already mentioned.

Original or Hobbesian liberalism asserted the freedom of the individual to do all those things that the laws do not prohibit: to follow the occupation that his own judgment indicates to him; to buy and sell at prices reached without encumbrance by notions of justice; to consume whatever he likes without interference from sumptuary restrictions; to govern the education of his children according to his own lights; and more in the same vein. (*Lev.* chaps. 21 and 15) Again there is a tacit criticism of the many legal systems or at least legal enactments that have ignored or violated these liberal precepts which derive their authority from the primacy of self-preservation, the premise from which also the valid restraints on natural liberty and equality may be deduced. As one might say, liberalism began with a perception of a natural impulse as having so much authority stemming from its intensity that that impulse gives its direction to the law and at the same time necessarily defines the criterion by which the law itself may be judged. As will be seen, in the course of the evolution of liberalism, the erosion of the respectability of self-preservation as a human motive will make it imperative that some other basis, and even some other basis less bound to nature, be found on which to rest the law, the criterion for passing judgment on the law, and ultimately society itself.

In the background of the three liberal benchmarks – relativism, constitutional legality and individual liberty – lies the axiom of natural equality, expressible also as natural liberty or the perfect and thus equal right by nature of every man to everything. Natural equality, in the sense of the non-existence of a natural right to rule, at the same time indicates the urgency of a conventional or arbitrary foundation for political society and also points to another familiar ingredient, the egalitarian, of the current liberalism.

While the four Hobbesian elements have survived thrivingly, they can give only an impoverished conception of actual liberalism, which consists of opinions and dispositions on a multitude of concrete political and social matters, some of which it will be instructive to probe as we continue in search of liberalism's human meaning. In the liberalism of our time, minorities, women and the poor command active solicitude, a reserved attitude towards business, patriotism, military forces and established authority is normal, and the causes of labor, the "environment," peace and foreign "movements of national liberation" are held in sympathy, although "nationalism" itself, encompassing patriotic enthusiasm (perhaps considered to be ethnocentrism), militarism and the altogether rejected imperialism, is repudiated. In addition, there is the often noticed stance of moral permissiveness and a tendency to consider culture, conditioning, or "history" as governing the formation of human beings rather than "nature," even or especially when the latter is understood in terms of technical genetics. Does this set of postures, which is of course not exhaustive, indicate the essence of liberalism and its human meaning? If so, it must first be ordered under headings.

Before proceeding, the difference between liberalism and interest-group activism should be recognized. Migrant fruit-pickers acting on their own behalf are not, as such, liberals. The middle-class intellectuals and professionals who support them are, to that extent, liberals. Keeping this point in view, a considerable difference opens up between liberal partisanship on behalf of minorities and the poor on the one hand and feminist advocacy on behalf of women on the other. The difference is between activity on behalf of others and on behalf of self. As a refinement of this distinction, liberal activism on behalf of others is either neutral to the interest of the agent or positively disadvantageous to it. As will appear, liberalism consists to a notable degree of attitudes and opinions conceived on behalf of others, so often to the detriment of the liberal's own as to attract attention. The conceptions, dispositions and sentiments that induce men to oppose or even to despise their own range from the base to the most elevated and may be sound or pathological, but are in either case of interest for the insight they give into the character of the men and the worth of the position they occupy.

It is a matter of common experience, if not of measurement, that there is a pure liberalism of white, middle-class intellectuals and professionals, for whom the adoption of an attitude on behalf of racial minorities, the poor, and the working class as distinguished from the middle class and its culture or morality is a repudiation of itself as a group or interest or even class. So far as liberalism entails a disavowal of one's native or adopted social class, an embarrassment at patriotism, an automatic suspicion of the military and a dedication to peace at exorbitant prices, it has the appearance of resulting from a judgment that one's own, and one's self as the self is reflected in the group or nation, are compromised.

That liberalism has a concessive or self-deprecatory aspect has been well understood since at least the time of Nietzsche. For the better comprehension of liberalism, though, it must be perceived that alongside the self-abnegation there runs a strain of self-assertion or self-affirmation that shows itself in such movements and beliefs as (on the part of females) women's liberation, the self-expressionism of progressive education and of so-called moral permissiveness, and the vague but not for that reason inconsiderable antipathy to authority as such. This is to say nothing about the cognate tendencies toward the breaking of traditional constraints in literature and the arts with a similar emancipation of utterance in view, and finally of the legal absolutization of the rights of expression in verbal and other media. The signs of self-assertion are not petty.

The content of liberalism is not exhausted by those features of it that arise directly from effacement and assertion of the self. At present, liberalism includes such beliefs or tendencies as persistent suspicion of private enterprise, immediate sympathy for labor and labor organization, consumerism, environmentalism, acceptance of the historical rather than "static" basis for human existence, and a rather uniform inclination to regard social domestic, and economic, in general external, conditions as preeminent in determining human character and conduct and to consider as weak or irrelevant the autonomous and the natural causes, especially the genetic. If these can fairly be brought under the headings of antipathy to capitalist enterprise and interest, and subscription to a theory of economic-historic conditioning, then they point to a component of liberalism that is borrowed from or vibrates sympathetically with Marxist left theory; or in some immeasurable degree with so-called populism; or in even more tenuous ways with remnants of Scriptural heritage. Since populism is not as such associated, and Biblical religion is even less associated with theories of social determinism, while liberalism is historically linked with the Enlightenment background of the socialist left, it is more plausible to explain the left tendency of liberalism through its complex relation with socialism than through a religious or even a populist influence.

The materials of liberalism that have come to sight are a tendency to self-abnegation and to self-assertion, together with a vague and incomplete sympathy with the socialist left. What are the sources of these divergent dispositions and what might be their meaning as they coexist in one political posture notwithstanding their apparent disharmony?

Let us consider first the possible source of the self-effacing ingredient of liberalism. To do so, we return to Hobbes in whom seeds of liberalism as a whole were found. Hobbes is in the position of maintaining that the drive for self-preservation is invincible and that precisely because of its intensity and because of the ease with which it and the desire for precedence join hands to make everyone's life precarious, it is supremely important that men's aggressiveness, their wish to rule but not to be ruled, and in general their pride, be humbled. Perhaps the largest practical element in the structure of Hobbesian protoliberalism is the rational (calculating) renunciation of claims or rights in which every man has the same title by nature, for the sake of life on a higher level than that of the brutes.

Rousseau, who criticized Hobbes so severely for his superficial construction of natural man, had his own means of agreeing with him in the matter that concerns us now. Rousseau sophisticated the definition of selfishness by distinguishing within it a good and a bad variety. He cultivated to a high degree of elaboration the belief that a natural politics could be erected on the good, simple, pristine sort of egoism, thus initiating or encouraging the modern resurrection of communism by suggesting that there is a form of society in which the socially-bred amour-propre will not arise. He remained free to denounce the harmful selfishness, which is essentially pride or vanity, and to add his voice to the chorus of objurgation that has helped frighten modern man into a mood of self-deprecation. It hardly needs to be said that the inner convictions of Hobbes and Rousseau with regard to Christianity are beside the point when one observes that, however different their premises might have been from those of Scripture, their conclusions accorded in this respect with those that followed from the pious comparison of man with God to the diminishment of man in his own sight.

There are profane and sacred sources of the human sense, and emphatically of the modern sense, that self-abnegation is the proper posture for a man.

But just as Scripture teaches man also that he is made in God's image and only a little lower than the angels, so the philosophers too have shown mankind to itself as having the right, indeed the duty, to stand with dignity so long as no one presumes to stand with more dignity than the rest. Like the self-denial that has entered liberalism, the self-affirmation has penetrated it from various directions. Very early, Spinoza found means of replacing the aggressiveness of Hobbes's crude passion of self-preservation with the form of activity that he identifies with freedom, and "intellectual love" of the whole that raises man to the peak of entelechy and thus to the summit of self-assertion. Rousseau depicts an Emile whose formation has made him proof against every vicissitude of nature and society, emancipated from necessity so far as may be within citizen life, a bourgeois hero. Hegel projects a picture of man translated out of the realm of nature and into that of Spirit, which is the realm in which humanity asserts its will in the purest and freest because most rational fashion. To detach the question from individual formulations and state the case differently, one may wonder whether any scheme for arranging human affairs would more effectively inculcate in human beings a sense of their power than does the modern combination of democracy and technology.

Kant's system is especially notable because it displays a link or concord between the doctrines of self-affirmation and the Marxist left ingredient in actual liberalism. Kant, for whatever larger reason, declared the absolute worth of every human being and therewith the absolute wrong of despising the will of a man by treating him as a means. It is wrong to use a man, which is a step away from saying that it is wrong to employ a man. Kant is among those who prepared the dogmatic vision of a society of innocently assertive men, bound together without the corrupt mediation of competitive aggression and unstained by the coercive exploitation of human beings, a dream that has contributed to the socialist inclination of contemporary liberalism.

If one were to recapitulate the development of modem thought along the line defined by Spinoza, Rousseau, Kant and Hegel, one might do so with the formula "flight from nature," meaning, respectively, to escape from the thrall of nature as ubiquitous cause by contemplative exhaustion of nature; to take advantage of the plasticity of nature in order to give nature an artificial rather than haphazard history; to enter the realm of freedom and morality, thus rising above the realm of merely natural causation; and to participate in the social world in which Spirit or will proper takes practical precedence of mere nature or unreason. If one were to extend the supposed line to Nietzsche, it would reach the will to power, the radical rejection of the drive to mere preservation of life, that is, the merely natural instinct, as the decisive human impulse. My contention is that this line forms one axis, the self-asserting, of the two that give shape to contemporary liberalism, the other axis being the contrary one of self-abnegation already described and related to the offense of pride. The figure formed on these two axes might at first be thought to be an anomaly because constituted by mutually contradictory impulses. That judgment would be in all likelihood a mistake, as experience and doctrine agree in suggesting: practical arrangements only too often benefit from the reciprocal tempering of opposite impulses, as the Founding Fathers might have argued and as Plato seems to have conceived in proposing a music and a gymnastic education. The present point is not at all that contemporary liberalism is an anomaly of contradiction but rather that it has grown into a shape so remarkably different from that which it had to begin with. The transformation that has given our liberalism its cast has been the result of a centuries-long effort on the part of modernity to find a moral basis for social life different from, and by some standard more rational or more noble than, the merely natural drive to self-preservation in Hobbes's sense. It is perhaps impossible to know the deepest source of that effort – whether it is forever spontaneous in the human mind or has been generated or transmitted and then kept alive by the influence of Scriptural religion, or has come about in some other way. However the need to transcend mere life and to strive toward living well might have entered the modern mind, liberalism appears to be an expression of that need. The characteristic defect of liberalism is not the contradiction but the peculiar political effect produced by the collaboration of those understandably present tendencies to self-abnegation and self-affirmation. It is to this that we turn next in trying to assess the human meaning of liberalism.

In the background of the argument to be made now is a historical fact, namely, the link of liberalism to the left, as has been suggested, from which follows a political fact, namely, a certain confusion of purpose in liberal deliberation when faced with threats from the left. Although it is surely impossible to know with any certainty how far the left inclination of liberalism might enervate the self-preserving disposition of a free society, the famous formula "better red than dead" encapsulates the liberal posture at its most hopeless, indicating the worst prognosis for liberal determination to survive. While this motto might gravely overstate the indifference of liberalism to its own fate, it does point unmistakably to what might, once again, be a crude contradiction in the content of liberalism: self-preservation at the highest price, namely, the price of the destruction of liberal life. If this is in fact a contradiction, it is nothing we have not already encountered in this brief discussion. To explain it, two points need be made. First, when the details of the liberal self-affirmation are looked at, they prove to be in the service of the assertion of the private individual as such in protest against the norms of the "bourgeois" state. Second, when the details of the liberal self-abnegation are considered, they prove to be expressions of depreciation of the collective – class, social or political – self rather than the natural individual self. This pair of facts should not be confused with an ordinary tension between the citizen's regard for his private interest and for that of the nation, which is familiar enough and surely not peculiar to liberal society. What gives our liberal egoism its peculiar, and peculiarly political bearing is its doctrinal tendency to resist and depreciate "bourgeoisdom" in a wide range of its political, social and moral manifestations. How has this come to pass?

Liberalism has evolved from its Hobbesian form through a flight from nature, from the uncontested primacy of the natural instinct of self-preservation, through a long period in which the will – a locution for freedom from natural necessity – was installed by philosophers as the legitimate animator of social as well as private man and as the favored object of liberal political solicitude. As opinion and sentiment have developed, the advancement of the will has eventuated in a political asthenia compounded of self-abnegation and self-assertion, in the manner described. Why has a doctrine of the will eventuated in a politics of diffidence rather than the more plausible opposite? The question is especially vexing in light of Nietzsche's formulations according to which the primacy of the will is intrinsic to a notoriously anti-liberal politics. But the will to power as Nietzsche apotheosizes it is not a mere contradiction of the natural impulse to preservation; it is a purification of it in the terms of an injunction to listen to the deepest murmurings of nature rather than abandon those promptings that are evidences of health. If an investigation of contemporary liberalism may decently be brought to its point by reference to Nietzsche, then one might say that our liberalism is one of the possible political results of the attempt to rectify the relation of nature and will or of necessity and the arbitrary, and that the Nietzschean doctrine of will to power and eternal return of the same is another. The former, which is in content the concurrence of self-abnegation and self-affirmation with emanations from Marxism posited above, has tended to bring liberal constitutional politics into a state of what I have called asthenia. The Nietzschean alternative for adjusting nature and will to one another has shown signs of being eligible by the most vicious forms of fascism. It appears that the hope of liberal constitutionalism must lie in the discovery of a liberalism that resolves in its own understanding and in a way conducive to its justified self-respect the reasons it has both for criticizing and protecting its own. The political weakness of liberalism, which arises not from the so-called displacement of the soul by the self but rather from an unhealthy attitude toward the self, stands revealed as shockingly close to liberalism's human meaning.

If at last one wonders how liberalism has become exposed to such dire reflections, one reaches an issue that transcends liberalism itself by far, namely, the question of history. I have implied throughout that the clue to the grand movements of opinion and sentiment is to be found in philosophy, or at any rate in thought, including the Scriptural. But there remains something mysterious in the political careers of the great systems of thought, or in the arrival of new modes and orders among men. What makes the conceptions of philosophy suitable for public acceptance or, not to prejudice the issue, for vulgarization? Is the human heart always in wait to applaud and to confirm with belief whatever gratifies its deepest and strongest if not loveliest impulses – envy; rage; love of pleasure; indolence; fear; as well as a capacity for awe, a remote sense of limitedness, or other more deeply buried stirrings? Even or especially if so, the original impulse has the form of thought. Fortunate is the political society in which the healthiest instincts resonate to the deepest insights.

3
Providential Care for Democracy

It is my melancholy duty to present these remarks to you as a lecture in memory of James Steintrager, professor of politics at Wake Forest University, once my student at Chicago. There is something as unnatural about a teacher surviving his student as there is about a parent outliving his child. It is unnatural, it is against the order of nature. That in fact has something to do with the subject I want to discuss. One might say that when a man in the prime of his life and with a promising career ahead of him is cut down, there is something irrational or something unreasonable about it. This implies that there is some basis of reason, care, or thoughtfulness in the nature of things, that is to say in the constitution of the whole world. Without planning it this way at all, it occurred to me that the subject that I want to discuss is in a way the same subject as the one that comes to mind when one thinks about the untimely death of someone like James Steintrager.

We sooner or later say to ourselves that our comings and goings both as individuals and as nations seem to be the product of forces and influences that are inscrutable to us. We speak, in fact, about the inscrutable ways of Providence. Yet we cannot entirely suppress our human inclination to ask, what are the ways of Providence? Why do we come and go as we do, when we do? Is there a reason to it? Is there something in the nature of the universe that could be said to be reasonable, or that could be said to favor one outcome over another? Particularly to raise our present theme: could there be imagined such a thing as a Providential care for democracy? Could it be thought to be true that a higher power has us in its view and somehow cares not only for us individually but cares for our prosperity as a nation? I will begin with a remark from a famous source which seems to dispose of the question of the Providential care of democracy and which, I confess, continues to fill me with perplexity. This is a short statement from the introduction to Tocqueville's *Democracy in America*. He writes as follows:

> The gradual development of equality is a Providential fact. It has the principal characteristics thereof. It is universal, it is lasting, it escapes day by day from human control. Every event, like every human being, has been subservient to its development.

And also the following:

> As one traverses the pages of our history [Tocqueville means by "our history" the history of France or the history of Europe], he does not meet, so to speak, with any great events during the 700 years that have not advanced equality.

I take it to be Tocqueville's conviction that something about the nature of Providence pervades the world in such a way as to induce a development in the direction of equality of the kind that he has detected, lasting in his day seven hundred years and in our day another hundred or so more. I ask the question: What could or would account for this cosmic support of democracy? By this I mean the support of democracy not only as a viable institution internally but, as one must necessarily mean, also support against its external enemies. It would say little if one were to affirm that Providence has somehow or other sustained a democracy and have in mind only the internal consistency of its constitution, leaving out of account altogether the threat to democracy from the outside. By "democracy" I do not mean the United States, but the principle of democracy and the principle, though somewhat different from the principle of democracy simply, of liberal government in the world. What could be meant by a Providential support for this or any regime?

I am going to suppose that what one ought to mean by the support of Providence is a pervasive conjunction of mind or reason or intelligence on the one hand, and will or intention on the other, that characterizes the constitution of the entirety and permeates it. If this support by the principle of the universe for such a thing as democracy means the support of a universal reason and a universal will, that support, it seems to me, would be incomprehensible if it were not true that democracy is the regime which is most compatible with the demand of reason, and with a reason which itself drives and at the same time is driven by the absolutely comprehensive will. Democracy would qualify, on those terms, as being most rational, most consistent with the Providential reason. It and God's reason – or wisdom, as we are more inclined to say – would support one another. I think there is no way to escape the inference that democracy would on those terms be entitled to think of itself as the best regime, to use an expression which is traditional in the history of political thought. For democracy to be supported by divine Providence I think it would be necessarily true that the conjunction of goodness and durability and those other characteristics that Tocqueville enumerates would lead to the identification of democracy as the best regime.

I will mention parenthetically that if one recalls the enumeration by Tocqueville of those qualities that indicate the Providential source of the development of equality, one finds something missing. The principal characteristics of that development are that it "is universal, it is lasting, and it escapes day by day from human control." Missing, for one reason or another, is good. Tocqueville somehow neglects to say that it is also good. If we had Tocqueville here to question we would of course want to know how he could have ascribed the support of democracy to Providence without enumerating among its qualities also goodness as a testimonial to that support. I am supplying on my own authority the inference that democracy would have to be good if it were to qualify as the regime that God's Providence particularly supervises. Could it be that good means or means only the rational? So far I have maintained that if this support exists, it would exist by virtue of the existence of a divine wisdom as well as a divine will; and it is impossible to conceive that the divine wisdom would sustain a regime that was not itself in a fundamental way rational. I raised the question whether rational takes the place of good in the list of qualifications that Tocqueville provides us. I followed that with the question: Does good necessarily mean only rational?

There is another possibility. When people speak about good and when the thinkers about these things addressed the question of good, they sometimes found themselves compelled to address the question of nature. The relation between the good and the natural could be formulated as follows. Is democracy good by virtue of its being not the most rational, but the most natural of the regimes? I will not here take up the implications of a distinction between the natural and the rational, but something along that line will emerge in the course of what I will now try to put before you.

In the course of the evolution of thinking about human life in the political medium, a disjunction was either invented or discovered roughly in the time of the 16th and 17th centuries. That disjunction was between the good and the natural. I can best explain this by indicating a novel sense in which the natural was interpreted by men to one another. Examine the natural environment, the surroundings to the outermost reaches. Consider the smallest things and the largest things. You will be struck by something that we loosely call regularity. One could also be struck by something looking like randomness. The people who think about these matters, however, are able without distortion to reduce the randomness to a form of regularity. Regularity more precisely characterized is reducible to the relation between causes and effects – generally speaking to the phenomenon of causation.

What does one observe when one interprets the natural whole in terms of causation? The formula that describes it better than any other is the one which arises out of the thought and writing of Spinoza. Spinoza spoke about an infinite chain of causation, meaning by that a sequence arising infinitely remotely and proceeding infinitely remotely and in the course of doing so passing through the human being who is, according to this formulation, no exception to the influence of that infinite chain of causation. The natural chain of causes produces an impression of necessity. Causation itself became a theoretical problem in the 18th century, most famously in connection with the work of Hume, although it had become a moral problem a century earlier in the work of Spinoza.

Without going into the way in which this understanding of nature became a metaphysical problem, it is important to take notice of how it became a moral problem. If the natural and the good must converge, but the natural and the necessary are indistinguishable from one another in the sense that this chain of mechanical causes passes without interruption through the human being, then morality among men is threatened through the elimination of what looks like their freedom. It would be important to trace this out if we were to examine the question entirely, but I want rather to focus attention on the following aspect of the enormous problems that arise through this development by which nature has been interpreted as the infinite chain of causes against which human beings have no shield.

So far as nature becomes identified with necessity, it becomes possible and perhaps necessary to identify the good by nature with a phenomenon that, for want of a better conception, I am going to call mass – the massiveness of effect, the massiveness of influence. One could say that the rule in nature is for the more massive to preponderate (and the word gives itself away), to overcome by weight. If it were to be true that nature as the instrument and the creation of divine Providence favors the preponderance of the more massive over the less massive, then I think it would be obvious that the Providence that looks out for democracy would be looking out for it through the medium of the power of democracy to preponderate, or to reflect within itself the preponderance of superior mass. In a way, all that I am saying is that if God through nature favors the more massive and democracy is the political instrumentality by which the more massive, i.e. the majority, preponderates over the minority, then we can find in this a rather peculiar ground for assuring ourselves that God's Providence is indeed directed towards democracy. This would be a circuitous demonstration of the validity of the Latin saw *vox populi, vox dei*, the voice of God is the voice (or vote) of the people or of the majority. In order for us to be satisfied that this is a sufficient testimony to the support for democracy that arises through the character of the cosmos, we would have to satisfy ourselves also in the conviction that God favors the stronger. This is a way of saying that justice is the advantage of the stronger. This is an argument that is well known through the first book of Plato's *Republic*, where it is soundly rejected as incompatible with a decent understanding of justice. Leaving that awful difficulty aside, let me state in a somewhat formal way the implication of this much of the argument. If democracy were to have obtained or earned cosmic support (the support of divine Providence) through the argument I have just now presented it would indeed still have to be true that democracy is the best regime and in it wisdom or reason would have to be preeminent. But wisdom and reason would now have to be so constructed as to be indistinguishable from necessity. We would have proved to ourselves that God's Providence is simply the care that the self-caring assure for themselves by the success with which they care for themselves. This is an elaborate way of saying that God takes care simply of those who take care of themselves successfully.

If we are conscientious in the way in which we ascribe to Providence a care for democracy, then it is our duty to consult those places where God has most authoritatively spoken his own intentions – that is to say, through the works of revelation. As far as I know, what God reveals of himself through the old and new dispensations says nothing about democracy or about democracy as the best regime. Obedience and faith under any regime, including monarchies and indeed including tyrannies, are what save – both here and hereafter. The Messiah is promised, not popular sovereignty. Out of the word of God as revealed in scripture, it would be very hard to make the case that God looks out particularly through instrumentalities, to say nothing of directly, for a democratic regime. In any case, God's purposes are inscrutable, certainly to us; his works are miraculous and therewith arbitrary in a certain sense, and that sense is conveyed altogether in the term "transcendent." If God is, strictly speaking, transcendent of the whole, that is to say not immanent in nature or in the world, then it must be true that his doings are from this limited point of view of immanence miraculous and arbitrary, and his teaching is, of course, through prophecy and inspiration. Somewhat differently put, the transmission of the heavenly dispensation to earth has to be by miracle or by grace and not by desert. This being said, I conclude this part of my argument with the observation that we cannot but be left in doubt with regard to the extent to which the whole, i.e. God, simply favors democracy. I think the case for the Providential care for democracy cannot be regarded as having been definitively made out.

The assumption of my last remark has been that reason is transcendent and that the rational, omniscient being who could be thought of as favoring democracy through his Providence is transcendent of the whole: he does not belong to it, and presides over it in a way that has to be considered mysterious when we reflect on what we mean when we say the words "the whole." How to say "the whole" and mean also that there is something outside of it is a very great puzzle that can only be understood in terms of miracle and revelation. Leaving that great issue aside, I raise the question: What if reason were not transcendent of the whole but were immanent in the whole? That mysterious saying means something like the following. Imagine that there is a bounded universe, a universe that indeed has a limit. It is very hard to specify the sense in which the whole has a limit, but we must try to conceive it. (It surely would be inappropriate to say imagine it, for it is absolutely unimaginable and can only be conceived.) Conceive that entirety as having the following character. Since it is the entirety, nothing can be conceived of other than it. Add to this the one simple empirical fact which is undeniable: there is change of flux within that whole. We cannot deny that we come into being and pass away and that this is the rule of all the things of which we have any knowledge within the whole. Add only that fact and you will have conceived this entirety in which there is a universal flux, a coming into being and a passing away, but always under the influence of something that could be called the law of commutation or the law of the conservation of the whole. Nothing can arise unless it arises out of something that has had to be sacrificed in order for that new entity to come into being. Think of this entirety in that state of commutation – of internal, constant commutation – and consider the possibility that everything within it is supervised by something that (for want of a better word) we have to call mind. Consider, in other words, that we have before us the scheme of the whole which is alluded to in what we know of the writings of the ancient Greek, Anaxagoras, who said that *nous* governs all – that mind, reason, governs all. This is what I would propose as the meaning of the notion that reason is immanent in the whole. There is no entity outside of the whole in whom reason and therewith will resides, but reason is of the essence of the being of the whole itself and governs that eternal commutation, that eternal flux.

There is a well thought out philosophic position which would have us understand that the political state is that agency in which reason manifests itself most emphatically and most unmistakably on the plane of humanity, of the human substance, that subset of substance altogether. It is reason at work that eventuates in the state or, more particularly, in the modern state or the state in which, by virtue of the working of reason in this human substance, freedom and reason come to govern the relations of all human beings, the sign of which would be that the will which drives the reason has taught itself to will only that which is worthy to be willed. This is a thumbnail sketch of Hegel on the state. If democracy were to enjoy the special Providential protection that we are contemplating, then it would have to be said that democracy would be that regime which stood in the position of the state as the perfected medium in which the good comes to man. If we were to employ the argument which provides the assimilation of reason and freedom it the state beyond Hegel and, without reference to his peculiar characterizations of the excellent state, focus it on democracy, we might produce a way of specifying the condition under which it could be said that democracy enjoys a special dispensation of protection by virtue of the nature of the whole. I do not know of any argument which has produced this conclusion, which Tocqueville may be considered merely to assert. The argument of Hegel does not produce this conclusion. The state as described by Hegel, that human form in which reason and freedom converge, is certainly not democracy. This is not to ascribe any extraordinary authority to Hegel but rather to point out that if anybody could be described as having characterized the state in such a way as to embody heaven on earth, it must be Hegel. The strongest argument I know of (namely that of Hegel) which apparently apotheosizes the state does not identify the state with democracy. I persist in the insecurity, which I expressed on grounds of reflection on God's will, that I feel in attributing to the nature of the whole a special care for democracy.

I will now go out of chronological order and mention the third and last of the great schemes within the framework of which it would be possible to reflect on the question of the Providential care for democracy and therewith the care of Providence for all things great and small in the world. Plato is known to us popularly as a rationalist. What that is generally understood to mean is that Plato presented a view of the whole in which being and intelligibility collapsed into one another. The instrument by which he produced this collapse was the doctrine of the Ideas as invented by Socrates. It is an immensely difficult and complicated matter and I can only refer to the consequences of the argument rather than go through anything resembling the grounds of the argument. We are given to understand that there are "things" called Ideas – Ideas with a capital "I" – which are not concepts. An Idea is not something in the mind of a man. Something about it has to lodge in the mind of a man, but the thing itself is not in the mind of man. The Idea has an existence. It is that One which collects the many and makes them intelligible. It is that which is eternal, that which permeates or supervenes over all the things that come into being and pass away and makes them intelligible. The understanding is that those things that come into being and pass away recommend themselves to the senses, but the things that are eternal recommend themselves to the intelligence. It is only on the plane of the intelligence that being can be recognized. Everything else must be consigned to the category of becoming. According to this famous Platonic-Socratic orthodoxy, the intelligible and that which is, and that which is herewith eternally, collapse into one another, and all of this is assimilated to the proposition that mind governs all. We should remember the place in the Platonic corpus where Socrates is, in a manner of speaking, reviewing his life. Socrates is about to die, and he recounts his intellectual autobiography. He mentions Anaxagoras, who produced the formula, mentioned earlier, that mind governs all. Socrates thought that this was what he had been looking for all his life, for it explained everything that hitherto had been unclear to him. For various reasons, Anaxagoras's formulation did not prove ultimately satisfactory and its unsatisfactoriness could be said to have given Socrates the reason for continuing to live, to work and to think. At any rate, *nous* and its affiliates of being and intelligibility permeate the whole. One could refer to the immanence and rule of mind throughout.

To understand what this dictum of Plato means for our context it is of course necessary to look at his political works. Consider for a moment the

Republic in its barest outline. From one point of view, the *Republic* could be said to have as its intention the production of the schema of the best political order, the best regime, or the best city. (It is called the best city, which is sometimes translated as the ideal city, but, literally speaking, the Greek words mean the best city.) The best city comes into being in the conversation between Socrates and the young men who are with him in the course of an attempt to say what justice is. The thought is that it is somehow convenient to look at the large embodiment of justice which is in the city rather than to try to detect it in the small medium in which it exists when it is the property of a single human being. With much trouble the speakers describe the institutions of the just city. It happens that the just city is rarely to be seen among men. "Rarely" is something of an understatement, for it has never been seen among men. It had not been seen by Plato's time and it has not been seen up to our time. This is not at all to say that there have not been decent and sensible and wise forms of government. But if it is true that the just city means what Plato thought it to mean, it must be said that that conception of the immanence of wisdom and being in the whole under the auspices of the Ideas has never produced the good city in actuality. The question is raised among the interlocutors whether it even could be actualized, and Socrates' answer to that is instructive. It is given in several locations, and in each case it is equivocal. In the sixth book of the *Republic* Socrates says, when pressed, something to the effect that there is no reason that it shouldn't occur even among barbarians somewhere, were philosophy – i.e. wisdom – but recruited to politics. Other things, some of which are very terrible, are said about what would have to be done in order to bring this theoretical city into practical existence. Such existence is rare, to say the least, and, according to the account that is given, it would not even be durable. The story of the best city is the story of a rather meteoric life, a coming into being and a passing away rather early. This makes us wonder deeply about the relation between good and the natural on these terms. Good and, indeed, being itself seem to come into a state of conflict or tension with existence. When referring to being and existence I refer to the difference between that which is essential and that which finds an expression. Existence is always taken to mean that which has come to be phenomenally. It is connected with coming to be, coming to be in the world or coming to be accessibly. Being is from every possible point of view at the opposite end of the ontic scale. Being is that which men to this very day are in pursuit of. Under the influence of such a thinker as Heidegger, questions about the validity of traditional understandings of being have come to the surface and are reasonably active. Being, we are still in search of. Existence is all around us. It is in that sense that I say the Platonic formulation indicates an amazing disjunction between the tendency of being and the tendency of existence.

To make matters worse, the *Republic* is followed by another book, the

Timaeus, which is its explicit sequel. The *Timaeus* is the story of the universe. It is literally the story of the coming into being of the whole. The purpose of it is ostensibly political: to say something about good cities, starting with the men who are their components. But you cannot start with men unless you discuss the coming into being of men, and you cannot discuss the coming into being of men unless you discuss the coming into being of the whole in which they are. In that way the sequel to the *Republic* is the story of the generation of the universe – an absolutely stunning performance. Socrates initiates the *Timaeus* by saying that we had a discussion yesterday, meaning a recounting of the conversation of the *Republic*, in which we generated in speech the good city. Now he would like to see the good city in act. He would like to see it do that thing which is most characteristic of its action, which most trenchantly indicates what a city does. And that turns out to be war. Socrates would like to see the city at war.

In the first place we are disturbed by the thought that the most active act of the city and even of the good city is war. In the second place, there is a very long account of the coming into being of the visible universe, an account that argues for the primacy of reason in the whole. The reason within the whole can be observed to be at work when you consider that the smallest elements of the whole are triangles. These are right triangles which, when put together with the hypotenuses converging at the apex, form an equilateral triangle, a triangle of sixty degrees all around. Those basic triangles are said by Plato through the instrumentality of his interlocutors to be really at the core of the visible world. But very simple geometry reveals that these particular triangles imply a term which we in English and they in Greek called irrational (*alogos*), exemplified by the square root of 2 and of 3. This concept arises in various places in the Platonic corpus, one of them being in the *Meno*. Exploring the Pythagorean theorem – the square that is erected on the hypotenuse of a right triangle has an area which is equal to the sum of the areas of the squares which are erected on each of the other two sides of the right triangle – you arrive occasionally at numbers which are not numbers. They cannot be expressed as a ratio of one number to another. These numbers which cannot be expressed as ratios (a word that embodies reason) are irrationals. To make the point as starkly as possible, present near the core of the visible world is the irrational – the square root of 2, if you like. Intrinsic to geometry is an infinite term, a term without a specification.

From all of this I would extract the semi-conclusion that here is some sort of resistance within nature to the reasonable and to the best. There is a resistance within nature to the best regime and there seems to be a resistance within nature itself to the strictest and most comprehensive hegemony of the rational. If there is such resistance of the natural to the best, one might say that even or especially if democracy were the best regime, nature would not particularly favor it. The immanent reason would fail to support the best regime, if democracy is the best regime, as the transcendent reason might not support democracy even if democracy is the best regime. Does this in a peculiar way strengthen the case for the survival of democracy?

If I argue that there is within nature some resistance to the best and I deny that democracy is the best regime, am I in a complicated and somewhat unappetizing way suggesting that democracy gets its support from nature precisely as not being the best regime? I would not depend on it, because if there is something in nature that supports the regime that is not best, it will support equally well all the other regimes that are not best, many of which are our enemies. For that reason I would not count on this. I then have to come to a conclusion which is less than perfectly consoling for those who live a democratic life and wish it to prosper and to survive. I do not think that God promises us our prosperity. I do not believe that one can trust to the care of God through Providence for the prosperity of democracy. Philosophy cannot reassure us. Neither modern philosophy characterized as Hegelian, nor ancient philosophy in the form of classical Platonic-Socratic philosophy can reassure us, whether we think of democracy as the best regime or not the best regime. I wonder what this tells us in the end about who or what cares for us. I am driven to the simple conclusion that we really have to take care of ourselves. There is no way that we can convince ourselves that we will prosper in the end if we do not do the best we can for ourselves. What does that mean? Ruthlessness, a concentration, not to say an obsession, with our security, with our well-being, with our strength, our wealth? I would hope not. I would think that a proper understanding of caring for ourselves cannot omit from view some notion of what virtue, morality and decency require of us. I think that if we care for ourselves properly, we will eventually be driven back to a very ancient understanding that relates virtue and happiness. I grant that that conjunction of virtue and happiness is not unequivocal. It is problematic. But I think that a view of life that disregards it is bound to be shallow, empty, and eventually unsatisfying. I have not dwelt on this, but it is the project certainly of a significant part of Plato's *Republic* to show that justice, and virtue more generally, are not only eligible for their own sake but they are indispensable to the happiness of a human being. In some difficult sense, they are indispensable to the happiness and prosperity of states as well.

What then are we called upon to do? We are called upon to balance the demands of our survival, our prosperity, our preservation on the one hand, and the demands of our fellow human beings, of our regard for them, our concern for them, our recognition of them as human beings, on the other. We must recognize that they are different from us and that it is our duty to take care of ourselves with a view to that fact. And we must recognize the higher fact that we belong to the same kind – we belong together. Humanity is a one and we must respect it and regard it and have a concern for its preservation. The task of balancing these two, of making a defense of democracy which would be the nearest thing to a Providential defense for it that we can persuade ourselves exists in the world, is the task of wisdom in power. That conjunction of wisdom and authority has been on men's minds as long as there has been reflection on political things. It appears in Plato's formulations in the well-known institution of the philosopher king. It is repeated as matter of concern in the thought of Machiavelli, who sees no prospect for political well-being if power and intelligence are disjoined from one another. One sees it in the reflections with which Rousseau closes the *First Discourse*, concerning the conjunction of power and intelligence or wisdom which he deemed indispensable. Perhaps everyone who has speculated responsibly on the political life of mankind must come to the same conclusion.

I leave you therefore with what you might think a somewhat jejune conclusion, namely, that for want of a clear testimony that either the transcendent or immanent reason of the whole can be depended upon to safeguard democracy, we are thrown back on the only intelligence and reason and goodness which it is within our human power to command, and that is the reason and goodness that lie within us and that find an expression in the form of statesmanship. Statesmanship is often discussed and very seldom conclusively defined. Through the medium of a rejection of the certainty that we are being protected by Providence I offer this suggestion about the character of the statesman: he is that human being who faces without vainglory the fact that he stands *in loco providentiae* to his own people, which means that he must care for the well-being of a part of humanity without losing sight of the claims of mankind as such. He must discharge his duty without the benefit of the perfect power and wisdom possessed by a god whose image he would be well advised to keep before him as an object of emulation and a source of approval. In striving to imitate the highest wisdom in the course of caring for a part while knowing that the highest wisdom could not but have in charge the care of the whole, he would perhaps perceive himself as repeating in his office the paradigm of reason and the irrational that lies near the government of the whole. And that perhaps is how we too should perceive him.

4
On the Mutual Compatibility of Democracy and Marxian Socialism

Much of the high politics of our time is affected by the hostility and suspicion that pervade relations between the Western democracies and the socialist world. Is it possible that the hostility and suspicion are misplaced, and that the two world systems can find a common ground on which to acknowledge each other as compatible co-denizens between whom there is no difference so potent that the being of one must be a reproach to the being of the other? With a view to this question, I wish to ask whether it is possible for a Marxist society to be democratic or for a democracy to elect Marxism or to elect to remain Marxist. Putting the question in the form, "Is it possible . . ." would enable us to answer it by pointing to even one example of a Marxist democracy, thus to dissolve what seems like a theoretical matter in an empirical medium. This expectation is encouraged by the existence of Marxist regimes that call themselves democratic, but it is, at the same time, frustrated by the obvious unwillingness of the non-Marxist, pre-Marxist democracies to concede to them the propriety of that appellation. In the self-understanding of countries that were democracies before any state was Marxist, democracy is defined by the wide availability of significant choices which cannot be expressed with impunity in Marxist countries or, if they are available at all, then only to a microscopic elite. In the self-understanding of democracies which have at the very least a prescriptive right to be so called, choice or election is decisive for the definition; but can even a well-established self-understanding settle the issue of definition between parties with an interest in contradictory definitions? There is an obvious danger that the question will prove in principle incapable of being answered univocally in a way that is acceptable to both non-Marxist democrats and Marxists who claim to be democrats. This outcome, if it materialized, would furnish evidence of an irreconcilable difference between pre-Marxist/non-Marxist democratic understanding on one hand, and that of Marxism on the other, which would in its own way bear on the original question of their mutual compatibility. It would make clear that each, in its own efforts to embody democracy as it understands democracy, must live by a rule that the other cannot accept. This would leave unresolved, except by appeal to prescriptive right, the legitimacy of each side's claim to the name of democracy; but we may well stipulate the separability of that issue from the one that is of thematic importance to us and proceed directly to the matter of the compatibility of democracy and Marxism by adopting, with the temporary appearance of some arbitrariness, the viewpoint of the side with prescription in its favor, namely, that choice or choosing is of the essence of democracy and freedom is of the essence of choice. That is to say, democracy is a certain condition of choice: where (free) choice is present, democracy is present. This thought points to two somewhat different avenues of further reflection. One is that the theory of democracy is the theory of choice. The other is best put in the form of a question: can democracy be adequately conceived as politics reduced to terms of procedures, rules, or criteria governing the act of choosing, or must it be conceived in terms of the objects of choice, what one might call the substantive ends of the regime, properly to be called democratic. (It is difficult to avoid every resonance of the controversy over which side can rightfully appropriate the name.) How long the two avenues of reflection continue to be distinct from each other remains to be seen.

If democracy is a mode of choice, then the theory of democracy would be the theory of choice, and much if not all of our quest for the proper definition of democracy would have to be seen as already completed in the work of the sophisticated writers on the logic of public choice and collective action. Can democracy be adequately understood as the regime whose members' actions are the logic of collective choice converted into practice? It is not necessary for the present purpose to distinguish the economic, strategic, psephistic, and abstractly logical choice-theoretic effluents from the original theory of games because they all participate in a single predominant characteristic: they all pertain to the behavior of agents whose purpose is gain, advantage, or preponderance in relation to one or more similarly motivated actors who presumably have the same equipment for calculation. That the theory of choice has its origin in the theory of games tinctures it not at all with the levity of play but, rather, confers on it all the gravity of the passion for winning.

It might be held that the abstractness of the pure logic of choice renders the theory of collective action marginal to any field of human activity, such as politics, in which the empirical or "pragmatic" is, if not everything, then at least inseparable from everything. For the present purpose, the same point might be made somewhat differently by noting that the pure logic of choice is, *qua* pure, no more democratic than oligarchic, no more peculiar to an American election, for example, than to a maneuver in the Kremlin. This criticism is oblique to my present point, but the objection to choice theory draws attention to a difficulty that we have an obligation to address.

If we think about modern democracy, especially as it is known in the West, we find ourselves contemplating the political setting for the pursuit of private gain, advantage, or preponderance on the part of individuals and groups very much in the spirit of choice-theoretic behavior. But if we ask whether this reveals the essence of democracy itself, we may pause before saying that it does, because it is impossible to ignore the simple definition of democracy as rule by the people or the great multitude, which from ancient times has been supposed to be the poor who will press for their gain and their advantage through their preponderance, but who cannot be thought immune to influences that might deflect them from their egoism. In the interest of not prejudging the question of the mutual compatibility of democracy and Marxism, I should like to leave open the possibility that a people can be influenced significantly by creeds, theories, situations, and doctrines, that they can become practitioners of a divinely commanded self-mortification, or patriots imbued with a sense of imperial mission, or victims of strategic weakness who surrender to vulnerability and fall thence into hedonism. Who will insist that a people as such must inevitably rule itself according to the dictates of a busy egoism, probable though it may be that they will?

I should like, therefore, to distinguish the *demos* which has come under the influence of some force that is strong enough to turn it away from what I will venture to call the natural ends of the political mass, and the *demos* that in its forthrightness aims at gain and advantage through preponderance. I will venture further to maintain that those goals of self-preference, so familiar through their insistent appeal as to be called natural, are normal to democracy to the point that they seem joined to its essence; that the *demos* can be turned away from its spontaneous inclination only by the application of enormous pressures that arise outside itself and thus imply a divagation from autonomy; that such deviations from the essential tendency of democracy are to be distinguished from those canalizations of self-preference within democratic life such as are indicated in the tenth *Federalist* and that promote the mutual accommodations and concessions that enhance gain. If such a distinction is accepted, then democracy can be understood as directed essentially to certain ends fit to be called natural. Democracy, then, appears as a system of choice or election under the formal principle of autonomy; but it proves to be more than that – a system of election, indeed, but one in which the freedom implicit in election is inseparable in essence from the natural status of the objects of choice. Whether the tension between autonomy and domination by the attractive force of natural desiderata will escape the notice of Marxist or other critics of democracy's self-perception is a question to be kept in mind. For the present, it suffices to observe that undistracted democracy is not essentially a system of means for making choices but, rather, a regimen for superimposing or applying such a system upon or to a substratum of natural ends or the desires for those ends, ends which democracy has no impulse to subvert or replace and which should be considered intrinsic to pristine democracy itself. As Scripture testifies (that it is better to give than to receive is a precept requiring the support of faith in contention with impulse) and as anthropology vainly seeks to deny (with the evidence of the unusual practices of faraway tribes) and as publicized lapses of communists high and low strongly suggest, there is something only too painfully natural about the self-preference that so commonly displays itself as acquisitiveness and that can be confidently regarded as defining the ends that dominate the acts and the machinery of democratic choice.

In proceeding along the two paths indicated at the outset by the reflection that democracy is a certain condition of choice, we have discovered that the two avenues opened thereby – the one indicated by the question whether the theory of choice is not in fact the theory of democracy and the other indicated by the question whether democracy contemplates only the instrumentalities and not the substantive ends of choice – in fact converge on the thought that the means embedded in democracy are peculiarly complementary to the natural ends that those means subserve. This convergence will enable us to progress in our effort to judge the mutual compatibility of democracy and Marxism.

The question of whether or not Marxism and democracy are mutually compatible is vitalized by the empirical fact that the subjects of Marxist governments have hitherto lacked the opportunity freely to express their political judgments, preferences, or choices. It must be understood, however, that what is perceived by liberal democrats as a fact is seen by Marxist advocates as a tendentious interpretation imposed on an undeniable fact that happens to have a meaning contrary to the one attributed to it by liberal democrats. Marxists have no need or desire to deny that they insist as far as possible on one-party government, which is a system that distinguishes a politically favored minority and a passive mass. It is unnecessary to rehearse the arguments of the orthodox and revisionist theoreticians over the role of vanguards, just as it would be irrelevant to impugn the motives of those who justify or lead the one-party elites associated with Marxist government, unnecessary and irrelevant because our attention should be concentrated on the conception of choice, and hence of freedom, on which the visible institutions of Marxist government are erected. For that purpose it is enough to reflect on a few of the best-known tenets of Marxist doctrine, such as those which follow. Society has hitherto been plagued by division; the great One has failed to rise out of the alienation that chokes the happiness of the Many, a multiplicity that is an aspect of the system of property. Multiplicity and alienation are empirically inseparable from the concrete miseries of mankind: massive poverty and loss of freedom among many, and dehumanization of all – a paradigm of slavery. At the bottom of this well of degradation is unreason. Marxism is a doctrine that promises the reign of One over Many and that sees a salvation in the concomitant triumph of Reason over abominated Passion. But this is a victory that will occur only when the world's business of production and distribution is no longer left to be conducted under the signs of greed, hedonism, and combativeness – passions that generate the outcomes mediately which are accessible to reason immediately – but rather of reason itself and thus necessarily of philanthropic principles: reason over passion and One over Many.

The way to this immense consummation is to be led by those who have been made wise by their wretchedness (abstracting entirely from the paideutic influence of Marxism itself). This is an astonishing proscenium to frame a drama that lives by rejecting the reason that flows indirectly from passion; but that difficulty is immaterial to our purpose, which is to find the principle of choice or election that lies immured in Marxist politics. Led however restively, by a vanguard however instructed, humanity is to arrive on the plane of a freedom that goes far beyond emancipation from wage-labor exploitation and political disfranchisement, and on the plane of a reason that far transcends the state planning which replaces the balky effectiveness of market spontaneity. The freedom and reason contemplated by essential Marxism are revealed as the obverse and reverse of a single coin. They are so revealed by the meaning of the decisive slogan of Marxism: from each according to his ability, to each according to his needs. The human community in which that aspiration had materialized would be a One in which the Many had effectually caused themselves to vanish in a concrete realization of Humanity as such – one for all, all for one. The implicit abandonment by each individual of his pristine self-preference is the deepest sign of the radical rationalization of life envisioned in Marxism, which in this way appropriates the moral-political ideal of universality inherited from Rousseau (the general will) and Kant (the categorical imperative). The rule of reason in this sense could be also the zenith of despotism if it were not accompanied by, indeed generated by, autonomy. To reason must therefore be added a freedom conceived so that there is no disparity of radical depth between freedom and reason. This is accomplished by construing freedom as that condition of will that has disciplined itself to will freely only what is worthy of being willed, which is precisely the rational. It is of no concern to us for the present purpose that the self-discipline of the will is the determined, i.e., unfree result of a purely material condition, namely, the abolition of the private ownership of the means of production. What matters is that there is an undoubted ground of choice elaborated in the theory of Marxism and available for invocation to repel the charge that the subjects of a one-party regime are simply the victims of oppression.

Here we may abstract from such practical and gravely serious issues as are implicit in the dogma of a transition period (how long can an unredeemed promise retain its plausibility let alone its validity?) and concentrate instead on the meaning of the principle of choice that lies within Marxism. To be considered first of all is the fact that the Marxist principle of choice entails the defiance of the claim that the transcendence of self-preference on a massive scale implies or is the subversion of nature and, accordingly, has never been seen. Marxist orthodoxy may not simply demur to the bill of entailment; it must positively insist that widespread transcendence of self-preference is possible, and, hence, that Marxism is invulnerable to the charge of utopianism that is often leveled against it. The social transcendence of self-preference is indeed the subversion, but far more than the subversion it is the outright explosion of nature, of that nature to which has been attributed those human qualities such as egoism which are, as Marxism must affirm, in fact generated in history and replaced in the same medium. We might note in passing how widely this teaching of victory over nature differs from that enshrined in Christianity (with which Marxism is routinely compared) and from that which is prominent in the modern scientific philosophies of "conquest of nature" from Bacon to Hegel. Christianity and science, to use the latter term broadly, understand the effectual reality of unchanging nature and conceive of a victory over it through faith or reason as in no way identical with its demythologization. One is entitled, therefore, to speak of the Marxist conception of choice as being radically anti-natural in the sense that it is hostile to the ideology of nature rather than to the nature whose reality is impugned. I leave for other occasions any judgments of the plausibility or utility of such a conception.

What is one to say about the mutual compatibility of two social systems, both of which claim to embody freedom, but one of which attaches its principle of choice to a well-worn universal, namely, nature, inferred from observation and the other of which derives its principle of choice from the rejection of that universal as outworn and imaginary? That each might adapt itself to the other in ways that, although marginal are yet noteworthy, is not inconceivable. But in order to conceive a democratic Marxism or Marxist democracy in the fullest sense, one must be prepared to tolerate one paradox or another: a democratic mass free to respond to its natural impulses arbitrarily renouncing them and seeking only the good of the whole, or a thoroughly socialized mass conducting its affairs according to the rules of a game whose purpose is to win. (The inappropriateness of game-theoretic analysis of choice to activities in a Marxist society *qua* Marxist seems to follow directly from the expulsion of winning from the ends of a socialist mass more than from the political modes of a society of democratic self-seekers.) It might be argued in favor of the compatibility and, indeed, the veritable synthesis of naturalistic democracy and Marxian socialism that such decisive equilibria as are manifest in the equality of marginal revenues and costs, developed spontaneously in egoist market models, can be simulated and reproduced by the machinery of socialist planning; or one might argue more broadly that the conditions of rivalry and friction can when necessary be introduced in facsimile in a society that exists in order to transcend all effectual disunity. The argument would be weak, however, for even the perfectly effective replication of an outcome of the activity of the democratic animus would signify nothing for the affinity of that animus with the contrary spirit and aspiration of socialism. As much could be said regarding the numerous measures of regulation and redistribution adopted by the democracies, in apparent mimicry of socialism but across the grain of the undiluted egoism of primordial naturalistic democracy.

After all has been said that can be said in a speculative vein, there remains a question that can be answered only empirically. It runs as follows: granting that the principle of democracy is the egoism, even the natural egoism, of the many relatively poor, is it not possible that the preponderant poor may be made to perceive their salvation in the supreme welfare society projected by Marxism? Cannot Marxism promise the most successful satisfaction of the natural desires of individuals by offering the conditions of the hive or the herd? Has modernity in some way brought mankind within sight of a social order in which the *demos* seeks the satisfaction of individual, irrepressible, and natural desires through the instrumentalities of a state in which "nothing and no one can free a person from the compulsory demands of society, its laws that are obligatory for all."[1] There is no way to dispel the empirical possibility of such an outcome; but that eventuality would leave in its wake a question about the society in which the aggressive animus that suffuses individual autonomy and that subserves individual autarky has either become atrophied or, at the very least, is outlawed constitutionally. Is that society not *ipso facto* non-democratic? Nothing that has been learned about human society could justify the conclusion that friction and rivalry belong so singularly to democratic life that democracy is present where and to the extent that they are present; but it is plausible to maintain that where they are absent or banned, democracy – and perhaps politics altogether – has been superseded.

The foregoing points to the second theme under which I propose to consider the mutual compatibility of democracy and Marxian socialism. This theme is identified by the ruling question that arises under it: can we discern with the necessary responsibility and sufficient clarity a primary human temper that animates democratic life and the comparable one for socialism; and will they if they emerge, be mutually compatible?

The issue of the correspondence between a particular political order and some human temper, animus, character, or type has engaged the thought of writers known to us since Plato, who connects each regime with the pre-dominant influence of a certain human capacity or passion, or some equilibrium among a number of them. Montesquieu writes of the spirit of laws and is much occupied with "the spirit of monarchy," "the spirit of democracy" and so on,

1 K. Chernenko, quoted in translation, *New York Times*, September 26, 1984, p. 6.

by which he means the deep human drive or motivation that prevails over all others in the specific regime and thus gives its overriding character to the society itself. Kant, at the end of the long footnote on Professor Schiller early in *Religion within the Limits of Reason Alone*, trenches on a related subject when he reflects on the psychological substratum of goodness in man, though admittedly not man *qua* citizen of a particular regime. When Nietzsche looks beyond good and evil, he discovers in *ressentiment* what he takes to be the deep animus that inspires or pervades all mass politics. And when other writers refer to a democratic and an authoritarian personality, they may have in view certain human propensities or impulsions that are not themselves political, that are primordial in relation to the overt political opinions, choices, and acts, but that have a decisive political influence. I wish to consider in a preliminary way whether or not there are subliminal or, at any rate, affective and, as such, subpolitical correlates of democracy and socialism, with a view to considering the mutual concord or discord of those correlates and, thus, of the concomitant political systems.

From the outset, we must agree to deprive ourselves of the apparent evidence of certain concrete experiences, namely, those of the democratic and Marxist countries, because of the difficulty, insurmountable at least by me, of distinguishing what may be attributed to national character or tradition, what to the peculiarities of British, American, Soviet, Chinese, or Cuban rule, and what to democracy or socialism itself. But part of my concern will be the human traits that are fostered by, as well as the impulses that are drawn upon by, the alternative social systems, and it would be impossible to discuss those plausibly while refusing on principle to observe the available specimens. For example, one might speculate that some cognate of self-assertiveness finds expression in naturalistic democracy, and the social expression of that deep animus is bound to encourage either belligerence or cupidity. But which, in fact, is it? We must leave open the possibility that we shall be unable to dispose of the issue before us – the mutual compatibility of socialism and democracy – without empirical materials that are very elusive.

Setting all such difficulties aside, I will begin my inquiry into what ultimately animates the two regimes with a question: what is democracy? The formal, familiar definition of it as rule by the people is, of course, not incorrect or, not *simply* incorrect, but it is nearly useless for the present purpose. Surprisingly, the respect in which it is close to incorrect proves to be helpful for us now: "the People" in the abstract may be thought to rule but in fact very few people rule, strikingly few seek office, and relatively few manifest a desire to participate in the selection of those who do rule. From this it may be gathered that the decisive human impulse defining democracy is not the passion to rule, but rather, perhaps, the refusal to be ruled by any man or men who claim to rule without the *explicit*, not the merely tacit consent of "all." This is an indirect expression of at least one formula for equality. The animus within this claim of equality is a species of pride, an ambivalent expression of self-regard: each is as worthy as every other, and no other is more worthy than the first. This pride of jealousy or of invidiousness relies on an opinion of the self and of the other that may be rendered cardinally as well as ordinally: to be as worthy as others who themselves have no such ambition as drives them toward rule and no such merit as raises them above "equality" is to make a proud claim to a modest estate. Lest it be thought that this judgment constitutes an instant disparagement of the dignity of the democratic spirit, it should be pointed out that the generalization of so unassuming a form of pride accomplishes the conjunction of the effectual political impotence of each individual with a sense of his human worth. This notable conjunction could, it is true, be achieved by universal religion, in the absence of each man's political significance, but only where religion might be made to count.

Abstaining from further judgment of the worth of the sense of worth that accompanies the democratic claim of equality, it is easy to see the element of spirited self-assertion that infuses democracy, and to see also the convergence between the self-assertiveness so uncovered and what was previously argued to be the self-asserting end of naturalistic democracy viewed as a medium of choice. It is equally easy to see the similarity, if not identity between the animus of equality and that of marketplace competition, which evinces in behavior a simultaneous self-assertion and other-denial, or "out-doing," as Socrates might have said.[2]

What, in the same vein, is Marxist or modern communism? It is a project for the human condition that, to speak negatively at first, cannot be defined in terms of relation between men and ruling or being ruled because it aspires to the transcendence of rule properly so-called in the classless and, therefore, stateless society. Positively put, communism is a project for uncoerced life. Since the elimination of coercion in the political sense is a concomitant or by-product of the abolition of subordination in the sphere of production, a sphere considered primordial in Marxian socialism, the removal of exogenous constraint or coercion may be considered all-inclusive as encompassing the transcendence of politics and economics alike. The formula "From each according to his ability, to each according to his needs" is in its own way an announcement of the transcendence of economics, and may serve as such until a conception of economics becomes available that is free of the implication of scarcity, actual or felt.

The removal of coercion, specifically of state and economic coercion, presupposes the highest degree of conscious sociality among the denizens if the Marxist project is to materialize according to plan. It is imaginable that the

2 Plato, *Republic*, 349 b-c.

socialization of the ownership of the means of production would operate as a mere condition modifying the behavior of the denizens and causing them to respond to needs and desires in a manner that would have the outward appearance of cooperative good will but was in fact automatic. This outcome would frustrate the intention of Marxian socialism, which is precisely to humanize the members of society, to free them and above all to make them live as human beings do who are conscious that there is no conflict between themselves and any significant "other" in their environment to impose on them and to which they must feel strange. It would be misleading to say that no self would define itself by reference to anything other than itself, but it would not be misleading to say that to the extent that every conscious and self-conscious self must distinguish and thus define itself with reference to others, the socialist self would do so in the consciousness that no other, however distinguishable, is hostile. The condition of the socialist man might be freedom, understood as freedom from coercion and thus, to speak loosely, freedom to live; but the animus or spirit is not freedom but, rather, some state of the soul correlative with that peculiar and peculiarly based freedom. One can only speculate, for every aspect of what we are discussing is in the realm of the projected: there are no empirical materials that would not offer dubious data. One may speculate that the human being living in the absolutely hospitable medium, relieved of every significant frustration or strangeness, would exhibit a vigor of high activity, a spiritedness of productivity in all directions (by hypothesis, compatible with social living). One may equally plausibly speculate that activity presupposes resistance or a monitory other, even if only in the form of a recognized contrivance such as the production quota which must acquire the meaning of a scrutinizing authority and under whose discipline the affected human beings would become intimidated, routinized, or conscientious, depending on the effects of other causes.

It may be a serious defect of the socialist vision that the human product which it projects as its goal simply cannot with any confidence be connected with the causes that are supposed to produce it. The failure of that connection greatly weakens the possibility of comparing empirically the animus of democracy and that of socialism, but it leaves intact the comparison on the plane of aspiration. On that level, it is safe to say that, in envisioning the unalienated man, the man who is at home among humanity, socialism envisions the man whose environment is parental and fraternal (with no sophistications of sibling rivalry relevant) or, in other words, a man whose *sense* of his own dignity, as distinguished from any claimed objective basis for it, is caring or a species of love. The environment from which alienation has been removed is dominated not by justice – to each according to what he deserves – but by caring. I propose, therefore, this second ground on which to reflect on the mutual compatibility of democracy and Marxian socialism: naturalistic democracy tacitly presupposes and without conscious intent may even project the human being in whom the self-preserving and self-serving aggressiveness evoked by Machiavelli and Hobbes is the irreducible, characteristic animus, while modern communism projects the human being in whom the decisive animus will be a species of affectionate sociality. While I freely acknowledge the great lacunae of information that impair the foregoing, I conclude that democracy and socialism conceive of two different and opposing states of man, indeed, of two different kinds of men, and to that extent or in that sense the two systems are mutually incompatible. I leave out of consideration what must be included in any discussion that could claim to be conclusive: how far can the aggressive animus and the affectionate be added to one another to form, in this peculiarly modern milieu, the aggregate of *thymos* and *eros* sought by Plato for the guardians of the excellent city?

That there is room for both of these dispositions in each human being is beyond doubt, but that more than one of them could be primordial is offensive to logic even if not refutable by experience, leaving the synthesis of democracy and socialism possible only in a weak sense, i.e., as the mixture of the two in various proportions but always with one in the ascendant: witness, for example, the Swedish and Israeli societies. There are indeed terms on which the reconciliation of democracy and socialism can be only too easily posited, but they are terms which will outrage the partisans of each and the projectors of their synthesis. According to the famous account of liberalism, both democratic and socialist, presented by Nietzsche, they are equally mean-spirited excrescences of the Judaeo-Christian morality, sharing as their common denominator neither spirit nor love but, rather, the hate-driven resentment felt by the base for the noble. This line of argument favoring the compatibility of democracy and socialism is to be rejected as irrelevant to the practical situation and of little positive help in answering our immediate question.

Finally, I shall take up the theme of the mutual compatibility of democracy and Marxian socialism in a third mode, that of the history of the thought that finds expression in the two social orders. I shall reason from a composite premise that needs to be made explicit, namely, that liberal democracy and Marxian socialism define the essential political possibilities for the modern world into the foreseeable future, and that these concrete political orders can be understood – I will refrain from saying must be understood – by the light of the concepts that are decisively active in each. Those concepts and the arguments in which they are embedded are an important ingredient of modern political philosophy. Thus, the effectual modern political alternative can be referred to and conceived in the terms of modern political philosophy. From this it follows that the mutual compatibility of democracy and Marxian socialism would be the rational consequence or expression of the mutual compatibility or even the unity of the corresponding strands of modern political philosophy, while the mutual incompatibility of democracy and Marxian socialism would indicate a discord and, hence, a disunity within what is called, perhaps simplistically, "modern political philosophy." By a species of logistic metonymy, replacing each regime by its rational surrogate, I shall sketch an argument in which will be considered the relation to each other of the elements of the effectual modern political alternative through a brief presentation of certain modern political conceptions that I take to be preponderant.

It would not be misleading to declare that such classic moderns as Machiavelli, Hobbes, and Locke discovered in nature no higher duty for mankind than to take care of themselves and no more comprehensive freedom than the unlimited right to do so. A conception of rights or freedom in the service of duty and of duties that rest on the same natural ground as rights produces a formidable moral construction, one that seemed problematic only in a few manageable respects, all growing out of the need to explain the origins of civil society out of natural freedom. By the use of explanations that differed from one another in ways that need not concern us, Hobbes and Locke showed the reasons that and the devices by which men gave their consent to be governed. Inseparable from those explanations was the notion that the primary rights of man are not only natural but also inalienable. They accompany man into civil life, in which freedom means nothing less than the exercise of those inalienable rights to life, liberty, and estate. The Hobbesian proposition that the right to the end implies the right to the means thereto was not rejected by Locke, who, in elaborating the evolution of the right of property, the means to life, traced rightful possession to the mixing of one's labor with that to which no one else had a rightful claim. Appropriation is the algetic projection of oneself onto an object through the act of "mixing one's labor" with it, infusing it and thus indelibly marking it with what is, without further analysis of the self, essential to oneself.

Questions of a larger possible meaning of freedom, specifically of freedom of the will, were of course recognized, but they were disposed of by Hobbes and Locke in a naturalistic way, by identifying will with a mental function under the control of a subject capable of suspending judgment. This particular assimilation to each other of will and mind was naturalistic in the sense that it looked in the opposite direction from, for example, Hegel's similar identification which served the intention of Kant, namely, to emancipate the will and thus the subject from natural necessity. This is worth saying, in the present context because it directs attention to Spinoza's exposure of the naturalized will as highly problematic. It was Spinoza's task to reconcile with each other the dictum of "no *imperium in imperio*," no human enclave of exemption from natural causality, and the existence of a true human freedom, that is, a freedom from mere responsiveness in a mechanical whole. He performed this task in the last part of his *Ethics*, by distinguishing activity from passivity, the act of mind from the response of body, having first erected the structure of the unicity of substance within which he could defend himself against the charge that he arbitrarily deprived nature of simplicity. After Spinoza, the articulation with each other of nature and a will compatible with requirements of freedom had to preoccupy Rousseau, Kant, and Hegel in ways that prepared the work of Marx. It may be added in passing that the scrutiny of natural causation undertaken from the perspective of morality and freedom was joined by the scrutiny of natural causation undertaken by Hume from the perspective of epistemology and metaphysics. The Kantian contribution to the patrimony of Marx should be understood as including what Kant owned that he had received from Hume, namely, a disparagement of the empirical, which Kant and then Marx could reconcile with the exalting of history through teleological reasonings that I cannot now take up.

The preparation for the work of Marx that was contained in the thought of his predecessors may be collapsed, for our purpose, into the Hegelian doctrine of personality and, thus, of autonomy. The fulfillment of the human condition requires the conjunction of freedom and reason that emerges when the human subject asserts his subjectivity while or in cheerfully willing all those outcomes whose rationality is evinced in their perfect harmony with the requirements of society, i.e., of the state. The utterance of the human subject in an external thing that is called his property is a stage along the ascent to the ethical life. The classic modern conception of property as being in support of freedom defined by reference to life has been replaced by a conception of property in support of freedom defined by reference to autonomy of will consummated in perfect rational sociality.

Marx's efforts to emphasize his originality and, especially, to widen the distance between Hegel and himself, are not relevant to our present purpose, which is to judge the mutual compatibility of naturalistic democracy and Marxian socialism. My intention in sketching certain developments in modern dogma has been to suggest that the democracy and socialism in which we are interested are the concrete expressions of a set of conceptions that may for some purposes be regarded as the modern unity, and for other purposes must be regarded as a duality. Modernity has been unified in its formulation of the human problem in terms of the mutual adjustment of nature and freedom. It has been deeply divided through the efforts put forth to elevate the conception of freedom out of the gravitational field of mere preservation. Naturalistic democracy grew out of the senior line and Marxian socialism out of the cadet branch of modern political philosophy. Such a purely formal statement of the case gives the impression that they are divided by a family quarrel; but some family quarrels become known as civil wars, and Marx, for whatever his opinion on the subject is worth, inclined to the view that his system is so radically different from what went before that the issue between them must almost inevitably be resolved in violence.

There is a sense in which Marxism may be perceived as itself a synthesis of contrasting elements. Locke's doctrine of property puts heavy emphasis on the mixing of labor, of something irreducibly one's own, with the unformed or unappropriated, and in so doing gave inspiration to the labor theory of value. Marx could not and did not wish to escape the labor theory of value, but he adapted it decisively: he envisioned labor as being transformed from toil, the painful and degrading servitude of wage earners, to the satisfying, because uncoerced *activity* of the productive animal destined under the right conditions to actualize in the concrete external all the latent human power otherwise doomed to suffocation within. The scope of Marx's adaptation of the labor theory of property and value, and the dubiousness of the claim that Marxism is an effectual synthesis, may be gathered from the realization that the primordial labor theory tacitly accepts while Marx rejects as a presupposition that man will forever gain his bread in the sweat of his face, i.e., painfully, just as women will bring forth the product of *their* labor. The extent to which Marx fell in with the spirit of revisionist modernity in projecting a human condition unfettered by nature is a measure of the incompatibility of Marxian socialism with naturalistic democracy.

Testing the mutual compatibility of democracy and Marxian socialism by the three criteria proposed in this paper – choice, animus, and genealogy – has produced a signal that is negative, but not overwhelmingly so. I have argued that a human mass left free to express its inclinations could not be expected to choose a social organization dominated by principles that include the need for overturning the very inclinations that rule in the electing mass. I have tried to show that each of the two systems grows from and is nourished by a primal human thrust, and that the aggressive animus of the one contradicts the specific eroticism of the other, leaving aside speculations on the reducibility of hostility and affection to one another. And, finally, I have sketched the developments in philosophic thought that can be regarded as delineating the being and becoming of the two social systems, and find that Marxism and liberal democracy are the phenomenalizations of theoretical projects whose differences are so great, notwithstanding a common parentage, that the compatibility with each other of the respective social orders can only be doubtful. I believe that the weight of evidence available by the means I have used is against their mutual compatibility. Much persuaded of this, I am nevertheless anxious to avoid proving that the bumblebee cannot fly.

5
Activity, Philosophy, and the Open Society

The coiner of the expression "open society" is, of course, free to appropriate those words to the meaning that he has in mind in inventing the term; but when he uses that freedom, he stimulates us to wonder about the meaning of that combination of words in itself and apart from his intention. Here, I propose to look at the expression "open society" naively, as if to ask without partiality what an open society might be.

In what way or ways can a "society" be "open"? The question may be approached through openness itself: what are the ways of openness? A flower, a door, and an eye can be open, but each only in its own way. The flower, as open, is an entity that has undergone a change which we think of as a development, that is, an ascent, in the course of which a fullness that was potential and concealed came out into the open or into the light of day. Obedient to influences hard to define, the flower has disclosed either itself or those "influences" that are at work on itself and has arrived at an openness which is, by the way, the necessary prelude to its decline out of the light of day. For a society to be open in this sense, it must have reached a fulfillment implicit in its kind, either *qua* society or *qua* particular regime, or merely *qua* individual state; and that in turn means that societies, regimes and countries belong to the class of entities that unfold, stand forth in revelation, and then shut down towards death. History appears to confirm beyond doubt that political beings belong to that class. It seems, then, that an open society is one whose truest, most inward being has come to light in a concrete efflorescence, fated some day to dissolve.

Is it possible to say precisely and concretely what would stand forth revealed in the fullness of society's openness? Would one recognize that fullness in a moral fact? In a condition of high culture – music, literature, the arts? In a perfection of religious life? In a plenitude of wealth and power? Or perhaps in a state of perfect concord among the inhabitants of the realm? In groping toward the indispensable concreteness, we find ourselves in need of an answer to the question, "What is society?" Thus, if it were true that the essence of society is a bondedness, a being drawn together, a likemindedness, mutuality or "integration" of members, then the fully opened society would be the society that is most nearly a One. When Aristotle criticizes the Platonic scheme of communism he shows reasons for rejecting this conception of society, although when he insists that there be a friendship as well as a justice among men who form a polis, he seems to require that a society possess exactly such a bondedness if the members are to be free men rather than slaves. For the present purpose, it is sufficient to say that society is some kind of a one that has emerged from a many. The open society, then, is the one that has reached and disclosed the proper *concord* of unity, participation, and distribution that lies in the essence of society itself.

It is impossible to come to that conclusion without putting aside all the other suggested ends or goods of society – aesthetic, moral, imperial, religious, or still others. For example, it is conceivable that a society has opened to its fullness when human productivity has reached a peak within it: when its musical tradition has produced a Bach, its literature a Shakespeare, and its sculpture a Michelangelo; or rather, to follow another road, that its moral practice has reached the austerity of Geneva. How may the society be judged with regard to its openness if these various fulfillments are not synchronous, as in fact they need not be? Perhaps the problem can be solved only by ordering these regions of perfection, which means referring them all to the meaning of society itself and ranking them according to their proximity to that core of society's being. Even this will not do, because it implies that it is by virtue of the nature of society that, for example, unity stands highest, art next, and morality next in the order of fulfillments – that it is more important that a society be one than that it be artistic or moral, if it is to be considered open. The actual order of these criteria is irrelevant to my purpose, for I wish to maintain only that the conception of open society that assimilates opening to efflorescence eventually falls back upon some definition of essential society, society-in-itself, a thing that does not effloresce but without which the efflorescence of society is incomprehensible. To be as explicit as possible, the essence of society determines the openness of society not so much in that the essence is the definition of society but rather in that it is necessary for knowledge or recognition of the openness of society. Openness as efflorescence is derivative from essence: the concept of "open" *in this mode* is therefore not available to anyone who rejects the reality of an essence that stands in the background to vouchsafe a meaning to the word "open" so used in reference to society. The investigation of that essence is philosophy.

Even without claiming to be thorough, we saw at the outset that there are three apparently quite different modes of open: as a flower, as a door, and as an eye. While we say commonly that the door is open, we mean that the doorway is unobstructed and that the house is open. An open passage is a neutral access to some space that is receptive to being filled with what is outside yet capable of being inside. Our next task is to think about a society that is open in the way in which an open house is open. We know what an open house is open to: it is open to strangers, outsiders, anyone outside who prefers to be inside, and it is open to whatever is in the air. Eventually we will have to ask ourselves what class or classes of things are free to enter – or in principle to leave – the open society without hindrance. It is obvious that more is involved than the migration of people. I should like to put off the consideration of this point until later and to take up instead the question, "What is the meaning of the condition of openness in a society?" with a view especially to the related question, "By what agency or means is the openness of a society brought about?" The restriction of these questions to the mode of openness indicated by the figure of the house and its door is always to be understood. In terms of that image, I am asking something like, "What is the state of a house with an open door, and how can one understand the coming to be of that openness?"

An open house is one whose master does not have control over the relation between what stands without and what stands within. An open society, correspondingly, would resemble to use another image, a living cell in which the osmotic process had gotten so far out of order that material passed arbitrarily in both directions through the cell wall. This would kill the cell, but I do not wish to say straightaway that the same condition would kill the society; I wish rather to think about the masterlessness of such a state or the utter passivity of it. In order to understand the passivity of openness, we must grasp the determination of the society, just as we would have to conceive clearly the walls of the house or the cell, if we were to think profitably about the comings and goings between the thing and its externality. What determines or constitutes a society? (I should make clear that I have in mind society in its most intense form, namely, political society.) I will accept as well established the proposition that what constitutes the political society is its constitution. That being stipulated, the passivity of a political society, and therewith its openness in the present sense, would mean the uncontrolled movement of extraneous material into the body of the constitution, say by amendment or simply through usage, and the similar elimination of material from it through desuetude, interpretation, or in any other way.

The imputation of deliberate agency and therewith of active conscious choice, in this remark on constitutions in flux, will be weakened as soon as we make explicit that the constitution need not at all be written. Thus, amending the constitution might have very little in common with our own well-defined procession of steps for proposing and ratifying an amendment. Where the constitution is unwritten and the flux of the constitution is not governed by any identifiable agent's intention, the question arises immediately: Who is responsible for the change? And that question points to the larger one: Who or what is at the source of the constitution as a whole? These questions come into view through our interest in the openness of society as equivalent to the passivity of society. In order to defend the open society from the imputation of passivity, we are searching for an agent whose active choice determines the society, i.e., its constitution, and determines also the changes of the constitution. We are perhaps searching for the self of a political society. If we fail to find such a thing, we shall have to entertain the possibility that the open society is an object at the mercy of history, whatever that proves to mean. That, were it to eventuate, would be worth noting, if only for the reason that a famous advocate for the open society considers it to be rationalized exactly as the antithesis of historicism, of theories proclaiming a necessity in history that must stifle the freedom and reason of open society. But without an autonomous society-self determining the flux into and from the constitution of the society, the open society appears heteronomous, adrift, and passive – especially passive.

In order to avoid that conclusion if possible, let us boldly suppose that what we call metaphorically the society-self is non-metaphorically the likemindedness, concord, or consensus of all those who associate. Then this likemindedness is the active regulator of the egress and ingress between open society and its externality. But besides the dubiousness of personifying Concord and making of it an active being, a god of sorts, there is the vexing question of the *origin* of that likemindedness. In the first place, it might be attributed to something simply present in all the associators, something that they share and that makes them see the decisive political things in one and the same way. This breaks down as soon as we recognize that such an explanation is tantamount either to maintaining that there are innate, natural insights regarding constitutions – in which case, presumably, these would be shared by all men and there would be a single constitution for all of mankind – or that there are local concords of limited duration, generated by what we loosely call circumstances, such as the climate, the soil, the sea, the mines, and threats or opportunities offered by neighboring populations. In this latter case, the likemindedness would be a simple product of the external circumstances acting as causes to determine a group of minds in a single mold. Such a concord would be merely the indirect means by which the external circumstances would operate as remote causes of, in the present case, the adoption and alteration of constitutions. In no way, then, does anything we have yet uncovered point to the autonomous society-self whose activity would secure the open society against the imputation of passivity.

There is yet another path on which to seek the source or nature of the common mind of society, and that is the one indicated by the old notion that the laws and constitution are the educators of men. It is obvious immediately that the truth of this adage would seem to remove all support from the proposition that there is an *autonomous* social concord that regulates the gate through which migrations into and out of the constitution take place. We would be asserting that the constitution forms the men and the men so formed allow a free flow of alien material into the regime and of domestic material out of it; that is to say, they then form it *after* it has formed them. The circularity of the influence of regime on men and men on regime significantly weakens the argument for the existence of an autonomous and hence active agent in the open society as such; but we must be careful not to exaggerate the scope of that circularity. It would be such an exaggeration to deny, for example, that the open constitution might teach men that they are free to deform the constitution in any way they like. Astonishingly, the constitution might form its pupils to betray it by deforming it according to their own independent lights. Rather than that, it might admonish them, indeed form them in the belief, that the one thing they are not free to reject or modify is the openness of the regime. Such a restriction would not offend logic but it would certainly deprive the successive generations of men of their absolute freedom or autonomy as agents. Stated otherwise, it violates the premise of openness in the society, understanding openness as analogous to the removal of the door from its hinges at the entrance to the house with the concomitant freedom of *every* element of the constitution to depart the structure.

Perhaps the last word we need say on this part of the subject is at once the simplest and the most inclusive: the very notion of the *formation* of men by an instrument which they legislate only in the weak sense of consenting to it is on its face a derogation from the autonomy we are seeking. Until we find that autonomy, we have not found the self-activation that can save the open society (in the mode of the open house) from the imputation that it is passivity masquerading as freedom.

Mindful of the passivity that permeates the openness of the open society in the present mode, we return to the question posed earlier, namely, "By what agency or means is the openness of a society brought about?" Surely there is no reason to accept as truth the mere prejudice that a passive progeny must have been engendered by a passive progenitor, whatever that might mean: perhaps there is decisive activity at its begetting. Let us begin again by returning to our image of the house and noticing the simplest fact about it: it consists of, it *is*, four walls and a roof. By its nature or essence it is an enclosure. The door is an exception to the enclosing integrity of the wall. That it is an indispensable exception or breach without which the house could serve no practical purpose does not affect its being an exception or breach. To correspond with the (openable) house in its enclosing integrity there is the constituted society, whose constitution distinguishes the order of life lived within its space from all orders that lie outside. Men live within a social space that is determined, given its boundaries and thus its shape or form, by the constitution. The tautologous cast of this statement – the social space is formed or constituted by the constitution – might be excused if the remark draws us closer to the perception of the constitution, and therewith the political society, as, respectively, an artificial horizon and the territory encompassed within that horizon – to borrow a famous metaphor. If we are in fact asking who draws the horizon around the open society, we find ourselves asking who defines the world for those who live within that horizon and that society, for beyond the horizon there is nothing on earth, though an infinity aloft. I will assume for purposes of the argument the answer most favorable to the presuppositions of the open society, namely, that the horizon is inscribed not by a stylus activated by any mechanism, whether historical or natural, but by an active human agency that is free in the fullest sense possible. Without any attempt to defend this, I will suppose and assert that speculative reason is that consummately free human agency whose act and expression is philosophy. Granting this, if only to strengthen the case for autonomy and eventually authentic openness, we have arrived at the thought that it is philosophy that draws the horizons that constitute, define and bound or enclose the society whose possible openness is our problem.

Let us accept that the society capable of openness, of a certain kind of freedom, is the creature of philosophy or of unconditioned thought. What would be the status of that unconfined thought in the life lived within the horizon that constitutes the (open) society – the society of freest egress and ingress of all things? We may envision two possibilities: first, the migration of elements in both directions across the horizon is absolutely random, arbitrary or senseless, unaffected or unnoticed by a philosophy that looks elsewhere. Second, the power that drew the horizon continues ceaselessly to exercise the same power, continually revising its original draftsmanship, regulating the ingress and egress of elements, standing effectually as the freest or indeed the only perfectly free agent – free by virtue of reason – in the open society consecrated presumably to freedom and reason throughout. The alternative as presented means that the open society is either chaotic and forever in danger of decaying into its opposite without premeditation, or it is subject to the uninterrupted superintendence of its architect, who never surrenders his prerogative as re-creator. There is no apparent reason to presume that the recreation will strengthen rather than replace the open society, unless it be argued that the open society is and must be known to be the best political order. But the best political order, *qua* best, is immutable, closed, and of eternal or at least natural definition rather than being bounded by a horizon drawn by autonomous human agency. The autonomy of the human horizon-drawer would in the latter case be wholly accidental to the generation of the open society, which would then rest on chance rather than freedom.

The relation of philosophy and the open society is a precarious one, not because philosophy is traditionalist and confining, but for the opposite reason that it is prone to inquiry and thus to dissatisfaction except in the barely imaginable case that it finds itself in the absolute polity. In brief, the activity we may posit as generative of the open society and thus as clearing it somehow of the imputation of passivity so derogatory to it is an activity of speculative thought, of philosophy whose friendliness to the open society is as fickle as it is to political societies generally. Were the *continuing* activity of philosophy to be the token of the open society's own activity, that society would stand exposed as a mere formality or shell, an occasion for the activity of a thought whose own true love is a restless philandering rather than a fidelity to the system that shelters it in its butterfly peregrinations.

The imputation that the open society, in the mode of the open house, is decisively passive seems hard to shake off; but we have yet to think about another mode of openness, that which is figured in the image of the open eye, that might be more favorable in this or some other respect. Our question now is, "What should we think about a society that is open in the way in which an eye is open?" An eye is open when a certain barrier is removed between an outside and an inside. That barrier is not like the door of a house, for the door obstructs movements in both directions while an eyelid can restrain only the inbound movement. Moreover, the inside in the case of the eye is not only or primarily the eye itself, but rather the brain and then the mind. Thus, if we were to be able to understand the openness of society by a parallel with the openness of an eye, we would have to be able to find equivalents to the unidirectional movement and the peculiar capacity of the open eye to be struck from without but also to inspect, that is, to take the initiative. Let us abstract from the inertness of the open eye under impacts from without as having been sufficiently considered under the heading of passivity. That leaves for reflection openness that only admits, and that admits not only the unsought but the actively sought as well. On these terms, the open society would be the chronic ingester of a thing or things we have not named, for the benefit of something residing within which we have not identified. We must try first to understand what class or classes of thing enter or are drawn into the open society, or, to simplify the issue, to what is the open society open? Let us say provisionally that it is open to the ways of others and to the thoughts of others, and it is open also directly to all those things that it might encounter indirectly through the thoughts of others – call this somewhat grandly the whole.

What can be meant by being open to the ways of others? It means to be interested in and curious about the manners, politics, culture, history, and so on of other people, "other" being understood in any way at all. This is genuine but lukewarm openness. Being fully open to Buddhism, for example, would include a disposition to think earnestly about adopting it – taking it in the practical way. In this demanding sense, a serious scholar of comparative religion might have to be described as open to the objects of his study only in the limited or lukewarm sense. In which of these senses can or must the open society be open to the ways of others? I will assert arbitrarily that if it is the essentially open society, then it must be open in the strict or demanding sense. I will not comment on the evident impracticality of openness in this perennially destabilizing sense, were it to prevail in the absence of some influence that would preserve the sheer identity or continuity of the open society. What would the nature of such an influence be? It would be a critical power, capable of distinguishing those alien things that are fit to be chosen and those to be passed over or blamed. It would resemble Plato's ability to contemplate Dorian institutions and find them choice-worthy, perhaps even for Athens. This brings us sharply up against the fact that the power to judge the alien things in a spirit of strictest openness could not function if it were not reflexive, turned inward as earnestly and probingly as it is turned outward. Intelligent strict openness must include introspection: openness to others is defective if its obverse is not a competent openness to itself on the part of the society. Thus we learn that we must make an addition to the list of things to which the open society is open: itself.

What can be meant by a society's openness to itself? I shall take it to mean capable both morally and intellectually, of the skepsis of its own full experience. But skepsis is a looking, a mere looking as one might say, which is to be perfected in an act of judgment, a pronouncement of good or bad. Judgment entails the availability of standards of judgment. Whence do they come? From the vantage point of the open society – open in the mode of the open eye – they can come from anywhere within or without the society: from strange philosophy, from true or false prophecy, from intuition, and so on. Is there no valid judgment on the validity of the standards for judging experience? The question is not any more pertinent to the status of an open society than to the condition of society altogether. The answer is, I take it, philosophy – again speaking with a limited purpose and thus profanely. Philosophy, or thought, provides the criteria of the criteria.

We have stumbled on a considerable difficulty. Stated briefly, the open society must know itself; it must scan its experiences with a view to their replacement if need be by alien things to which the society is open. We have made the suggestion, so easily as to be condemned as complacent, that philosophy sit in judgment and preside at the port of entry. But if any one thing has ever been made clear to us by our experience, it is that we habitually construe our experience, give it a meaning, under the influence of a system of thought or at least prejudice, and maybe even of philosophy. In the worst case, then, our very experiences would have a meaning that is imparted to them by some system of thought; and we would then go on to interpret and evaluate those same experiences by the application of criteria of judgment supported by some system of thought. Unless we are tacitly referring to two mutually independent systems of thought, we are talking nonsense. And if we are referring to two systems of thought, we are talking about the creatures who subscribe to them, beings who regularly apply criteria to their criteria. In saying these things, I mean to imply nothing about the soundness or the practicality of open society, but rather to say something about the conditions of meaning and existence of such a society not necessarily understood by those who argue for it. I do not believe that the difficulty I have just sketched is in principle insuperable. It seems to me not only possible, but desirable, that there be two concurrent systems of thought simultaneously active in the society: one, the prevailing political animus that embodies and prescribes the social ideal to and for the citizens, and which stands in the highest place as the criterion of experience and the rule of political orthodoxy sometimes called ideology; the other is philosophy proper, the criterion of all criteria. There is no difficulty in conceiving the co-existence of such so called systems of thought as long as one understands clearly that their co-existence is in one and the same society but not, *qua* supreme, in one and the same mind.

Thus it appears again that the open society is not clearly conceivable without the supposition of the activity of philosophy within it, this time in order to preserve it by imposing checks on what may enter it from without and to assist it in its openness to itself. Philosophy preserves the identity of the open society by providing it with the indispensable closure. The open society belongs to a class of things whose preservation depends on the mitigation of its own essential principle.

Having in this way introduced philosophy as a condition of the open society, I will take advantage of its presence as a means of explaining that society's openness to the whole and to the thoughts of others about all things. Considering the isolation of philosophy from the plane of political orthodoxy as a basis of openness in society, I would say that the open society is sanity incarnate. It is also indistinguishable, in this respect, from good society irrespective of openness. So far as open society does not perceive this about itself, it lacks what I believe is a necessary condition for its own existence, namely, a clear conception of the place of philosophy in political life altogether.

To conclude: In this very brief sketch, I have tried to show that society may be thought of as being open in the way of a flower, a door, and an eye. Its openness in the manner of the flower must be understood as dependent upon a recognition of essence, which means philosophy. Its openness in the manner of the door is tainted with passivity until cleansed by the presence of philosophy as the principle of activity within it. Its openness in the manner of an eye is dependent on the judging and hence closing power of philosophy, without which the open society would for yet another set of reasons lose itself.

It would appear that the preservation, to say nothing of the formation, of open society would depend upon the infusion of a constitution or of a social order with philosophy. Does this mean that men will not live openly until their governors become philosophers or philosophers become their governors? If so, it challenges Plato, whose Socrates gives reason to believe that such a success of philosophy would accompany or serve the closing of society. The authority of Plato is not as such decisive; neither can it be dismissed. The status of the open society might best, therefore, be regarded as uncertain as long as there is any reason to consider philosophy as both indispensable and antithetical to its existence. If the infusion of society with philosophy means the active presence therein of the deepest thought about humanity, one can conclude that the indispensable will not prove to be also the antithetical only by presupposing that open is best, which may not be merely presupposed. That the status of the open society is equivocal might mean that it has something in common with the worst and the best both of which are destined to precarious existence. We are thus brought to the threshold of the judgment that philosophy alone is competent to render, a judgment to which we cannot here proceed.

6
On the Dramatic End of Plato's Socrates

How does the structure of a philosophic exposition contribute to the meaning of a philosophic argument? I shall try to say something about the question in a context that is special and limited but not trivial – the context of a segment of the Platonic corpus. The dialogues to which I want to draw attention are those between the *Theaetetus* and the *Phaedo*; and before doing anything else, I must explain what I mean by "between." That explanation will serve to introduce the particular meaning of structure that will appear in the rest of this paper. The dialogues "between" the *Theaetetus* and the *Phaedo* would be, by one conventional reckoning, the ones that Plato wrote in that order. Of course, the order in which the dialogues were written remains largely conjectural, and whatever depends on a firm determination of that order is equally in doubt. There is, however, another order into which a number of the dialogues, especially those "between the *Theaetetus* and the *Phaedo*," can be placed with much greater certainty, namely, a dramatic order. If the order of composition may be called the poietic order of the dialogues, the order in which the conversations are depicted as occurring may be called the dramatic order. Of the poietic order one might say that it reveals the author's intellectual development; the dramatic order reveals his intention. I am going to suppose not only that Plato's intention is more distinctly inferable from the dramatic order in which he placed his inventions than any poietic order is inferable from any evidence that survives, but also that his intention is more important to our comprehension of his thought than is his development as a thinker. I concede with regard to the latter point that significant truths about an author's intention may lie concealed within his development; after all, his development is the growth or decline of his intention; yet even if only to follow the course with the less speculative premise, I shall throughout consider "structure" to mean dramatic order.

The *Theaetetus* is a Socratic dialogue that is recounted by one man to one or more others, some number of years after the words being reported are represented as having been spoken. The dialogue ends with Socrates' saying that he must go to the *stoa* of the king in order to answer to Meletus's indictment, but that he expects to meet the company again in the morning to continue the conversation. By ending the *Theaetetus* with this brief passage, Plato indicates that the trilogy of *Theaetetus*, *Sophist* and *Statesman* is at least a quartet that includes the *Euthyphro*, the dialogue that takes place at the porch of the king. The same concluding passage makes plain that the quartet occurs within weeks or months of the end of Socrates' life. (Also indicated is the need to interpret the *Euthyphro* as a component of the quartet into which Plato cast it. This means that the argument on the civil and theoretical implications of piety toward gods and fathers should be articulated with the arguments presented in the neighboring dialogues.)

It follows from the connection of *Theaetetus*, *Sophist* and *Statesman* with the trial of Socrates that that group of dialogues is linked in dramatic time with the other famous trilogy of *Apology of Socrates, Crito,* and *Phaedo*. In crowding these seven works upon each other in time, Plato signifies his conception of them as a unity of some kind, a unity that it is convenient to call the dramatic end of Plato's Socrates.

Of course one wonders how the supposition of this "structure" could contribute to the interpretation of the texts and the disclosure of Plato's thought. An easy conjecture is that Plato has devised an account of Socrates' end – his indictment, defense, condemnation and execution – that transcends the limits of the *Apology, Crito,* and *Phaedo*: an enhanced version of the trial of Socrates. This speculation assumes that the quartet should be drawn towards the trilogy for interpretation, that the center of gravity of the seven dialogues is the judgment of Socrates in a sense that is dominated by his civic indictment even though it transcends his public accusation and his own defense. I shall try to show, in the bulk of what follows, that useful though this conjecture may be, it needs to be stated differently. When the seven dialogues are examined concretely, they point to a still larger structure of Platonic dialogues, a larger structure that interests us because it does contain a judgment of Socrates, but on so broad a plane as to leave the trial as such shrunken by the expansion of the horizon within which it is viewed.

Specifically, the reader of the first trilogy will be aware that the three dialogues are, in different ways, penetrated by the presence of two famous rivals of Socrates, Protagoras and Parmenides. Protagoras is important to the argument of the *Theaetetus*, so important that Socrates impersonates him in a long speech in which Socrates does justice to Protagoras's views on perception, motion and knowledge with such success that Theodorus expresses his enthusiastic admiration. Theodorus, an active if sometimes reluctant interlocutor, is himself a Protagorean though apparently with reservations. His pupil is Theaetetus, who also appears to be Protagorean, although very docile to the argument of Socrates, perhaps because Protagoreanism is not a bad preparation for Socratism. (Of Simmias and Kebes, the Pythagoreans, similar things will be said below when we turn to the *Phaedo*.) As one might say, the *Theaetetus* is suffused with the spirit of Protagoras; but it is not for that reason an un-Socratic dialogue, rather if anything the reverse: Eucleides reports that he wrote this conversation down and that in the course of doing so, he would consult Socrates whenever he needed help in clearing up a doubtful point. This consultation would have to have taken place in the short and presumably preoccupied period between the indictment and the execution of Socrates. Besides embodying the active collaboration of Socrates in its written preservation, the Theaetetus contains an autobiography of Socrates, what one might call his obstetric autobiography, with a view to its content and also in order to distinguish it from the autobiography in the *Phaedo* – another superficially un-Socratic dialogue.

A point has been made of the Protagoreanism of the *Theaetetus*; but there is a dialogue called *Protagoras*, in which the thought of Protagoras is obviously prominent. Do the Protagoreanisms of *Theaetetus* and *Protagoras* harmonize? Why are two Protagorean dialogues necessary? Whatever the answers to these questions may be, the *Theaetetus* and *Protagoras* gravitate toward one another, and the *Protagoras* becomes attached to the basic structure of the septet by a line of filiation. In the same way, a line of attachment develops between the *Sophist* and *Statesman* on the one hand and the *Parmenides* on the other, for Parmenides is as actively present in the latter dialogues through the Eleatic Stranger as Protagoras is in the *Theaetetus*. The recurrence of themes in the Platonic dialogues is a familiar fact that would lead to the attachment of the *Meno* to our growing structure by the link of the doctrine of anamnesis, employed prominently in the *Phaedo*. Many other examples could be given. If carefully pursued, the dramatic, thematic, and personal ligatures would include some large part, perhaps all, of the Platonic corpus.

I have not come so far in order to suggest that there is a Platonic cosmos, but rather to speculate on what guided Plato in the construction of it. Raising the question is meant to set aside the routine reply that the shaping of the Platonic cosmos was governed by the shape of the real one – not because that is not true but because it is not what the already discerned structure indicates most pointedly, namely, that a great weight of non-Socratic thought presses on Socratism and must be reckoned with. The presence of non-Socratic thought defines the horizon in which the transpolitical or philosophic critique and apology of Socrates may be found. The cosmos to which the Platonic cosmos corresponds is to a surprising degree the theoretical, not the natural cosmos.

Taking advantage of the privilege claimed by introductions, I will introduce the body of the argument to come with an as yet unsupported assertion: it would not be wise to assume that Plato fashioned his world and populated it with non-Socratics merely to mirror the intellectual milieu that Socrates inhabited and, while sketching that world, to set the scene for Socrates to deflate every living and dead pretender to understanding beginning with Homer. It cannot be denied that Socrates is shown slaying his thousands; but his antagonists often have little enough to say for themselves and are not of great stature. Plato does cause his Socrates to put the armies of the fee-takers to the sword, but he also shows him at times occupying their towers without a proclamation to announce the appropriation. Most surprising, Socrates occasionally goes into direst battle armed with weapons borrowed from unidentified armories that belong to other champions whom Plato's contemporaries could and did name and who are recognized even by us. I have in mind, to give one striking example, the doctrine of invisible and most real intelligibles by which and by which alone the phenomenal world is to be understood. This was Pythagorean tradition by Socrates' time, though likely to be thought of by us as Socratic idealism. It is worth recalling that, in the *Parmenides* (130b), when Parmenides asks Socrates whether the ideas are his own invention and whether he thinks that there is likeness and unity and plurality apart from the concrete things that participate in these ideas in themselves, Socrates says yes, but his response appears directed to the second question, the first going unanswered. When Aristotle sets out, in *Metaphysics I*, to give the history of thought about causes, he sketches a picture of Greek intellectual life that should remind the reader of the mosaic panorama of the Platonic dialogues. In Aristotle's history, Plato looms large, as Socrates does in Plato's. Aristotle says that Plato was a Heracleitian both early and later in life, for he saw the world of phenomena as always in flux (*Metaphysics* 987a34). Is it not surprising that one could construct Plato-Socrates out of Pythagorean idealism and Heracleitian flux? In brief, there is a view of Plato and Socrates, and Aristotle is the greatest depictor of it, according to which Plato and Socrates are intimately bound in with and must be discussed as belonging to the milieu of that host we call pre-Socratic. In that view, the recognition of Plato-Socrates' preeminence does not sever their historical connection with their predecessors, nor does it entail their freedom from debt to those predecessors. The Platonic corpus seems at first like a depiction of the same pre-Socratic landscape, with Socrates included in it, but in a completely different perspective from Aristotle's. Those thinkers whose thought Aristotle diligently distills and criticizes appear, when they exist as personae of Plato's dialogues, like mere foils for the virtuosity of Socrates. Plato's perspective seems to make Socrates a giant among mediocrities and a luminescence among the dim or semidim. Did Plato not see Socrates on a human scale even as Aristotle saw Plato, who was called divine in his own lifetime? I believe that Plato's perspective was not less detached than Aristotle's, and I shall try to show this. But if it was thus clear-sighted, why was it given the appearance by its author of being the apotheosis of Socrates, the perfect philosopher with no debts, no peers, no errors, the man who cannot even proclaim his ignorance without adding luster to the testimonials of his wisdom? What was the unprecedented achievement of Socrates that justified so extraordinary a portrayal? The closing words of the *Phaedo* do not constitute an adequate answer. What follows here is an attempt to move toward an explanation, through the interpretation of a few elements of the *Theaetetus* and the *Phaedo*. My general intention is to argue that the Platonic corpus contains – perhaps simply is – the appraisal of Socrates; and that one of the instruments of appraisal is the depiction of Socrates as a man in the company of all those with whom it is useful to compare him, whom he taught, whom he could not teach, whom he refused to teach, and from whom he learned or conceivably even refused to learn.

The *Theaetetus* is recounted in Megara (whither Plato is said to have gone after the death of Socrates). In the recounted dialogue proper, Socrates is engaged in conversation with Theodorus, who is a geometer, an associate of Protagoras, and a teacher of Theaetetus. According to the tradition, he is someone with whom Plato himself studied in Cyrene. Theaetetus is introduced into the dialogue as the youth in the middle of a group of young men who are approaching. It becomes known that one of the others in the group is Young Socrates, the interlocutor of the *Statesman*. There must have been at least one more youth in order for Theaetetus to have been "in the middle," but no other youth is named or otherwise identified. Theaetetus is described as resembling Socrates in appearance; Young Socrates resembles him of course in name. Plato maintains silence in all respects about the conjectured third youth. Socrates begins his interrogation of Theaetetus by enumerating, in the form of a question, the subjects that he supposes Theaetetus to be studying with Theodorus: geometry, astronomy, harmony, and arithmetic (145c, d), which the youth confirms. This list is the same ("music" being substituted for "harmony") as the list of arts that Protagoras recites when, in the *Protagoras*, (318e) he derides the vulgar sophists who force their pupils back to the distinct conventional arts rather than teaching them, as he himself does, good counsel in domestic and civic affairs so that they may be as effective as possible in the city both in action and in speech. Protagoras is said to look at Hippias while speaking; it may be understood that he would look as pointedly at Theodorus. In pursuing the interrogation of Theaetetus, Socrates asks whether the increase of knowledge is the same as increase of wisdom, and whether knowledge and wisdom are the same. Now arises the chief question of the dialogue: what is knowledge? Theaetetus answers by referring to Theodorus's curriculum of the arts, adding also the productive arts such as shoemaking. Socrates turns this answer back because it gives examples instead of saying what the thing itself is; it adduces a many where a one is wanted. This is the same objection with which Socrates confutes Meno's definition of virtue (*Meno* 72a, b). What might be called the routine position of Socrates, namely, that the intelligible is a unity to which the multiplicity must be referred, bears an unexpected resemblance to Protagoras's apparent reason for disapproving of the ordinary sophists; they offer an assortment, he purveys wisdom itself in its unity.

Theaetetus admits to a concern over the meaning of knowledge and

Socrates encourages him to take heart and go forward, offering to put his own peculiar powers at Theaetetus's disposal during the investigation. This becomes the occasion for a lengthy statement by Socrates about himself, a statement that might be called his obstetric autobiography because he discloses in the course of it that he is a midwife of thoughts. His self-description is a curious mixture of depreciation and pretension, for he appears as a barren god, incapable of generating a thought but able to deliver a man of those he has within, distinguishing the pregnancies that issue in progeny from those that have spurious fruit and, like a god in his beneficence, fostering the true and exposing the false offspring. It is worth noticing that this characterization of his dialectic pedagogy differs from the one set forth in the *Meno*, where Socrates claims to be able to elicit all knowledge from all men by appropriate questioning: everyone knows everything by virtue of the immortality of the soul, and needs only to be reminded. There is a tacit withdrawal from that doctrine in the *Theaetetus*, where memory plays indeed an important part, but the memory in question is of the ordinary, earthly kind and depends on perception rather than on immortality of the soul or on the availability of ideas as objects visible in a realm above. This is the more in need of consideration because the *Theaetetus* begins the sequence that ends in the *Phaedo*, the place where Socrates argues the immortality of the soul partly on the premise of anamnesis. In any case, the *Theaetetus* ends inconclusively, aporetically, for the question what is knowledge is not answered. Socrates does not repeat the success of the *Meno*, where he induces the boy to discover, i.e., to discover in himself, an application of what we call the Pythagorean theorem. If the *Meno* tends to argue that through the application of the right method all normal men can be shown to possess all knowledge, the *Theaetetus* can be said to show that the quest for knowledge even about knowledge itself staggers through an arduous process of trial and error and reaches the edifying conclusion that failure in the investigation will make Theaetetus gentler with others and better able to avoid believing that he knows what he does not know. How important this wisdom might be is demonstrated in the immediately subsequent conversation of Socrates with Euthyphro, in the next dialogue. Whether the practical circumstances surrounding Socrates' end and the willfulness of the men who brought it about have anything to do with Plato's intention in closing the *Theaetetus* with aporia would require a separate investigation. For the present, it is necessary to inquire into the path by which Plato brings the *Theaetetus* to the conclusion it reaches.

Stimulated by Socrates, Theaetetus replaces his first suggested definition of knowledge with another, which is that knowledge is perception. Socrates immediately identifies this as Protagorean, and as tantamount to the formula of Protagoras that runs "Man is the measure of all things, of the things that are that they are and of the things that are not that they are not." Socrates interprets this to mean that each man is the judge of the coldness, hotness and other qualities of the things he perceives, and there is no way to go beyond the perceived appearance of things to their being in truth. In an unobtrusive remark, Socrates raises (152c) what will prove to be one of the most difficult points that he and Theaetetus will have to contend with throughout the dialogue, and which they will not be able to settle: What is error? The issue arises because, if what every man perceives is true for him and there is no truth beyond the truth of perception, or how things appear, no judgment about a thing can be wrong. By the end of the dialogue, the interlocutors have succeeded no better in accounting for or defining error than in defining knowledge. In this sense, "the problem of error" is an element of the discourse that survives to the end of the dialogue. This problem, which arises out of empiricism-relativism, survives the refutation in the dialogue of the original premise, namely, knowledge is perception (or "man is the measure") out of which it grows, which is surprising in the highest degree. Particular importance should be attached to whatever in the argument survives unrefuted or unresolved through to the end because, in an argument that ends formally in aporia, one must ask whether the work has in fact no affirmative conclusion or whether perhaps the conclusion consists somehow of whatever has been introduced into the argument but has not been eliminated from it by refutation. The *Theaetetus* especially calls for the consideration of some such hypothesis because the dialogue consists overwhelmingly of trial and error, of three major tentative definitions of knowledge, all of them overthrown when shown by Socrates to be untenable. It is possible that in such a case, some part of what survives must be sought in the negations, the statements of objections that effectually eliminate the affirmations which are cast out of the discourse. Obviously, a negative that eliminates permanently some factor of the argument and is not itself contradicted should be counted as permanently affirmed in the discourse as a whole. Collecting those negatives belongs to the full scale interpretation of the dialogue and not to the present paper. I note, however, that in reflecting on what an aporetic dialogue may be said to affirm formally, one might have to include the undisposed of issues raised by refuted positions, and the contradicting arguments by which refuted proposals are eliminated.

I doubt it will have escaped notice that this dialogue, in which the participants fail to find the meaning of error, was described above as proceeding throughout by trial and error – seemingly teaching in act what the obstetrician and his patient labor in vain to bring forth. If the dialogue were thus to present its teaching in act, then the judgment that the work as a whole ends in aporia would have to be modified: the genuine resolution of the issues would be embedded in the action or structure of the discourse as a whole. The dialogue has the appearance of being an enactment of error which fails in its efforts to articulate error or to define it in words. Because the definition of error and the definition of knowledge are mutually dependent, the dialogue inevitably has also the appearance of being an enactment of knowledge which fails in its efforts to articulate knowledge or to define it in words. If the *Theaetetus* were designed to present its own action or "structure" (i.e., Form) as the paradigm of knowledge, it would be offering a serious alternative to the doctrine of ideas as νοητά that are remembered by an immortal soul and that are drawn out of latency through a method of interrogation. It would be presenting knowledge and therewith learning as well as teaching in a purely terrestrial medium, within the realm of experience as one might say, linked to perception and ratiocination. However far this is from *defining* knowledge, it does indicate that the definition is to be expected to lie in some realm of being that is not out of touch with perception or appearance. One can only wonder if this speculation is to any extent supported by Plato's causing Theaetetus to reply with "it appears" (or, "it seems so") when Socrates argues provisionally, on behalf of the Protagorean view, that perception is always of what exists and, *qua* knowledge, cannot be false (152c).

Let us hold in abeyance the surmise that the aporia of the *Theaetetus* might be resolved in the retained elements of the argument and in the action or Form of the dialogue as a whole, and let us return to the progress of the argument. Theaetetus, as was said, proposes that knowledge is perception (151e). Socrates, unnoticed and without explanation, reverses the order of the terms and then proceeds to the identification of "perception is knowledge" as Protagorean and as tantamount to "man is the measure." By this understanding, each thing is as, and what, it is perceived to be by the one perceiving it, and error or falseness in apprehension becomes impossible. Socrates now asserts that this doctrine is the view that "nothing is one and a self-same thing itself" but everything proceeds from movement and the mixing of things: nothing ever is, but is always becoming (152d). On this, he says, all the philosophers except Parmenides – that is, Protagoras, Heraclitus, and Empedocles – concur, as well as the loftiest poets of the two kinds of poetry, Epicharmus in comedy and Homer in tragedy. It is surprising that there is no mention of Pythagoras. Socrates offers in support of this position, which he will attempt eventually to weaken, that motion does go with being and life, and rest with nonbeing and dissolution; and that heat and fire, the source and support of other things, is caused by motion. However provisional this advocacy might prove to be, a very important part will ultimately be played by heat or fire in Socrates' unretracted thought as brought out by the end of the *Phaedo*.

Socrates elaborates in considerable detail (156a–157c) the "Protagorean" doctrine that all perception is born of the motion of the endlessly moving percipient and object of perception. Attached to this "kineticism" is the notion that perception, the vital concomitant of motion, cannot be "wrong." One can only say about perception that it occurs. Apparently in order to refute the kineticism of Protagoras, Socrates moves to attack the infallibility of perception by referring to the state of dreaming, insanity, and illusion, arguing that we have "perceptions" in those states that can surely be called false. Socrates pursues the theme of dreams in his further refutation of Protagoras, asking Theaetetus how he would prove that the two of them were not dreaming their actual conversation. Theaetetus allows that the thing is too hard to prove. This paltry sophism is followed by the astonishing remark of Socrates (158d) that the previous point gains in weight because we are asleep and awake for equal periods of time. I take it that when an assertion is refuted by the use of feeble or false contentions, it may be regarded as having survived the refutation. In any case, the frivolity of this and other arguments in the vicinity is implied by Socrates when he begins to speak (166a) in the name of Protagoras, delivering a defense to which we will soon turn. For the present, two points seem to emerge: first, that in some indistinct way the Protagorean or materialist-kineticist ascription of special importance to heat retains its force, and with it so much of the Protagorean doctrine of motion and multiplicity in the all as must accompany it; and second, that for reasons at present at least equally unclear, the Protagorean view that man's perceptions are the measure of the being of things is also permitted to remain alive in some small degree. It should be made emphatically clear that nothing that has been said is intended to mean that Plato's Socrates is a crypto-kineticist. There is a very energetic denunciation of the Heracleitians or "Ephesians" (179a–180c), which happens by the way to be delivered by Theodorus, and which is mildly resisted by Socrates, who suggests that those sectarians perhaps speak differently in private and in public. He enlarges on the theme of dissimulation, distinguishing the ancients, who concealed their kineticism from the many with poetry (apparently Homer, 180d), and the moderns, who blurt out their wisdom so that the very cobblers will abandon the commonsense belief that some things are in motion and other things are at rest. He reminds himself that there are those who teach the opposite, namely, that all is one and at rest, a doctrine that can apparently be published without harmful effects, for nothing is said about the wisdom of concealing it. Whether this has anything to do with Socrates' own arguments and positions is exceedingly hard to judge. He goes on, however, to refute radical kineticism by showing the impossibility of saying anything about anything if all things are always moving and changing, that is, becoming rather than being. He concludes not only the critique of the theory of motion but of the associated Protagorean doctrine of "man the measure" by rejecting that formula *except if the man be sensible* (*phronimos*) (183b,c). To see how far this insight constitutes a rejection or refutation of Protagoras, we must return to an earlier point in the dialogue.

Beginning at 166a, Plato causes Socrates to deliver a remarkable speech in which he impersonates Protagoras rebuking Socrates for the levity of his disputation to that point and then going on to present Protagoras's understanding with unimpaired seriousness. "Protagoras" asseverates his belief that every human being is unique and will perceive and "know" idiosyncratically, in a literal sense "idiotically," but this flatly does not mean that there is no such thing as wisdom and the wise man. The wise man is precisely he who can so deal with us that when bad things appear and are to us, he can cause good things instead to appear and to be. The first illustration is the sick man and the physician. To the sick man, food tastes and is bitter. The physician will bring on a change in him to a condition in which food will taste and be sweet. The sick man is not ignorant nor is the healthy man wise because of the unwisdom or wisdom of their opinions; that is, the correction of the sick man is not a matter of rectifying his thinking: to make a man wiser is impossible, says "Protagoras." The required change is from a condition that is not good to one that is better. Physicians do this with drugs, teachers of wisdom (*sophistēs*) with arguments or words (*logois*). "Protagoras" argues that it is not a matter of making a man who thinks (*doxasai*) falsely think truly but rather of remedying a bad condition (*hexis*) of the soul so that the man will experience perceptions (*phantasmata*) that are better, but not more "true." The Socratic "Protagoras" now makes a remarkable observation: physicians are those who correct the condition of the body with a view to improving its perceptions or sensations, and farmers are the ones who treat sick plants, replacing bad perceptions in them with good, healthy and true perceptions (*aisthēseis*) (167c). Wise and good orators make the good rather than the wicked seem just to the cities. It is to be noted that in each case, the word for "good" in the expression denoting the perception of the better condition is not *agathos* but some form of *chrēstos*, which has an overtone of "useful." Socrates' impersonation of Protagoras continues with interesting assertions that we can omit from the present discussion. What has emerged is this: in the first place, Protagoras insists on the difference between wisdom and the absence of it. There is such a thing as a wise man, he differs from ordinary people, and his perceptions of the world might be the measure of it if his wisdom qualifies him as the φρόνιμος of Socrates' remark (183b,c) referred to earlier. While the wise man's wisdom far exceeds the vulgar understanding, the two have something in common. "Protagoras" sees the good as tinged with the beneficial, needful, useful as any man could readily understand those terms. There are good conditions, and health is a paradigm of them. So also is possession of abundance of wealth – Protagoras sees no reason to be apologetic about his own fee-taking. His moral standpoint is that of the ordinary man with his average perceptions, perceptions that would be called natural if natural means primary and unmodified by belief in any force or criterion higher than perceptible experience, either gods or eternal ideas. Nothing further from his thought can be imagined than

Socrates' depreciation of life and body in favor of death and soul, as in the *Phaedo*, which would seem to him demented. "Protagoras" speaks of soul and its *hexis* or habitual condition (167b1), but his curious references to the perceptions or sensations of plants are indicative of a strong tendency toward materialism in his doctrine, a tendency which would harmonize with his belief in motion as primary. He appears at first to alienate from each other Good, Truth, and Wisdom, which Socratic philosophy strives to reconcile or to amalgamate; but in fact his philosophy reconciles them, though on the plane of the empirical, terrestrial, and natural. His thought reflects energetically on experience, but it remains on the level of its own objects: transcending and even despising mere opinion, it does not hypothesize any entity that opinion – the prephilosophic conclusions from experience – cannot encompass. In an earlier passage, (162d) Socrates presents a reply that Protagoras or someone speaking for him might have given to Socrates' injection of the gods into the discussion. The reply is to the effect that the being or nonbeing of gods is excluded from Protagoras's speech and writing. One might say that he has no need of that hypothesis, nor of ideas either. No standard higher or more enduring than man and his experience comes to sight, and the soul itself has no pronounced primacy.

"Man is the measure" and "knowledge is perception" may prove to be untenable propositions, but they have so deep a foundation that they have reasserted themselves in one shape or another down to our own time. Socrates' numerous refutations of them and of their implications are uneven in their gravity, as he admits while impersonating Protagoras. To determine precisely the details of his judgment on Protagoras would be a considerable task, but it seems as if one might say that Socratism clashes seriously with Protagoreanism on the issue of the practicality of wisdom. Protagoras seems to replace "truer" with "better"; his wise man is a healer or improver of bodily or psychic conditions. One thinks of Socrates as teaching the natural impulse of the philosopher to recoil from the world of practice, beginning with politics and including acquisition and other affairs of business. The simplicity of this pattern is disturbed by Socrates' demonstrations in various places that the true king, the true rhetor, and – if Xenophon is to be believed – the true proprietor of an estate (and the true teacher of generals) is the philosopher. I believe there is another conflict between Socrates and Protagoras, a disagreement that might be called practical, that might serve to keep them apart as effectually as most other differences. Protagoras teaches that what seems good to the city is so for as long as the opinion holds, just as each man is the measure for himself. Whatever one might superimpose on this by way of distinctions between the wise and the others, this doctrine must put it into the mind of every city and every man that he or it *knows* (176d, 177a). If all the world were Protagorean, the hope of persuading anyone of the importance of knowing that or what he does not know must inevitably decline. How this point bears on the argument of the *Euthyphro*, the next dialogue, is too obvious to say. How it bears on the *Apology of Socrates* and on Athens itself is if anything more obvious. While the empiricism, materialism, and apparent atheism of Protagoras, and their underlying premise of universal motion, might not make it impossible to name or discuss anything, they do help to democratize the polis and obstruct the rule of the wiser sort. Protagoras's wise man is capable of becoming rich, a sign that his wisdom recommends itself to the many, or at least to those who can pay, as a thing of value. The wisdom of Socrates brought him of course a very different compensation, which is foreshadowed in the last lines of the present dialogue.

Is the relation between Socrates and Protagoras one of unrelieved disagreement? Probably not. The argument of the *Theaetetus* is much too complex to be summarized, and for the present purpose only a few points need be mentioned. After extensive efforts at defining knowledge, Theaetetus recalls (201c,d) having heard someone say that knowledge is true opinion together with reason, and that the things that are not subject to reason are not knowable. Socrates replies curiously, offering one dream for another, something that he thought he heard some people say, in exchange for what Theaetetus heard someone say. (A dream seems to have something in common with a rumor – speech emanating from an anonymous source. Cf. pages 96–97 above, on dreams.) What Socrates heard is that the primary elements or components of ourselves and of all composites are not subject to reason or to being explained or accounted for by reason. That is, Socrates addresses first that part of Theaetetus's formula that introduces the unknowable. Clearly, if there are things that are unknowable by virtue of being intractable to reason (whatever that might mean), then about such things there could be at best only true opinion. How one could know that the opinion about them is true is not clear, but that the argument is drifting toward the problems of the *Euthyphro* – piety and the gods – seems likely. At any rate, Socrates turns the discussion to the question whether the primary elements of things are unintelligible or are more or less intelligible than the composite things into which they enter. He concludes that the primary irreducible things (*prōta*), of which the letters of the alphabet and the musical notes are illustrations, are if anything more intelligible than the composites made up of them: the things of perception, the things we see and hear stand high in the order of knowability (206a, b). Socrates reaches the conclusion that the syllable, the paradigm of a composite, even if regarded as "some one indivisible idea" (205c) and "one idea," (205d; also 203e, 204a) is saved from unintelligibility by the intelligibility of the letters, those particles known to us in the only way in which they can be known, not by explanation but by perception. There seems to be some sense in which knowledge is perception and perception knowledge.

Socrates turns now (206d) to the question "what is reason intended to signify for us?" Without the formality of asking Theaetetus, he lays it down that reason – that which is to be added to true opinion to form knowledge – means one of three things: the verbal reflection of thoughts in speech; rendering an account of things in terms of all of their elementary parts; explaining something in terms of the characteristic that distinguishes it from everything else. Socrates proceeds not by supporting or refuting the claim of any of the three to be the definition of reason but rather by showing that no matter which definition prevailed, true opinion plus reason would not be a tenable definition of knowledge. He does this by showing that the possession of reason in the first two senses is incompatible with error, and that the third involves tautology (209c): the peculiar snubnosedness of Theaetetus will not enter into combination with my (true) opinion that that is Theaetetus until it has already been distinguished in my mind from all other snubnosednesses that I have ever seen – and this by its having been impressed on my memory in the first place in its difference from all others; and similarly with all the other characteristics of Theaetetus. Once that impression in terms of singularity has occurred, meeting with you again tomorrow, i.e., seeing you, will remind me and cause me to have right opinion of you. In brief, Socrates has come round again to perception plus memory quickened by a renewed perception. He seems to have rediscovered Protagoras's empiricism and terrestrialized collection.

We turn next to the *Phaedo*, a dialogue that shows Socrates demonstrating the immortality of the soul during his last hours, and in the course of that demonstration exalting the soul over the body while maintaining that death is preferable to life (59b). In order to accomplish his purpose, Socrates introduces his familiar theory of ideas, the intelligible and eternal archetypes, of which we retain revivable impressions as we pass through our disembodied toward our incarnated states. Contributory to his showing the immortality of the soul is an argument to the effect that things are brought into being by their contraries, as pleasure follows pain and life itself is consequent upon death. By the time the dialogue has run its course, the reader has been made to wonder how far Socrates himself believed the soul to be immortal, to what extent he considered the soul to be independent of the body, and whether he had not admitted ponderable variations of the orthodox idealism always associated with his name.

The conversation is related by Phaedo, who was present, to Echecrates, a Phliasian who is remembered as a Pythagorean and who shows a sympathetic interest in Socrates. Also present at the death of Socrates was a sizable group of Athenians and others, of a variety of philosophic persuasions. It is made explicit that Plato was not there: "Plato was, I think, sick" (59b). Whether or how this mention of Plato's absence is to be connected with Phaedo's remark, after Socrates' account of the ideas as causes, that "all who were there" thought Socrates had made the thing wonderfully clear, must remain more or less conjectural (102a). Eucleides and Terpsion, the Megarans of the recounting of the *Theaetetus*, were there. So also were Simmias and Kebes, two Thebans who are described by Socrates as pupils of Philolaos (61d). Philolaos is the Pythagorean who is said to have sold the written report of the esoteric tenets of Pythagoreanism to Plato himself. Simmias and Kebes are the principal interlocutors of the *Phaedo*, together with Socrates, and their reservations and doubts, as well as their unquestioning concurrences, are instruments that Plato uses in giving the argument much of its shape. As the thought of Protagoras moves in the *Theaetetus*, so that of Pythagoras affects the *Phaedo*, in ways that I can only illustrate here with great incompleteness.

I should like to begin by asking why Simmias and Kebes are made the partners in discourse of Socrates during most of the dialogue. I believe that an indication of the answer is to be found in the following places rather early in the conversation. First, at 64c, Socrates asks Simmias whether death is anything but the separation of the soul from the body. Without hesitation Simmias replies that it is nothing but that. This is a begging of the question that forms the context of the exchange, for if it were known that death consists of such a separation, it would be known also that the soul is capable of and has an independent existence, a point which Socrates in fact attaches to the question to which Simmias has given an affirmative answer. Simmias sees nothing arguable here.

Next, at 70a, Kebes wishes to hear dispelled the common fear that the soul disintegrates upon being separated from the body. He would like some assurance that the soul exists and has any power and intelligence (*phronēsis*) when the man has died. Socrates refers to "some ancient account that we remember" to the effect that the souls go from here to the infernal region and return and are born from the dead. And if this is so, he asks, if the living are born again from the dead, how might our souls not exist there? The support for the affirmative is to be found in the doctrine of the generation of all things from opposites. As pleasure is born of pain and everything that becomes becomes from the opposite of what it turns into, so also living arises out of being dead just as dying follows living. Kebes accepts this astonishing mixture of an old story and a flimsy analogy without a murmur, although he is not generally a passive interlocutor. Strengthening this argument with another, Socrates declares that if there were not a universal reciprocation between opposite states, the universe would collapse into ubiquitous death. Kebes is persuaded, and Socrates makes an unusually strong statement, declaring that it seems to him that it is altogether exactly thus, and that return to life and the birth of the living from the dead and the existence of the souls of the dead are the reality (72d). Kebes agrees and confirms all of the foregoing by introducing a favorite Socratic doctrine, that of anamnesis, as an additional proof. Of course, if the soul carries forth into life various impressions that it received before birth, it must have lived on somewhere. Simmias would like to be reminded of the proof of this position, and Kebes furnishes it with notable economy. Human beings can answer well-put questions about anything, which they would not be able to do if the knowledge were not within them. In order to reinforce Kebes' argument from anamnesis, Socrates refers without explanation, as if it were self-evident, to a man's knowledge of things as gained through seeing, hearing, or other perception (73c). The aporia of the *Theaetetus* seems to dissolve in the tacit acceptance of the spurned Protagorean suggestion.

Returning to the question why Simmias and Kebes are made the chief collaborators of Socrates in this ultimate dialogue, I think that Socrates' description of them as pupils of Philolaos, which means Pythagoreans, gives a clue that gains in plausibility by their conduct in the exchanges just summarized. Their easy acquiescence in the most problematic assertions apparently comports with their Pythagorean training, which would have put those conceptions, thought to be peculiarly Socratic, well within the range of the familiar or the authoritative. As one might say, Plato could not find more agreeable interlocutors with Socrates on questions of immortality and the migration of souls than Pythagoreans. The same indoctrination would prepare them equally well to accept the theory of generation of opposites by opposites, at least if Aristotle is to be believed when he ascribes to the Pythagoreans the belief that "contraries are the first principles of things" (*Metaphysics* 986b3). All of this is said without intending to minimize the weight of the objections that Simmias and Kebes will oppose to the doctrine of the eternal vitality of the soul as distinguished from its capacity to survive the body for a limited time. Perhaps Simmias and Kebes are imperfect Pythagoreans, as Theodorus was a deviating Protagorean. It is not possible now to try to clarify these relations of detachment on the part of certain members of philosophic sects when they contemplate their orthodoxies. It is well worth noticing, though, that Simmias and Kebes make objections to Socrates' doctrine of immortality, and that, upon the completion of the statement of those objections, the whole party is disconcerted by the inroads that have been made on what was thought to be an unassailable position, to such an extent that doubts about reason itself arise. Beginning at 88b, Phaedo breaks into the account in his own character with certain remarks to Echecrates. Phaedo relates how Socrates caressed him, and drew a parallel between misanthropy and misology: both arise out of misplaced trust too readily given, followed by repeated disenchantment until eventually hatred of all men or of all reason ensues. The lesson is caution, not dogmatic skepticism. What this speech that Plato puts in the mouth of Socrates betokens for Plato's own understanding of philosophic sectarianism is necessarily matter for speculation. At any rate, here at 90d, Phaedo concludes his exchange with Echecrates and resumes the report of the argument proper, ending what might be called the Phaedo section. If one were to wonder why this crucial work was named after a character who did nothing in the dialogue but serve as addressee of the admonitions just related, I think one might plausibly conclude that Plato attached much importance to the chief point of the Phaedo section. Those who find the location of a given passage in a text significant will wish to know that the Phaedo section divides the dialogue as a whole into very nearly equal parts.

Let it be supposed that Plato has injected Pythagoreanism into the elaboration of Socratism in a way that indicates some congeniality of the one doctrine to the other. By these tedious evolutions, we seem merely to be rediscovering the judgments of Aristotle on Plato's provenience, although doing so by concrete reference to the dialogues, which Aristotle does only on occasion. There is, however, another feature of Plato's critical method of constructing the argument to which one must pay attention in order to interpret the texts. It seems that with regard to some weighty issues, Socrates makes powerful representations which he himself unobtrusively qualifies, certainly presents with the utmost tentativeness, or perhaps even seems at last almost to reverse. In order to observe this, we must follow an argument that develops after Kebes has shown a need for a proof that the soul not only preexists the body but is altogether imperishable (95b et seq.). Socrates declares that this is tantamount to a demand for a thorough investigation of the cause of generation and corruption. Socrates now gives a remarkable account of his intellectual experiences as a seeker after knowledge about causes. He relates how his explorations into natural philosophy, apparently on materialistic principles, led him into confusion and discouragement, causing him eventually to forget even what common sense had plainly if insufficiently taught him. Then he discovered Anaxagoras, whose dictum that mind is the arranger and cause of everything delighted him. He reasoned that mind does all that it does with a view to the good: mind causes the generation and corruption of each thing in order to procure what is best for it. Thus the study of generation and corruption is really the study of good. Great was his disappointment when Anaxagoras went on to introduce air, aether, water and many other foolish things as causes, i.e., to vitiate his doctrine with matter, as if any such could explain why (that is, with a view to what good) anything came into being or happened. Anaxagoras, in mixing matter with mind, lost sight of the distinction between cause and the conditions necessary for the operation of a cause. He and others ignore the good, more powerful than any other power to keep the whole together. Now Socrates describes his second or post-Anaxagorean voyage in search of the cause. He begins by stating his method of inquiry. He adopts each time some explanation λόγος as a hypothesis that he judges to be the strongest, and he posits as true whatever agrees with it and rejects as untrue whatever does not (100a). Now he will hypothesize the existence of the beautiful in itself, and the good, and the great and all the others. "If you grant me this and concur in the being of these things, I hope to be able to demonstrate cause, and to prove to you that the soul is immortal." Astonishingly, Kebes grants the existence of the things themselves without a question. We might notice at this point that the doctrine of ideas, at least in the present context, is subordinate to the theory of cause and the demonstration of the immortality of the soul.

Briefly, each thing is, or rather is made to be, what it is by that "thing itself" in which it participates. A beautiful thing is made beautiful by beauty itself, by its "participation" in the beautiful. Socrates calls this "the safest answer I can give" to the question "what is the cause?" (It must be said immediately that a few pages later, Socrates will call this account not only safe but stupid. So we must not jump to conclusions about his naïveté.) Socrates praises the clarity of the results of his method, and Echecrates breaks into Phaedo's report to join in the praise. Phaedo replies, as was said above, with the remark that everyone there thought Socrates had clarified everything amazingly. Now Socrates shows how a man can be larger than one man but smaller than another: *he* can participate in the great and the small, which can simultaneously cause him or be present in him, but neither the great nor the small, the thing itself, can admit or participate in its opposite without being destroyed. When the opposite approaches its opposite, one of them must either withdraw or be destroyed. The importance of this for the life of the soul will appear soon.

Now an unnamed interlocutor notices that beauty's being the cause of beauty means that like is caused by like, which contradicts the earlier doctrine that generation is by opposite of opposite, as pleasure out of pain. Socrates easily distinguishes "things" from "things in themselves": the former are generated through opposition, the latter as has just been said are repelled or destroyed by contrariety. Socrates takes the next important step by distinguishing heat and fire, cold or coldness and snow. Heat and coldness are what they are in themselves, fire and snow are not heat and coldness but hot and cold. His point is that the things in themselves have surrogates which behave like them but differ from them. Thus, if fire approaches snow, one or the other must withdraw or be destroyed; neither can tolerate its contrary. Sometimes, Socrates says, "not only the idea itself αὐτὸ τὸ εἶδος deserves the same name forever and ever, but also something which, while not being that idea, always whensoever it exists has that form" (103e). For example, three may always be called three, but although it is not The Odd, it may also always be called odd. Now three will oppose anything Even just as strenuously and eternally as Odd itself would do, because three contains the idea of odd. Obviously, Socrates has prepared a position that goes beyond his first argument that something beautiful is made so by Beauty itself. Socrates now says (105b,c), "If you ask me, what causes something to be hot, I will not give you that safe but stupid answer that it is Heat, but rather out of our present work a more sophisticated reply, that it is fire; and if you ask what causes the body to be sick, I will not say Sickness but fever" (in Greek, something like "fieriness").

All this comes to an immediate head in a brief passage in which Socrates shows that the soul is to Life as fire is to Heat. Soul is not Life itself but Life's surrogate, and it and death are opposites that must flee one another or be destroyed. Thus it follows that when death descends upon the body, the soul must flee, and thus its survival of the body is proved. The reason that the soul must flee death and cannot stay to be destroyed by its opposite, as snow is by heat, is given thus: if the deathless is also indestructible, the soul cannot be destroyed when death approaches it (106b). One thought that the question was precisely whether the deathless is necessarily also indestructible. The demonstration now seems to take the form "if something is deathless, its vitality is the same as or is the sign of its insusceptibility to destruction." What must live must be. But does this formula mean, what must live must be alive as long as it exists, and it cannot exist once it no longer lives; or must the formula mean, life is of the thing's essence, it must be in life and there is no way to think of it without implying its life and thus its existence? This latter formulation will certainly remind of a particular kind of proof of the existence of God: if there is a being such that existence is of its essence, then there is no way to discuss it without acknowledging the necessity of its existence. In either case, as the demonstration is left by Socrates, it has something of the appearance of begging the question. "Is the immortal soul indestructible?" is answered with the assertion that what cannot die cannot pass out of existence. That this conclusion is as interesting to gods as to men is made explicit (106d). At any rate, it could have been asserted as well at the beginning of the argument as at its end, for nothing in the argument proper visibly addresses this issue.

The demonstration of the soul's imperishability is puzzling also in that, while the soul is characterized as the carrier or surrogate of Life, death acts for itself, capable of approaching and, presumably but only for a while, withdrawing. Is death the surrogate of a larger Idea, or is there a Death Itself, the Idea of Death? Is not death simply a negative, the privation of life? What is the ontic status of privations? Are they nothing? If death is ontically nothing, a nonentity, does it for that reason cease to be discussable or cease to be a source of anxiety? The dialogue never suggests that death is not discussable or that it is not a source of anxiety to man and perhaps even, if rarely, to Socrates. The status of privations is not an explicit theme, but it is an active one, in ways that I cannot take up here and of which I will give only a single example. At 106a, the cold is called the heatless or unhot and the hot is called coldless or uncold. Socrates says nothing about how far one can go in translating anything into the privation of its opposite. If heat and cold can be named by some process of reciprocating privation of negatives, can death and life be similarly named?

After all, the absolutely living is called in Greek as in English the deathless, and Socrates says of "the very idea of life" (*auto to tēs zōēs eidos*) that it is "deathless" (106c). There is a special reason for raising the question through the particular conjunction of the examples of heat and cold alongside life and death, as will appear. I think it is fair to infer from the foregoing that Plato presents Socratism as both affected with Pythagoreanism and as being developed by Socrates in ways that differ from the simple orthodoxies of Socratic idealism. A question opened up by this inference, but especially by the second branch of it, is how far the conjectured attributes of Socratism belong to Socrates' thought and how much to Plato's. On this difficulty I shall have nothing to say now.

In what direction does the Platonic Socrates seem to withdraw from the rigidities of the ideas and even perhaps of the superiority of death to life? I can give only one suggestion, one that arises out of the place of Crito in the world of Socrates. Crito is Socrates' interlocutor in a famous dialogue in which Crito tries to persuade Socrates to save himself from death. In the present dialogue, Crito resists Socrates' death to the very last moment, urging him to use any small means to prolong life – and this after the colossal efforts of Socrates on behalf of death. One inclines spontaneously to say in spite of, but I mean to suggest that one should perhaps say because of Crito's imperviousness to the radical depreciation of body and life, Socrates shows him a marked and touching affection. I wonder whether Socrates doesn't like him for his common sense, healthy humanity, and his unshakeable adherence to the simple dictate of natural experience. Nothing can make Crito see death as anything but fearful, bad, and to be avoided as long as possible, and he cannot feel anything but unashamed grief over the loss of one he loves. Socrates does not spurn him because, I suspect, for all his manifold abstractions from body and contradictions of natural experience, Socrates was not completely in accord with his own orthodoxy. Blinding ourselves to this, we will probably be poor readers of Plato's Socratic dialogues. I find some imponderable support for this speculation in two facts included by Plato in the *Phaedo*: when Socrates' bonds were removed from his legs by the jailers, he put his feet on the ground and sat thus until the time came for him to die (61d); and when his wife came to bid her seventy-year-old husband a last farewell, she was carrying a babe in arms.

However this may be, the argument of the dialogue is not yet over. Having shown that the soul is imperishable as well as immortal, Socrates desires to depict its fate after its emancipation from the body. This requires him to give a description of the nether regions, a description that unobtrusively becomes a description of the whole world. Socrates presents it as something of which he was persuaded by someone unnamed. To begin with, and stated conditionally, if the earth is round and is in the middle of heaven, it needs nothing to support it but the homogeneity of heaven and its own equilibrium or equipoise (ἰσορροπία). The earth does not fall because it is in a place and condition of perfect opposition of forces, and thus of rest. As for the earth itself, it is a body whose surface is indented and whose interior is hollowed and channeled with an intricacy of passages like a system of arteries and veins. The bulk of Socrates' myth of the earth describes the fluids – primarily water, air, and aether – that lie in and over the pitted surface and that circulate through the great passages within the body of earth. It is a scene of endless flux and oscillation brought on, as he says, by the bottomlessness of the fluids. The cause, he says, is that the fluids have, in the Greek term, no "basis" or step, nothing on or with which to stand. There is a reciprocating rush of fluids from side to side, and out of this mélange of fiery, muddy fluxions comes an equipoise. Socrates, who professed his dissatisfaction with Anaxagoras as a doctor of causes, appears to have lapsed into Anaxagoreanism or some form of Heracleitianism at the last moment. The subversion of body has drifted toward a hypothesis of body as cause. What he admits as cause is simple mechanism of matter, and it would be straining credulity to maintain that the cause of that intricate contraption of fluids in motion is the good, namely, the just accommodation of departed souls, rather than the equilibration of spherical earth that must hang without support in the heavens. The cause of the world order is certainly not the good if the good is tantamount to or implicated in the good of man.

There is one last conjunction of notions in the *Phaedo* to which I should like to draw attention. Early in the conversation, (63d) Socrates notices that Crito has been trying to say something, and he asks him what it is. Crito replies that the man in charge of the poison was trying to admonish Socrates to talk less because speaking warms one up and the heat counteracts the poison. Later (105b,c), when Socrates is transcending the safe but stupid dictum that the cause of heat in something is The Hot, he gives as an illustration of the improved conception the statement that what causes the body to be sick is not the presence in it of Sickness in Itself but rather of fever, i.e., fieriness, or heat to excess. In the last sentences of the dialogue, the effect of the poison on Socrates is described as a growing coldness beginning in his feet and rising, like death itself, through his limbs until it reaches his heart, when not only his members but himself died. I wish to suggest that life itself is portrayed as some condition of a man or rather of his body, indeed of any animal or its body, in which heat and cold are in a state of equilibrium or rest, an equilibrium that can be upset by things introduced from without such as drugs, and that can be affected, at least in some men, by an activity of the mind such as speech. (It is not clear whether Socrates in fact required the double or triple dose.) How far the life of man can be understood through the *Phaedo* as a mechanical thermal equilibrium, a microcosm of the fluid equilibrium of the world, is problematic. One would like to know what significance, if any, to attach to the fact that the Greek word for soul is ψυχή and for cooling ψύχω. Can one be certain that Socrates' last words, the reminder to Crito to pay the debt to Aesculapius, were not a mark of his gratitude to the great druggist for a painless death through cooling numbness rather than for release from life as if it were a disease? What the text does seem to make clear is that the intention of Plato cannot be discerned unless his Socrates is seen in his depth, free from the bonds of an exoteric dogmatism that is, after all, incompatible with his famous irony.

The Socratic dialogues of Plato portray a large variety of philosophic schools, human types, and professions. To understand Plato is to grasp the outcome of the many dramatic meetings in which those actors are brought together for talk. How the reader perceives the outcome of those many discussions should lead him to Plato's premises; but we are tempted to reverse the process and to derive the outcome from some prejudgment of Plato's premises. I have tried to examine some parts of Plato's work presupposing as little as possible about his judgment of Socrates; and I have done so for the sake of understanding what Plato's true judgment of Socrates was and therefore, from Plato's perspective, what Socrates was. I have tried to keep an open mind on the question whether Plato kept an open mind, and I was led to conclude that he had done so. I do not find that Plato blinded himself any more than Aristotle would do to the ligatures that bound Socrates to the thought of his predecessors, or that he believed that alone among men Socrates had no origins to speak of. Nor does it appear that the doctrines for which Socrates is most famous were held by him as dogma or without regard to their value as exoteric.

What entitles Socrates to the encomium of Phaedo at the end of the dialogue – that Socrates was the best and wisest and most just man of that time of whom those about him had experience? Perhaps the answer lies in this: that he achieved the decisive translation of Greek philosophy onto the plane of sobriety. He seems to have taken Pythagoreanism with its cultic and other extremes and domesticated it for prudent men. This domestication included a drastic reformulation, toward restraint, of philosophy's political pretensions. On the other hand, he appears to have elevated Protagoreanism by reminding it of soul and heaven, of which the Pythagoreans were only too frantically aware. Socrates seems to have moved among the schools and professions of the Greeks like a judge in the midst of enthusiasts, pedants, mountebanks, thinkers, climbers, connivers, poets and others. After he had done his work, the stage was set for the seriousness and restraint of Aristotle. That the achievement of Socrates was a historical achievement seems to be some part of the burden of Plato's Socratic corpus. How much of that achievement was in fact Plato's is an enormous question that must remain present to the mind of anyone who hopes to understand Plato.

Socratism appears as a turning point in Greek and thus in all thought, as the cautious deradicalization of its extremes of spiritualism, cultism, and metaphysical dogmatism, accomplished through a careful sifting of the best resources available. There is reason to think that the history of philosophy in the modern age has been a record of the radicalization or intensification of the primary conceptions, a course opposite to that which came to a climactic point with the philosophizing of Socrates. If this observation were to prove correct, it would indicate that the decline of society is compatible with the most contradictory evolutions of man's theoretical existence. One must be singularly devoted to truth, to be cheered by this discovery.

7
Religion, the Constitution, and the Enlightenment

It is a fact and an enigma of the American experience that the Federal Constitution is at the same time the definition of our national existence and an entity whose own definition is a vexed matter of interpretation. Few truths would be more generally admitted than that the meaning of the Constitution is continually in dispute and moreover that the very principles of constitutional interpretation, by the application of which anything that could claim to be that meaning would emerge, are themselves recognized as arguable: original intention, living document, natural right? The prosperous longevity of a country whose definition seems so problematic is a subject worthy of deep meditation, but it is not our present subject. The project of this paper is rather to pursue a particular mode of inquiry into the meaning of the Constitution regarding religion. The need for such inquiry arises not only out of the general difficulty of determining the meaning or the bearing of particular provisions of the Constitution but out of the indubitable importance of the subject in our national life and the remarkable reticence of the Constitution about a theme of just such importance. In that reticence there lies embedded, I believe, an intimation of an important fact of our national existence, namely, that this is overwhelmingly a nation of Christians but it is not and was not intended to be a Christian nation.

How may the attitude of the Constitution toward religion be recognized in the text? To begin with, there is the curious fact that, in the two places (Article I, section 9 and Article V) in which the Framers had reason to refer to a particular year, they did so by writing "the Year one thousand eight hundred and eight" although in the paragraph that immediately precedes their signatures, where they use the pronoun "we" and speak literally and purely for themselves, they wrote "the Year of our Lord one thousand seven hundred and eighty seven." Nowhere in the Constitution itself is there even so small an indication of public preference for Christian religion as the use of the conventional calendar formula would evince.

More explicitly, the Constitution requires that Senators, when judging of impeachments, be on oath or affirmation (Article I, section 3), tacitly conceding the eligibility of an unbeliever to sit in the legislature. The President himself is required to solemnize his loyalty to the Constitution by oath or affirmation (Article II, section I). Again, in Article VI, the formula of oath or affirmation is repeated, followed immediately by the clause that prohibits the requirement of any "religious test" "as a Qualification to any Office or public Trust under the United States." The Framers appear to have intended that the alternative of oath or affirmation was not subject to construction as a test that could distinguish believers and unbelievers, or among believers, and thus distinguish the eligible and ineligible for public office. Only so much in the original Constitution. Thereafter, the endlessly construed First Amendment clauses constraining Congress from making any law "respecting an establishment of religion or prohibiting the free exercise thereof."

The Constitution prescribes, in those few intimations, that a nation composed overwhelmingly of Christians shall require its enormous Christian majority to limit its Christian belief and practice to a private sphere of life, defined as a realm that the public authority will protect by guaranteeing never to enter it through favoring or burdening any denomination or by favoring Christianity itself. The abnegation of the public with regard to religion is an article of political conviction of such power in this country that it has, if anything, grown in strength rather than dissipated itself during the two centuries of our national life. This is in itself a notable fact incapable of being explained by simple appeal to "original intent" of the Framers as the authoritative principle of Constitutional interpretation, for there is absolutely nothing in existence that can vitiate the power of the living over the dead except the self-limitation of the living, which must itself be understood as a manifestation of the sovereign autonomy of the living, who say continuously, "I am what I am."

There is more that follows from the relegation of religion to a private sphere, namely, the protection of the public or the whole from the private in its partiality. No sect may receive such public favor as would put it in a position of authoritative influence over the laws or their execution: the wall that defends the private equally restrains it.

Moreover, in forbidding the requirement even of Christian confession as a test of eligibility to participate in public life, the Constitution gives public precedence to the quality "citizen" over the quality "God-fearing" and in so doing emphasizes the declaration of the public's independence of the religious-*qua*-private or partial.

In sum: the Constitution, regarding religion, premises a public and a private, separate and equally protected by their mutual immunity, the public consisting of fully privileged citizens and the private of voluntary communicants, with the understanding that the rule of the majority is suspended in any case in which the majority is defined by its religion. Concretely, Christianity was disqualified from the beginning as race eventually came to be in defining a recognizable majority.

How may we begin to understand the sharp distinction between public and private, the mutual segregation of religion and politics with the implicit demotion of the influence of religion on the way of life, and the studied impartiality of communicating Christians regarding Christianity in juxtaposition with other faiths or with no faith at all? I propose to consider these questions by looking to the realm in which the truths of politics must necessarily arise, that realm of speculation about man and his place in the whole which is occupied by political philosophy. As we scan the issues whose grounds are unclear to us, we can hardly fail to notice that every one of those issues received a striking and novel development in the works of the great thinkers of the Enlightenment. It would be impossible to read Hobbes, Locke, and Spinoza, to take only those examples, and fail to notice the ways in which their formulation anticipated, suggested or guided the prescriptions of the Constitution regarding religion and its place in the regime. I propose to attempt a sketch of the relevant portions of those authors' work with the hope of shedding light on the meaning of the Constitution's treatment of religion, without for a moment implying that the Framers were adept in political philosophy. I mean to go no further than to suggest that something had taken place in the European world similar to what Hobbes had hoped would happen, namely, that his doctrines would percolate down and into the general mind, thence to exercise a decisive influence in the lives of multitudes of men by riding into the definition of political communities.

By what means, and for what ends, was the exercise of religion and its non-exercise made a private concern, as much a private matter as the choice of an occupation, a dwelling, or a mate? The argument begins with exegesis and thus, in fact, with the critique of Revelation. The authority of scriptural religion rests on the authority of Scripture, and the authority of Scripture depends on the meaning and nature of any possible communication between God and humanity. But that nature and that meaning can be grasped only by study and interpretation of Scripture itself, and that necessarily by men who are enlightened by natural reason alone. The first task imposed upon themselves by the theologico-political writers of the Enlightenment was to interpret the Bible: to declare in plain speech what the Bible contains, in what mode it addresses its addressees, and certainly whether anything within it should be understood as making any claims to an authority that could rival that of the civil state. In beginning with exegesis, the philosophers undertook the most difficult task but also the one that promised the greatest prize, for no argument that defines the influence of the religious authorities could exceed in cogency one drawn from the only source accepted by themselves as unimpeachable.

Because of the broad agreement between the political philosophies proper of Hobbes, Locke and Spinoza, all founded on the premise of a state of nature that required to be transcended and accompanying natural rights that cannot be to the same extent transcended, it may be permissible to begin with the argument of Spinoza, whose theologico-political position is both radical and representative. Spinoza is aware that God makes verbal or explicit contact with man at the point of prophecy, and therefore that no question is of greater practical importance than what is a prophet and what is prophecy. He claims to show that a prophet is a man whose characteristic aptitude is not intelligence but imagination, and that prophecy typically is the report of a man of no intellectual distinction recounting those imaginings of his that are prompted and determined by his singular bodily state, his peculiar historical and private experiences, necessarily delivered to his particular contemporaries in the only language that they understand, in the peculiar idioms of his and their particular time and place. As one might say, Spinoza applies to the phenomenon of prophecy the whole thrust of his dictum, enunciated in the *Ethics*, that man is bound up in the infinite chain of causes that we know as nature, within which man has no privileged status as a dominion within a dominion. So situated, man is of course utterly and totally subject to the rule of the one overwhelmingly powerful substance which is God. What then is the authority of a prophet? Prophets, prophecy, and Scripture altogether do not disclose Truth, they pronounce in the mode of commandment with a sole view to Obedience. Truth is in the realm of Reason or philosophy, Morality or practice is in the realm of Theology or prophecy.

The naturalization of prophetic Scripture, in limiting theology to the mode of commandment and obedience, has profound consequences for the definition of a man's duty. When Spinoza argues that the prophetic statement that God is a fire arises out of the peculiarities of time, place, vernacular, and bodily state of the prophet, he is preparing for the conclusion that there is no duty to believe that God is a fire. Is there anything, then, that a believer is obliged to believe because it is a truth? The Enlightenment returns a surprising answer: a Christian – and for obvious reasons the emphasis is on the condition of Christians – must believe only that Jesus is the Messiah, and that so that he may be saved. As Hobbes and Spinoza point out, each man will believe according to his own understanding, there being no way to coerce belief although there may be many ways to affect it, and the retention of the freedom to believe is so involuntary that it must be recognized as an inalienable right of nature. Throughout the Enlightenment there runs the drive to reduce to a minimum the content of dogma, for two apparent reasons; first, as Spinoza has it, to frustrate the theologians whose authority is in direct proportion to the multiplicity and obscurity of the tenets of faith that only they can interpret and wield; and second, so that the law of works, of charity, of morality and, at bottom, of sociality may shine forth and take precedence of the law of faith. In any case, it is not subscription to any articles of dogma but rather the performance of the works of charity that testifies to faith, as Spinoza maintains in his way and Locke does in his own. This being so, and consent to doctrines being no basis for or criterion of fidelity, doctrinal conformity is in every way a personal or private matter, and faith must be understood as indistinguishable from sociality. There is no authority, assuredly not the civil authority, that may legitimately design to coerce the understanding by imposing on the will, that is, the will to believe. If freedom means, as modern authors teach, the freedom of the will from the weight of any other particular will, then privacy with regard to religious belief lies close to the heart of freedom itself. It is clear that the will of the political authority is not a particular will, and it is thus equally clear that the plenitude of freedom with regard to belief must be supported by yet another argument, namely, that the right of the civil authority to coerce is, like every other right, limited by the power to employ the alleged right in fact to coerce. The right of the civil authority is frustrated by the rugged intransigence of the mind, and the private freedom of the will is thus protected by what might be construed as the essence of the will itself, namely, to be equal to every other natural will and to be irrepressible by every other legal, fictitious, or political will.

As the rationalizing exegetes demonstrated the practical, moral and socializing authority of Scripture at the expense of its standing as the record of revealed truth about "speculative" matters, the issue of rivalry between the civil and the ecclesiastical authority with regard to power over the lives of men demanded resolution. To put the matter as starkly as ever it was posed by the political philosophers, the rivalry of civil and ecclesiastical authority was simply the rivalry between the public or political and a private or sub-political domain, and it belongs to the nature of political life that absolutely nothing encroach on the supremacy of our one and only bulwark against the miseries of the nonpolitical condition, namely the sovereign civil power. We know that our human salvation was brought by human means because we know that the divine law, the law of God almighty the overwhelming, inescapable and eternal, ruled in the state of nature as it must rule always and everywhere; and that it was by the rational device of political compact, not through the bearing of the law of nature, that the purpose of nature and of nature's God was given effect. The political entity, the one whole body of the nation concentrated in its sovereignty, is "the public," the supreme ONE, and to it every knee must bend. To speak metaphorically, the unity of God, the source of the divine and natural law, must be conveyed in the unity of the civil sovereign, the source of the civil law. If one notices that the primacy of the public or civil over the infra-public or ecclesiastical marches with the impenetrable privacy of individual belief, one perceives in outline much that lives in our Constitution: the public isolates itself from the religious in order to defend itself against its most potent rival, and in so doing it rejects forever any demand that it intervene on behalf of churchly shepherds whose flocks prove unruly. If these are indeed the purposes that animate the Constitution, then the Framers' *abstention* from

Establishment rather than *prescribing* Establishment must be explained and reconciled with the doctrine of civil supremacy.

To clarify this: Hobbes, in the interest of a single unrivalled public, subordinates the ecclesiastical authority by *establishing* it, and in so doing compels us to think again about the meaning of the First Amendment injunction forbidding Congress to make any law respecting an establishment of religion. Disregard as strategic that the Establishment clause protected Establishment in the states in which it existed. Consider only that Establishment lends itself to enhancing the ecclesiastical authority by arming it with the secular sword and also to draining it of its independent power by relegating it to the bureaucratic apparatus of the state. We might conceivably be in doubt whether the Framers intended to enhance or to annul the power of ecclesiastical authority by precluding Establishment of a national church if we were in doubt whether the Framers intended to restrict the churches to the protected realm of the private and, by so doing, to carry forward their project of forming a more perfect union, which should be the public ONE. It is my contention that the Framers elected non-Establishment rather than Establishment as the means for securing the public because non-Establishment is the device for protecting the public that provides the strongest guarantee of privacy in denying this nation of Christians the opportunity to become a Christian nation. This means that Christians have found a ground on which to accept the proposition that the constitutional arrangements for preserving the public and the private take precedence of defining this country as a Christian nation.

This leads us to the preparation for such a position of religious self-denial and private self-assertion as was laid down in the profane critique of Christianity that developed within Christendom at least from the sixteenth century on. Familiar from the thought of Machiavelli is the judgment that what Christianity claims as its greatest boon to mankind, namely, the redirecting of attention from this world to the next, is in fact damaging to the only life over which in principle men can have control. It is true that Machiavelli's imputation that Christianity is enervating is matched by Hobbes's that it is inflammatory and fertile in sanguinary civil disorder – anything but passive. That these judgments tend in opposed directions does not mean that they annul one another, but rather that they would combine to unsettle the simple confidence of Christians in their faith. But closer to our immediate concerns is another line of criticism, one that also presents Christianity as in a state of some tension with the view of man as a self-disposing being whose freedom is in his autonomy, whose offenses, atonements, and exonerations must be as much his very own as are those beliefs that no authority should presume to coerce. We might see on a remote horizon that image of man as a perfectly self-determining, self-legislating being whose will forms itself to a duty that it itself prescribes to itself and thus emancipates itself from every will, including the divine, that could impose itself on the human will. Before we could properly contemplate that Hegelian consummation, which is only anticipated in the Enlightenment as an environment of the Constitution, it is our task to consider the Enlightenment in its bearing on Scriptural Christian religion in the concrete.

It is Locke, in *On the Reasonableness of Christianity*, who insists that the revealed scheme of reward and punishment be understood as bound by the same criteria of justice as recommend themselves to human reason: that punishment proper be inflicted for guilt, and only upon the personally guilty. Can Christian religion be understood to teach that there is such a thing as the guilt of mankind as such, that the sin of Adam infected every human being and for that sin a just God, our supreme paradigm of righteousness, condemned him to punishment by death? The manner of Locke's refusal to accept this as authentic Christian teaching is instructive: that man may have been given over to death as a consequence of the sin of Adam must be granted, for to deny it would contradict the plain meaning of Scripture; but that giving over may not be understood as punishment. It must rather be understood as a deprivation of a good which had been freely given and might therefore be taken away by the grantor for his own reasons: it was not man's by *right* (sec. 6). Yet would such a deprivation be just, or would it have simply to be accepted because of the power of the one who gave and who took back? Locke (sec. 9) reinstates the claim of right in arguing that through the advent of Christ, each man may possess that good thing which his own deeds entitle him to by right. Locke's Christianity is not a teaching of the natural right to life. It is rather a teaching to the effect that man, when under the rule of God alone, before Christ's appearance on earth, was subject to death without remission, but that through Christ's intervention, men regained the elementary right of justice, which is to gain good for good done and to suffer evil only for evil performed. Not until much later in the book (sec. 175) does Locke venture to introduce the term "natural right," in a passage where he does indeed refer to a natural right to *eternal* life belonging to Jesus by "natural right" of inheritance as the son of his Father, and belonging to those whose faith makes them the brothers of Jesus and therewith the sons of God by adoption. It is made clear enough by Locke that within the scope of Christian religion, "natural right" must have an equivocal meaning in that it does not belong to man as man, to natural man, but, in the admittedly special case of right to eternal life, it belongs only to Christians. The marriage of the simply rational concept of natural right and the Christian doctrine of salvation in faith seems to produce an anomalous offspring: a natural right that does not inhere in man by nature.

Locke understands Christianity to make only few, and those easy, demands on faith. Few and easy as they are, and lying at the heart of the definition of Christian confession as they do, one might suppose that they take precedence of every other requirement for admission to the bounty promised in the new dispensation. It is not perfectly clear that they do. What the Lord has always required of us is to do justice and love mercy, or put otherwise to deal charitably with our fellow men. We are strictly enjoined to obey the law of works. We are most strictly enjoined to obedience. But it is beyond human ability to obey the law of works in every necessary particular, and as a consequence every human being would be given up on irremediable death if there were not a condign means of averting the punishment that each man merits on account of his own singular behavior. That means is obedience to the law of faith, the sincere belief that Jesus is Christ. Obedience to the law of works is in principle primary or sufficient, only empirically or accidentally insufficient. To believe otherwise would be to believe that God demands obedience of a creature whom he has made essentially incapable of fulfilling the law. What this would add to God's glory by way of power it would subtract by way of injustice, not to say misanthropy. Locke's construction of Christian religion leans strongly toward deeds as distinguished from faith, and at the same time, or therefore, toward the ultimate responsibility of each human being for his own fate.

If death does not come to a man by punishment for the sin of Adam, can life come to him by redemption through the death of Jesus? When Kant proposes to investigate religion within the limits of reason alone, and when in so doing he tests all religion, but especially Christianity, by the criterion of morality and not faith, he reinforces the Lockean promotion of the law of deed in ways that address our immediate question. Speaking of the clearing of the guilt of the offending man, Kant writes, ". . . only the supposition of a complete change of heart allows us to think of the absolution, at the bar of heavenly justice, of the man burdened with guilt; that therefore no expiations, be they penances or ceremonies, no invocations or expressions of praise (not even those appealing to the ideal of the vicarious Son of God), can supply the lack of this change of heart, if it is absent, or, if it is present, can increase in the least its validity before the divine tribunal, since that ideal must be adopted into our disposition if it is to stand in the place of conduct."[1] And, to the same effect, ". . . so far as reason can see, no one can, by virtue of the superabundance of his own good conduct and through his own merit, take another's place; or, if such vicarious atonement is accepted, we should have to *assume it* only from the moral point of view, since for ratiocination it is an unfathomable mystery."[2] The opposite would contradict the "spontaneity" that is intrinsic to morality, which, it must be understood, is the only true concern of the only true religion. From the suffusion of religion with morality,

1 *Religion Within the Limits of Reason Alone*, translated by Theodore M. Greene and Hoyt H. Hudson, bk. II, sec. 2, p. 71 (New York: Harper Torchbooks, 1960).

2 *Ibid.*, bk. III, div. 2, General Observation, p. 134.

and of morality with "spontaneity," which for Kant means freedom from calculation of ends to be obtained as reward for obedience to the moral law, there follows a powerful reservation against the very notion of an offer of a thing of value in exchange for compliance with a prescription of dogma. On these terms, popular religion stands accused of allowing itself to encourage a mercenary motive, to be reprobated in the name of true morality and true religion equally.

As can be learned in many places, true religion and true piety were conceived by the Enlightenment with the requirements of civil life uppermost in mind. Spinoza has it that ". . . piety towards one's country is the highest there can be" and ". . . the highest piety . . . is exercised in maintaining public peace and tranquility."[3] Kant expresses himself as follows with a view to the status of merely historical religion: "The true (moral) service of God, which the faithful must render as subjects belonging to His kingdom but no less as citizens thereof (under laws of freedom), is itself, indeed, like the kingdom, invisible, i.e., *a service of the heart* (in spirit and in truth)."[4] The true church is the Church Invisible that consists of those whose wills incline steadily and increasingly toward obedience to the moral law that they know before Revelation discloses it to them, and who are indistinguishable from the practitioners of charity and civility.

Inevitable is the conclusion that piety is the virtue of calm and reasonable citizens, determined to bestow and to enjoy the fruits of a sober life in common, never to be set at odds with their fellow citizens over affirmations that no amount of merely dogmatic conviction could confirm and no degree of doctrinal dialectic could ever put beyond dispute. Could it be imagined that "the Enlightenment" anticipated, or thought itself the instrument for procuring, a world from which unreason and disorder would be expelled? It is unlikely. Hobbes referred to men's disposition to seek the causes of things, indeed, but not necessarily to seek the natural causes thereof. Spinoza considered the multitude of men to be ignorant and unpromising with respect to their perfection. Kant was convinced of the constant presence of the principle of evil in man, meaning by that an ineradicable disposition to violate the moral law that dwells within.

Considering the evident veneration of Reason on the part of "the Enlightenment," is anything like the "rule of philosophy in the person of a philosopher-king" visible as the goal of the Rationalists' thought? Certainly not. Hobbes had hopes that his mind would govern if his book were adopted as a text in the universities and his revelations would disseminate themselves throughout the civil community, but the actual sovereign men and women could well be undistinguished. Locke advanced the claims of consti-

3 *Theologico-Political Treatise*, chaps. XIX and XX.

4 Kant, *loc.cit.*, bk. iv, part 2, General Observation, p. 180.

tutional monarchy, a species of republicanism supported by the consensus of ordinary people, the multitude of those whose rationality was manifested in their industry. Spinoza went furthest and acknowledged the superior naturalness of democracy, the rule of those for whose wisdom he had no sentimental admiration. Kant saw the future in its best light as republican, again under constitutional monarchy. "The Enlightenment," which was not possessed of a single voice, was rationalistic in a way that comported perfectly with public support for religious observance. It was not a project for the "replacement" of religion, a program for public atheism. It was the aspiration for a civil life in which religious practice would be deflected from the age-long course of aggressive dogmatism regarding the avowedly mysterious, and toward a truly godly sociality of obedience and good will among multitudes for whom reason in the full sense, that is, philosophy, was out of reach. There is perhaps no more practical link between the high thought of the Enlightenment and the spirit of the constitutional attitude toward Christianity and religion than is contained in a brief passage from Thomas Paine's 1776 pamphlet, "Common Sense:" "As to religion, I hold it to be the indispensable duty of all government, to protect all conscientious professors thereof, and I know of no other business which government hath to do therewith. Let a man throw aside that narrowness of soul, that selfishness of principle, which the niggards of all professions are so unwilling to part with, and he will be at once delivered of his fears on that head. Suspicion is the companion of mean souls, and the bane of all good society. For myself, I fully and conscientiously believe, that it is the will of the Almighty, that there should be diversity of religious opinions among us: It affords a larger field for our Christian kindness. Were we all of one way of thinking, our religious dispositions would want matter for probation; and on this liberal principle, I look on the various denominations among us, to be like children of the same family, differing only, in what is called their Christian names." With regard to religion, the American Constitution appears to protect Religion by transcending every phenomenal manifestation of it. In so doing, it appropriates to a political purpose the philosophic project of the Enlightenment for interpreting revealed religion as an instrument of civil sociality and nothing more.

The political project of the Enlightenment may be said to be the production on the subrational plane of politics, that is, among those multitudes who are incapable of philosophy, the diminished parallel to the life of the true lovers of God the one and unimaginable. The parallel to the truly free life is the politically free life, which is not available until historical religion is deprived of any ground on which to claim coercive authority. Thus the historical interpreters of Scripture must be replaced by the rational interpreters so that nothing unnatural or uncivil, which is to say irrational, enter the political order from Scripture. It is to be noted that the civil order is seen by the Enlightenment philosophers as an antithesis to the state of nature, yet the civil order is threatened by the human dispensation that appeals from the natural order to the order that claims to transcend it. Apparently, the true religion and the true polity are expressions of the truth of nature and not of anything outside it, but nature is mute. Only through reason, which is human reason, can nature be enabled to speak, or to pronounce those truths in whose absence men are confined in that prison of the state of nature from which nature tries dumbly to expel them.

When mankind has been expelled from that dubious Eden, philosophy or reason can at long last hope to prevail – not over mere "passion," as the pagans might have had it, but specifically over the moral and political disorder introduced into civil life by the recognized interpreters of Scripture. The Enlightenment saw itself as the Second Reformation, opening up the possibility that reason may be appealed to in the interest of and not as an antidote or alternative to free popular government. I believe that this formula indicates the sense in which the Enlightenment lies in the background of the American Constitution and the American experience.

The movement of modern thought that we know as the Enlightenment divided itself into a rigorous rationalism accompanied by an extraordinarily austere conception of true religion on the one hand, and a resignation to the irrationality and passion-bound nature of the multitude of humanity on the other. In brief, modernity reproduced a disjunction between the ordinary *is* and an *ought* in the heavens for which the modern writers sometimes blamed the ancients, although claiming that by aiming lower they avoided the fatal transgression of misplaced optimism. I suggest that the American experience exhibits a similar and parallel cleavage, between the Constitution's scrupulous sterility regarding religion and Christianity on the one hand, and the persistent fidelity of the American people to their Christian faith on the other. While the theoretical support for our liberal, popular regime lies in the modern doctrines, loosely rationalistic, that portray a nature whose mechanism does not include the distinction of just and unjust, good and evil, most of the members of our democracy believe, as Christians and Jews, that the essence of the Whole is a righteous God before whom every knee must bend.

Far from seeing this as a fatal contradiction, we would do better to regard it, at this Bicentennial in our national life, as a sign that a high Providence has enabled this last best hope of earth to endure, reaping as a reward for its generous spirit the privilege of enjoying the blessing of two separate worlds.

8
On Pleasure and the Human Good: Plato's *Philebus*

Plato's *Philebus* is said, under the encouragement of its subtitle, to be about pleasure; but how far it is from being simply about pleasure, or even primarily about pleasure, may be seen from the development of the argument toward and then vastly beyond the problem of species as that problem is brought to sight by the variety concealed within the apparent unity of "pleasure" itself. The discourse unfolds through the themes of finitude and infinity, of mind and cause in the whole, and eventually to the meaning and status of Good. Philebus's disclosures about Good emerge without thematic reference to regimes and politics or to virtues and morality. The Good, of course comprehending the human good, is brought to light in so comprehensive a way as to induce or compel an insight into the articulation of human existence with the nature of the whole in which man is fated to know, experience, and perform good and its privations. Man, Good, and the Whole are within the scope of *Philebus*.

The dialogue begins without indication of its setting in time or place and without any suggestion of a reporter who had participated in it or who had received the report of it from some other who had. It belongs to the world as a whole; and it is the effectually avowed product of its author, in the most emphatic sense Platonic, as a dialogue "reported" by Socrates himself is in an emphatic sense Socratic. There are three interlocutors, of whom Philebus is by far the least active. The exchanges, with few exceptions, are between Socrates and Protarchus, a young man associated with and influenced by Philebus. Philebus is a technical hedonist who says very little, having resigned from the discussion before the work itself begins, explaining himself as afraid of offending Aphrodite, most truly called Hedone, whose preeminence is about to be assaulted. The dialogue is named after the participant who has next to nothing to say and who contributes to the argument the proposition – pleasure is the good – which is edifyingly exploded by Socrates. As the discourse will make clear, though, the devastation of the claims of pleasure is not absolute, and in the resolution of the wider problem of the good, means will be found to harmonize conflicting claims, to produce a kind of *philia* on the plane of good that will reflect or repeat a reconciliation of opposites on the plane of the whole, a reconciliation indispensable to the constitution of the universe. Tentatively, one might explain the peculiarity of the title as an adumbration of Plato's view of the whole as a scene of indispensable concession to cosmic forces that enter into good but that can make their contribution as long and so far as they are subordinated to Measure. Thus Measure, or Number, will enter our field of view and will from time to time dominate it, as Number and the Numberless, Finite and Infinite, are drawn in their arrays into the search for Good.

Casual remarks (16a,b) reveal that the discussion is taking place before an anonymous audience of young males who seem to be pupils, friends, or associates of Philebus. Their youthful openness to hedonism would be understandable; so also their youthful enthusiasm for worrying the similarities and differences among things, to the distraction of everyone around them, gently ridiculed by Socrates but shown by the end to have a solemn significance. The youthful audience is a paradigm of apparent contradiction: out of the vitality of humanity spring the twin impulses toward pleasure or eros and reason or dialectic.

Socrates opens the conversation by stating for Protarchus's benefit the root of the difference between Philebus's position and Socrates' own: Philebus says that pleasure is the good for all living things while Socrates maintains the superiority of noetic facility, roughly wisdom, for all those to whom it is available. Philebus thus proposes a good that strongly draws to itself every living thing, the untaught and the unteachable alike, in a testimony to the unity of all animate existence and perhaps, as later speeches of Socrates himself suggest (42c *ff.*), the unity of all corporeal existence; while Socrates' conception of good points to disjunction, disparity, and fracture, humanity set apart and mankind itself divided against itself to a degree that becomes measureless when all "who are and will be" are had in mind as those who may or may not to one extent or another share in Good.

Socrates now proposes the general line of inquiry that will in fact shape the entire investigation: to consider whether enjoyment or thinking is most conducive to man's happiness, or whether it is not rather some combination of the two that is best; and in the latter case, whether pleasure or thought is more nearly related to the combination of the two of them. The form of this odd question should be noted carefully because it will reappear when Socrates joins the Finite and the Infinite in a combination without asking which of the ingredients more nearly resembles the sum of them, though the answer is clear and crucial. At any rate, Protarchus accepts this formulation of the terms of the argument and Socrates proceeds to the criticism of pleasure, apotheosized as Aphrodite – the name preferred by Philebus and the goddess – or as Hedone, the name by which she is most truly known. Socrates argues that the impression of unicity given by the word "pleasure" is illusory, concealing differences that verge on contradiction among the concrete pleasures. He might have made a similar point by referring to the two names of the goddess, but he tactfully refrains from doing so. Protarchus insists that pleasure is pleasure, regardless of differences which he evidently considers accidental. Protarchus's position is troublingly similar to the one we might expect to be taken by Socrates the proponent of the eternal Ideas: pleasure is One, the pleasures are Many, and the way to know the being and the nature of the Many is through the way in which they are One. For the first and not the last time in *Philebus*, the strong drift of Socrates' argument is away from the simple sovereignty of One and towards the serious authority of multiplicities even if those include mutual contradictories.

Socrates now makes plain that the importance of the differences among the kinds of pleasure lies in the fact that some are good and some are bad, thus tacitly indicating a reason for overriding the familiar issue of being and intelligibility conventionally associated with Socrates' teaching on the Ideas. (Compare this "Parmenidean" concession to the arguments against Socratic Idealism with the speech of the Eleatic [Parmenidean] Stranger in *Statesman* 263 on *eidos*, *genos*, *meros*.) More important for the purposes of man's happiness than participation in a single *eidos* or class is participation in Good. But is not Good itself a One in which all contradictory multiplicities will come to a harmonious beatitude through participation in it? It is worth knowing, at the beginning of one's reading of *Philebus*, that Good itself is left at the end as an amalgam of discrete ingredients dependent on a principle of combination (measure) by whose alchemy Good is constructed. There will be no uncompounded unity that dominates the universal pyramid of multiplicities by standing at its apex.

In order to elicit Protarchus's agreement that pleasure is heterogeneous with regard to its goodness and badness, Socrates offers to subject wisdom too to the question regarding its multiplicity. Protarchus is deceived and charmed by the appearance of equal treatment, not noticing that Socrates' concession regarding wisdom is limited to its possibly consisting of unlike parts, even mutually contradictory parts, with no reference whatever to the possibility that any of them could be bad. This small duplicity on behalf of mind passed over, Socrates continues by declaring that their purpose now must be to determine whether pleasure or wisdom or neither of these but rather some third is the good. He proceeds by bringing to the surface the wondrous (*thaumaston*) assertion, implicit in what they have been saying, that one is many and many are one. He dismisses as commonplace the illustration of unity and multiplicity in one thing's being both heavy and light, or its being compounded of many parts; but the dismissal itself appears problematical because at a later point the issue of the heavy and light or the great and small will loom in the form of the more and less, the Infinite or Numberless, while the composition of a presumptive One, namely, Good, out of a recognizable multiplicity will be at the peak of the dialogue's achievement. Still, for the present it suits Socrates' purpose to focus on the conception of unity not as it arises from things that come to be and pass away but as it comes to view when applied to such things as man, ox, beauty, and good. More striking in this selection of examples of eternal things than the inclusion of animal species is the obtrusive jumbling of things high and low, on the principle referred to in so many words by the Eleatic Stranger (*Statesman* 266d) when he speaks of the search for truth without heed to the dignity of the things considered. Of course the possibility must be faced that what will come to light through an investigation of the unities or even the Ideas will have a morally neutral cast, reflecting a neutrality of the whole itself regarding a matter of great human concern.

Socrates now sets forth what he takes to be the ruling questions about unity. First, whether it is to be accepted that such a thing truly is. Next, how these things which are forever one and the same, neither coming to be nor being destroyed, can be so firmly the same one. And then how this One is to be in one and also in the infinite multiplicity of the generated things – whether it is broken up among them or maintains itself in some sort of isolated distinctness: very much the question thrust upon the youthful Socrates when he must defend the Ideas against old Parmenides. But Socrates does not refer to Ideas here (15), rather to one and Many – not "what is?" but "how many," in anticipation of the emphasis on measure that will soon be striking. And the emphasis on measure or limit will itself be a response to the encroachment of the limitless or infinite on the One.

The order in which Socrates presents the serious questions about unity is notable for the fact that it places the issue of accepting the being of the One before the questions about the difficulties inherent in the character of the One. The existence of Unity may be prior to the character of unity, but the question whether we should accept that being before knowing anything about what in its being would testify to its being deserves attention. It appears to receive that attention immediately (15d) when Socrates remarks that we say that the same One and Many, generated by speech, circulate and have circulated, always, of old, and now in every single thing that is uttered, and that it neither ages nor dies in us, neither commencing nor ceasing but apparently inhering in speech itself. In light of this remark, the reason that we may or must regard the question of our accepting the being of One before considering or knowing anything concrete about it is easily understood: we accept it because, as speaking beings, we have no choice but to do so. As one might say, without the ever-present and ever-active One and Many, there could be no language and thus no speech. It is to be noted that this reason for human acceptance of the One is not tantamount to a proof of the One's cosmic or universal existence, for it is an argument from human convenience rather than from the nature of things.

More exactly, if a requirement for the human good could be understood without any doubt as having an existence dictated absolutely by the nature of the whole itself, then we could know positively that the Whole and Man are in a state of absolute unity and perfect articulation, beyond any mere "neutrality" of the Whole in regard to us. The case would be significantly different if the One existed in and for the human world rather than or even differently than it does in the world of the Whole. Socrates' answer to the first serious question about One falls short of indicating the perfection of the relation between man and the whole.

Saying nothing that bears visibly on the last two serious questions, Socrates moves on, presumably on a continuous path, to introduce a major element of the dialogue, a path of inquiry that is of the greatest efficacy and divine or human origin, and is indispensable to all the arts. It is that all the spoken-about things arise out of one and many and have within them innately the finite and infinite; and that, things being so ordered, it is up to us always to posit one idea in each case and to search for it and to find it, for it is there. Then if we grasp this, we must go on after one to two, if there are two, or to three or to whatever number until we can understand the original unity in its oneness, not only that it is one and many and infinite but also how many. We must not be satisfied with simply "many" but, he insists, we must arrive at a particular number between one and infinity before we settle for the infinity that accompanies the unity in things. Socrates ends this seminal discourse by criticizing the wise men of his time who pass heedlessly between unity and infinity, disregarding number, and in so doing fall into eristic and miss dialectic. The full import of this definition of dialectic will not become clear until Socrates, for the benefit of the understandably confused Protarchus, explains himself with the use of examples. The examples will show that dialectic is the art of answering "What is . . . ?" with "how many?"

The definitive example is sound, which is of course some one thing. It is also infinite, or as we would say a continuum of infinitesimals. One could break in on the infinity by designating a duality, namely, high and low; or a trinity of high, medium, and low, but with these alone there would be no art of music. Necessary to be known are the intervals and harmonies, and the movements of the body that follow – all of these determined in finite quantities by measure and number, including the rhythms of motion of the body, namely, dance. While our knowledge of anything is on the level of a sense of its infinity or infinite gradation, we do not understand it. Socrates does not make explicit the equally consequent conclusion from his illustration that we do not understand it when we know it as a One.

Starting with unity, e.g., the unity of "sound," one may not proceed to the infinity of sounds but must find the finite number of them that is the key to understanding. Likewise, starting with the infinity of sound, one must find the number of sounds before pronouncing a unity. Socrates' explicit reason for going through the argument in the reverse direction is that doing so will draw the discussion closer to the large purpose of the conversation, which has to do with pleasure, wisdom and good. How it does so is a matter of great concern. The reverse illustration is that of the infinity of sound and the transition thence to its unity through the finite number of the letters of the alphabet. This transition too is of divine or human origin. As Prometheus was the only one named in the musical illustration, so the Egyptian Theuth is the only one mentioned by name as the inventor of letters and the science of letters. He observed the infinity of sound, the multiplicity of the vowel sounds and the consonant sounds, and in a way not made clear, distinguished also the silent letters. He reduced all these to a finite number of letters and generated the science of letters, or grammar. There would have been no science or intelligibility in the One and the Many without the intermediation of Number.

We cannot take up the difficult question whether what an Egyptian inventor of writing generated was a true alphabet or was rather a system of hieroglyphs that captured the sounds of spoken words and then became meaningless symbols of those sounds, as letters are. But we cannot avoid the implications of the fact that the Egyptian alphabet, whatever it may be, is extracted from Egyptian speech, as the Greek alphabet would be extracted from Greek, and so on through Russian, Hebrew and Sanskrit. Alphabets are human inventions drawn from the multiplicity of languages, the conventional manifestations and exemplars of natural speech. As one might say, the natural One of "speech" would be unintelligible and of no effect if it were not reduced by human agency to a number, some finitude or measure, of actual languages; and there would be no understanding the sounds of each language as such, and of course no writing it down, if its sounds were not identified and reduced to a number. I wish to stress the arbitrariness of that reduction, a point that comes to mind as one notices the regional dialects into which the pronunciation of any language might be and every language probably is divided. The number between One and Infinity that is crucial to understanding is, in the definitive illustrations, a product of human determination affected with arbitrariness as well as with definiteness. As we learned earlier, out of the capacity for speech comes the primal drive toward or need for the One; and as we see now, out of that same speech, not as rational discourse but as sound produced through the mouth in the mode of utterance, comes the drive toward or need for the Number that fructifies the One as it reduces the One to the concrete intelligible. It would be going too far too fast to say that Number replaces Unity as the ground of intelligibility, but it would not be unreasonable to suggest that Number presses hard against Unity for the distinction.

At this point, Philebus repeats the question he had raised previously as to the bearing of the present discussion on the matter before them. Socrates replies that the issue is just how each of them, presumably pleasure and wisdom, is one and many, and how each is not immediately infinite but is of some number. Protarchus reasonably takes this to mean that Socrates might wish to go on to determine the number of kinds of pleasure and wisdom; but in his speech to Socrates, Protarchus opens the possibility of pursuing the inquiry in some other unnamed way, should Socrates choose to do so. Surprisingly, Socrates abruptly gives the discussion what appears to be a new direction. He vaguely recalls hearing that neither pleasure nor wisdom is the good, but that some third thing is. If that is so, then pleasure cannot triumph, and there is no need to distinguish its kinds (*eidē*), or as we would now say, its number. Socrates promises that what follows will help to explain this, to us astonishing, casting aside of the laborious preparation for a taxonomy of pleasures and wisdoms or the discovery of the number of each. As Unity was challenged by Number, that is, cardinal number (two, three, four), so cardinal number is now about to be challenged by ordinal number: which is second and which is third as pleasure and wisdom are ranked behind the other thing that is the good, which is identified provisionally as the combination of pleasure and wisdom.

Socrates begins the new argument by laying down that the good is the perfect in the sense that anyone possessing it would need nothing more in order to be happy. From this it is easily made to follow that neither pleasure without mind nor wisdom without pleasure is the good. If either were sufficient, it would be fit to be chosen by every plant and animal as its way of life, so far as possible, throughout its life (22b). From this remarkable pronouncement we seem invited to consider that there is some absolutely strict sense of "good" that removes it from the realm of the peculiarly human and that satisfies a demand that it apply, if not to every single object in the universe, then to every kind of thing that grows. On these terms, either mankind will have to settle for and participate in a good that is modest enough for the gnats and mosses of the world or it will have to find and dwell with a good that it prescribes to itself or is prescribed to it by some power that can or wishes to define a human good.

The explicit aim of the next part of the argument is to determine whether pleasure or wisdom is closer to the combination of the two of them, as, according to Socrates' illustration, wisdom would be if mind proved to be the cause of the combination. Mind would not then be itself the good but, as cause of the good, it would be its closest kin, as, mutatis mutandis, would pleasure. For his present purpose, Socrates declares that he needs a new instrument. That new instrument is a principle for investigating all things by quadripartition, according to the doctrine that everything in the Whole is either infinite, finite, a combination of both, or the cause of such a combination. This quadripartition replaces a tripartition, which in turn replaced the bipartition One and Many, which in turn could be regarded as the first analysis of the Whole Infinite. Socrates showed that neither Many, which he calls infinite, nor One is sufficient without the intermediation of Number, thus introducing the tripartition that guides all investigation on the way to the good. In the present quadripartition, the argument evolves away from Unity in two distinct ways. First, One is no longer an element of the taxonomy; and second, the number of elements in the taxonomy is now larger than ever. It might be appropriate to mention that the growth in the number of elements will continue until the good itself is reached.

Lest it be thought that the primal disjunction of One and Many has been simply superseded, Socrates proposes to move on by seeking the One and Many, i.e., the nature or definition, of the infinite and the finite. First, in what way or in what sense is the infinite many? The defining examples are the hotter and the colder, by which Socrates means to illustrate an endless more and less, the opposite and contradictory of a definite number or quantity or measure. The more and less are always advancing and not at rest, while definite quantity stays still. Thus the "many" or essential plurality of the unnumbered is not its being composed of an unimaginably large quantity but rather its being characterized always, unceasingly, by more and less. Otherwise stated, something that belonged to the infinite could, as such, be known exclusively as more or less, in the way in which hotter and colder may suggest but can give no clue to Hot or Cold. One may wonder whether Hot and Cold proper do not collapse and vanish into their unlimited comparative correlates. If at this point a witness to the dialogue were to be dissatisfied because the principle of explanation seems to apply only to adjectives and not to substantives, he might be reassured by being reminded that "good" itself is both an adjective and a substantive.

Socrates summarizes the discussion of the Unity of the Infinite by saying (25a) that whatever appears to us to become more or less, as more or less hot or cold, should be placed in the class of the infinite as in a Unity according to the earlier argument in which we said that we must bring together all things that are scattered and split up, as far as is possible for us to impress on them some one nature. In the earlier speech referred to at 16d, Socrates is preparing the mediation of One and Infinite by Number, and to do so announces that the division of everything between finite and infinite makes it necessary for us always to posit and search for the one idea of things that lies within. This relatively mild formulation for man's contribution to the positing of the One is strengthened by the transition from the use of the verb *tithēmi*, posit, at 16d to *episemainō*, to set the mark, seal, stamp, or sign of the One on the confused Infinite (25a). The same strong locution is used also in the *Statesman* 258c, as part of what emerges gradually as Plato's critique of the One.

Socrates claims to have arrived at the Many and the One of the infinite, that from which all limit or definiteness is intrinsically absent. It may be thought paradoxical that what is in itself without definiteness is subject to definition, as the Infinite has just been shown to be by having a unity assigned to it in the form of some one nature that we strive to impress upon it. Apparently, the Infinite in being can be transformed into the Finite in reason or thought or speech, in that or so far as a One can be imposed upon it. It is one of those things spoken about to which we are compelled as speaking beings to apply the dichotomy of One and Many. If there is some tension between what is in being and what is in thought, that tension can be managed, resolved, or overcome only by thought or from the side of thought, human thought brought to bear to the best of our power, as far as possible, *kata dynamin*.

What we now seem to know is that the Many of the Infinite is the more and less in the infinitesimal and innumerable manifold thereof, as well as the things that can exist only as more and less: while the One of the Infinite is the thought or the speech that utters the thought in words which report the membership in the class of the more and less.

Socrates finds it easy now to speak about the Finite. The things opposite to the Infinite – not subject to more and less, but rather to their opposites, namely, equality and the equal, the double, and all relation of a number to a number or a measure to a measure. By these illustrations and the locutions in which they are expressed, Plato makes clear to us that by the Finite he means what exists as a finite or rational number, a ratio between two commensurable quantities that are numbers, between which a relation exists that can be expressed as a definite number. By its opposite, the infinite, Plato then evidently means that existence of which the paradigm would be such a quantity as *pi*, the symbol of the relation between two such incommensurables as the circumference and the diameter of a circle, or the square root of two, Ö2, the symbol of the relation between two such incommensurables as the diagonal of the unit square and any of its sides.

As will appear, Socrates considers himself now to have discussed the way in which the Finite is many, which is to say that he has shown by example the many kinds of things that belong among the Finite. Instead of completing the explanation by taking up the unity of the Finite, he passes on to ask what sort of idea the third class has, the one that is a mixture of the Infinite and the Finite, which latter he now says has not been collected into its unity, although what is to follow might produce that effect. The mixed or third class of things contains those in which the definiteness of number has been added to and evidently predominates over the indefinitely large multiplication of possibilities between more and less courageous, more and less purple, and so on, in the sense of Socrates' examples from health, which is restored when "number" intervenes to banish the "infinite" or disorder that presents itself as illness; and from music, wherein the Finite is added to high and low (i.e., higher and lower), fast and slow, for the perfection of music; and from the moderation of cold and hot in the climate. To use the addition of Number to the Limitless Opposites as a trope for expressing the superiority of moderation to extremes would be to waste a great effort on a very modest outcome. But Socrates ascribes by name health, beauty, strength, and many great beauties of the soul to this limitation of the unlimited by number – a limitation that could come to be only if two mutually contradictory things, the Finite and Infinite, or measure and the incommensurable, could be combined under the influence of the harmonizing or moderating power of cause, which would impose measure on its opposite and thus apparently transform the third class into the Finite just as surely as the mixture of the colored and the colorless would inevitably be colored. We perceive now why Socrates hinted that the missing "unity of the Finite" might emerge in the definition of the third class of things, the combinations of Finite and Infinite. Apparently, it is of the nature of the idea of the Finite or of Number itself to exist as the dominant counterpoise to an opposite principle in the Whole, a Whole that is constituted by the Infinite incommensurable-irrational as well as by the principle of measure and control that brings things to their proper sizes, amounts, and conditions. Inevitably, if we are to understand our world, we will wonder about the power that brings together the contradictory reconcilables to form a combination dominated by, if not indeed converted into the more potent but still limited ingredient, yet under such conditions that the union must always appear precarious.

At this point (26b), Socrates gives the discussion a historical or political bearing by remarking that a goddess intervened at some time to put an end to universal insolence and wickedness and unlimited pleasure-seeking by imposing law and order, *nomos* and *taxis*, which belong to Finite. The universe is so strangely constructed that its powerful impulse, ubiquitous in all animals, namely, the innately unlimited thrust toward pleasure, requires to be restrained so that the happiness almost universally believed to accompany the infinite is in fact possible only when the seductive infinite is subdued to the finite, over heavy resistance. Law is the finite for us; it is also the alternative or even the antithesis to nature according to the distinction rendered venerable in classical political philosophy between *physis* and *nomos*. The very order of our world is deep in mystery, but mystery that would be greatly attenuated if the cause of the mixture of Infinite and Finite were manifest to us. Socrates will turn to the Cause next, but only after speaking of the Many, i.e., the concrete members of the third or mixed class: everything born of the limitation of the unlimited – perhaps all things. He does not stop to make explicit the One of the mixed class. There is little need to do so for once he has characterized the concrete many, the definition of the One would simply repeat that characterization: the One is what is seen in the Many and made into speech while the Many are the instances of that same observation and speech in concrete manifestation. The Idea as a separate being in which the concrete existences "participate" plays no part in the quadripartition Infinite-Finite-Mixture-Cause. The One as alternative to Many, in the formula One-Number-Infinite, is replaced by Mixture and the Cause of Mixture, by a duality and the cause of the duality, in the formula Infinite-Finite (or Number)-Mixture-Cause, as Plato's critique of the One continues.

Cause is what produces the members of the class of mixture, and the best life is a mixture of pleasure and wisdom. The interlocutors' task is not to determine the best life, which proved to be easy, but to decide which of its two ingredients stood in second place, that is, in second place behind the mixture itself. The mixture is a composite of infinite and finite. Pleasure belongs wholly in the class of the infinite. Socrates moves to make the argument turn on whether mind and wisdom are in the class of the finite or the infinite and he proceeds by gaining assent to the proposition that the whole itself is ruled and ordered not by unreason or chance but by wisdom. Protarchus, appalled at the thought of denying this, agrees to it so hastily on the evidence of the heavenly bodies that Socrates cautions him against adopting thoughtlessly the acceptable received opinions. This noted, Socrates begins the investigation of Cause by himself referring to the nature of the bodies of all living things, that is, the nature of fire, water, air, and earth. His point is that fire as it is in us is the paltry counterpart of the great fire of the Whole by which our fire is nourished, out of which it is generated and by which it is ruled; and similarly with water, air, and earth. We are, in other words, naturally, spontaneously, automatically in perfect and absolute concord with the Whole on the plane of body. As somatic beings, we are one with the Whole and are ruled by it unqualifiedly. Now it is Socrates' task to establish our relation to the Whole on the plane that is relevant to soul or Cause. His proof of the presence of soul in our body is achieved with no difficulty by the simple means of asking Protarchus whether they should not say that our body has a soul. That admitted, Socrates moves next to a surprising position: instead of arguing that, as the quadripartition of body to us must be understood under the identical quadripartition of body to the Whole, so the presence of soul in our body must be understood by reference to a universal soul, he reverts instead to the quadripartition of Finite, Infinite, their Mixture, and Cause, the fourth which is in all things and which provides us with soul and with those things that are good for the body. As Cause replaced One at the earlier stage, it now replaces soul in the forward movement of the argument. His argument for Cause goes beyond soul to what provides both soul and the good of the body, to what he calls the totality of wisdom. How, he asks, could there be missing from the other components that exist throughout the heavens, that single one which he calls the most beautiful and glorious nature? Would it not be better if we said that in the Whole there is much infinite and enough finitude, and a not contemptible cause which orders the times and seasons and is most justly called wisdom and mind. But wisdom and mind could not come into being without soul. And in the nature of Zeus you would say that a royal soul and a royal mind were brought into being through the power of Cause, and other noble things in the others according to how each likes best to be spoken of. Thus we know that mind always rules the Whole, as the ancients said.

The totality of wisdom that rules so widely is not soul but is prior to soul, and it is not the wisdom of the god but is responsible for the soul and mind of a god, is prior also to god. But Cause, or Wisdom and Mind, could not come to be without soul, although soul does not produce Cause, rather the reverse. Soul must therefore be a condition of the existence of Cause if Cause, *qua* wisdom and mind, were to come into being. Cause, in any ordinary signification of the word, and according to the meaning given it by Socrates, is prior to its product; but that product is here presented as necessary to its own productive cause, if the productive Cause *qua* wisdom and mind is such a thing as comes into being. Cause *qua* productive is primordial; but if productive of a cosmos it must have and depend on mind. Absolute Cause should be both different from mind as being its producer, and it should be guided by mind, perhaps while being coextensive with mind, to the end that its product be a cosmos, and order. If there is no mind without soul, and the cosmos is a product of intelligent Cause, then soul must be coeval with Cause. Then it would be misleading to represent Cause as unconditionally primordial.

Our perplexity will not subside if we do not clarify to ourselves what we mean or should mean by Cause. We might mean a mere efficiency or power or capacity for producing an effect or a product or change in the state of things. If we meant this, and in doing so meant to adhere strictly to the notion of an efficient cause, which is an entity distinct from any other to which the form and the end of its products are intellectually present, then we should have to admit either the separate existence of such an intelligent companion or the activity of mere chance, were our axiom the orderliness of the cosmic product of Cause. But if by Cause we were to mean not mere efficiency but the totality of whatever is primordial to an orderly cosmos, not admitting the need for a collaboration between efficiency and any other indispensable separate adjunct entity, then we would have adhered to the strictest because absolute sense of Cause, and in so doing would have made unnecessary, indeed repugnant, the hypothesis of soul which bears intelligence and is opposite to body. If an escape from the difficulty were sought by ensouling the cosmos itself, making it an animal possessed of its own self-directing intelligence, then Cause would be rendered superfluous immediately by what would amount to a denial that the cosmos was in need of a power that both transcends and precedes it for its coming into being. Socrates does not here choose to take that direction but, on the contrary, as was said above, he unexpectedly fails to argue the existence of soul in the All by analogy with our somatic integration in the

Whole, moving instead to Cause as the amalgamation of the Infinite and the Finite. As he previously moved cautiously toward presenting the One as if replaceable by the mere characterization of the Many, so he now appears to de-emphasize a discrete soul of the All, a separate intelligence external to and decisive for the good of the cosmos but not of the body of the cosmos, installing in its place that which makes possible or accomplishes the harmonious conjunction of irrational and rational that are the inmost irreducibles of the universe. Whatever it is that is the ground of, reason for, producer of that reconciliation of opposites, solely by itself whether in the capacity of agent or in the capacity of an essence shared by the reconcilable opposites that drives them into mixture because they are what they are, that "whatever" is primordial self-subsistent Cause. If, however, Cause is not to be understood, cannot be understood except as working in the presence of mind as distinct from the intelligible essence of objects, and mind for all purposes means soul, then Cause can never be conceived as unconditional. In presenting Cause as both unconditional and dependent upon soul, Socrates is not so much contradicting himself as compelling us to look directly at a question that stands before all serious theology.

Everything said is intended to conduce to the conclusion that mind rules and that mind belongs or belongs more or less or virtually to that one class of the quadripartition that is called Cause. Hence it follows that mind or wisdom lies closer than pleasure to the highest of the four classes, and thus stands in second place ahead of the life of pleasure the infinite, which is what was to be shown. Socrates has determined the order of goodness between pleasure and mind not by establishing first what is meant by good but by erecting Finite or definite number as the criterion of superiority and arguing as if the decisive quality of mind is its power of limiting the unlimited or imposing number and thus reason on the unnumbered and irrational, represented by *pi*. It is not at all clear how *pi* can ever be mastered, for it belongs in the nature of things; but that it can be somehow subdued is demonstrated by the simultaneous existence, in a condition of evident reconciliation and mutual dependence, of the circumference and the diameter of a circle. Perhaps the numbering power of mind is demonstrated in the fact that the irrational "number" is made by mind to appear as if it were a number, namely "*pi*," through an act of mind that cannot be better denominated than by use of the figure used earlier by Socrates: stamping upon some plurality the idea of a rationalizing unity. At any rate, number or Finite is at the present stage of the argument the surrogate for Good.

For reasons not stated, Socrates moves next to investigate the coming into being of pleasure and mind – in what, and through what passion or affect (*pathos*) each of them comes to be. The satisfactory discussion of pleasure is said to require the inclusion of pain, and the inquiry will begin in fact with the genesis of pain. Socrates opens the investigation with the assertion that both pleasure and pain have their origin according to nature in the third class, the class of the mixture of Infinite and Finite. Since he argued earlier that pleasure belonged to the class of the Infinite, his assertion here has the clear implication that its being in one class is compatible or consistent with its becoming through another. Whatever that might portend in general, Socrates' immediate point is that the third class is the locus of harmony and of health, which are subject to disruption and restoration according to whether dissolution or a repletion is taking place, or a displacement or restoration – a movement against the natural condition or a movement towards it. Since a movement of return is unintelligible in the absence of a movement of displacement, it is clear that the discussion of pleasure is impossible without considering pain if, as will soon appear, pleasure originates in bodily motions of a natural direction. Every ensouled being comes to be according to nature out of the infinite and finite, so that its natural state is also its harmonious or measured state in the sense that each is present in some right amount. In light of what has gone before, that must mean that some number has been applied to something capable of being present as more or less. The illustrations of this highly abstract doctrine indicate an intention on Plato's part to explain pleasure and pain as counterparts of somatic states: hunger is a dissolution and a pain, eating a repletion and a pleasure; excessive cold brings on a painful congelation of the moistures, the return of the parts to their natural places and separation is pleasure. Plato has provided an account of pleasure and pain in terms of how they come about or come to be – "what it is" as what is its coming into being, as before he explained the One as the Many and as he continues to speak of the living and other things as compounded of Infinite and Finite rather than of body and soul.

But there are pleasures and pains of other sorts and origins. There are the pleasures and pains that arise within the soul itself, those that come to be when the soul looks forward to pleasures and pains that lie ahead. In the briefest of remarks, Socrates lets it be understood that the pleasures and pains of the soul itself are mere shadows of anticipation derivative from those aesthetic accompaniments of small bodily motions already described as pleasure and pain. Before leaving the subject of their genesis, Socrates characterizes both kinds of pleasure as "pure," that is, unmixed with pain, by which he cannot yet mean arising independently of pain since pleasure has been defined in terms of the hedonic movement that follows the perturbation of pain.

Still inquiring whether pleasure as such is simply choiceworthy, Socrates asks Protarchus to consider whether a living being in whom neither the disrupting nor the restoring motions were occurring would not be free from pleasure and pain at the moment. On this basis Socrates affirms that there is a condition devoid of pleasure and pain alike, and takes the next step of asserting that there is nothing to prevent one from living a life of the mind in that manner. For this astonishing assertion nothing resembling evidence is offered, only a reminder of the point made much earlier that anyone living such a life would be entirely without feelings of pleasure or pain. In the earlier passage (2Ide), Socrates made the joylessness of such an apathetic life a reason for rejecting it in favor of the mixed life of pleasure and mind. The reasoning that argued against its desirability is now adduced in support of its possibility – a non sequitur made conspicuous by the recent definition of pleasure and pain in terms of bodily motions, harmonious and inharmonious with nature, that could cease only in death. In fact, the impossibility of such a cessation of the flux in a living body will be granted freely by Socrates at a much later point in the dialogue (43a). At any rate, that gods probably feel neither joy nor its opposite is the weakest of arguments for the possibility of a human life without either.

Socrates reverts now to the pleasures of the soul itself, connects their origin with memory and declares it necessary to clarify perception (*aisthēsis*) before grappling with memory. According to Socrates, the body is affected in two ways: in one, what the body suffers never reaches the soul for its awareness, while in the other, the vibrations (*seismōn*) of the body reach the soul's consciousness to produce sensation, which Socrates defines as the shared experience and shared motion of body and soul united. The soul does not "forget" those things of which it was never aware, it is simply oblivious of them, while it is only the perceptions that it has once entertained that it can either remember or forget. Memory is the preservation of perception, which involves the body's motions. Memory seems to constitute a pool or fund of such stored perceptions, from which the soul can on its own initiative draw when it wishes to do so, and when it does so, it "recalls" rather than "remembers." Socrates stresses the importance of the distinction between remembering and recalling for the bearing it has on the pleasure of the soul apart from the body, and also the soul's desiring. Socrates guides the discussion next to the subject of desire, what it is and how it originates.

Desire is exemplified by hunger and thirst, emptiness calling for replenishment. Desire means a yearning for opposite states, for example to be filled while being actually empty. Since it is the body that is empty, the locus of desire must be the soul, for the body cannot and the soul therefore must envision the state opposite to its actual one. This is possible for the soul because it has the power to recall the perceptions or sensations of past states, in the present example the sensation of the body's being full. It belongs only to the soul to be cognizant of a state other than its actual state, but that other state is one that must have been experienced as actual at some other time. There is no question of a free or speculative intelligence at work. From all this Socrates infers that all desire is of the soul, not of the body, although, as he fails to mention, so far as hunger and thirst are typical of desire, to that extent the body commands the soul's desiring. Socrates remarks, as if casually, that every living thing is always striving towards the opposite of its actual state (35a), a statement that, if true, would mean not only that Socrates had been converted to the doctrine of flux in a significant degree but also that the wise desire to be foolish. It would be better to understand this remark, which helps to present the soul as always seeking to make of the future a copy of the pleasant past recollected, as referring particularly to states of the soul and body in their intense symbiosis. Socrates now proclaims that the discourse has shown that the appetite, the desire, the rule in every living thing belongs to the soul by virtue of its having the power of recalling. For the second time, Protarchus does not point out that the soul's recalling and desiring are responsive and ministerial to the states and needs of the body. Had he done so, Socrates might have been induced to make explicit that soul, whose hegemony is now being argued, differs in a significant respect from Cause, the ruling element in the quadripartition that preoccupied him and that seems to have dropped out of sight. Soul is not *nous*, or mind, reason, wisdom, or intellect. It is only that capacity for participating in, retaining, and recalling the vibrations of the body that it experiences as sensations and that it can transfer from the past, as the discourse will soon show, to the future as an image of things to come. If, therefore, Socrates will leave unqualified his assertion that the argument has shown that soul rules every living thing because the memory that projects our delights and thus rules us belongs to the soul, then he would have found an extraordinarily pregnant meaning in the argument: we are ruled by our propensity to pleasure and to avoid pain, more fundamentally, to seek our preservation and avoid our destruction.

For the stated purpose of drawing an inference regarding the way of life, Socrates turns to the sensations of pain and pleasure that relate to being full and empty and all the others connected with the preservation and destruction of living things. He considers the transition between being empty and being full, elicits the thought that one may be pained by his present state but cheered by the anticipation of his coming relief. Socrates describes one who is affected by a pain that is expected to be followed by a pleasure as "between" (*en meso*) pleasure and pain. It is noteworthy that he does not adduce such a being in the middle to illustrate the freedom from both pleasure and pain to which he referred earlier when speaking of the present subject, namely, the way of life, maintaining that the most divine way of life would be the one free from both pleasure and pain. Here, in the rather pointedly somaticized discussion of pleasure and pain, he describes the man or other living thing who is in the middle condition as partaking at once of both (36b). The distinctions of soul and body, man and beast, become blurred as the mechanical etiology of pleasure and pain progresses. Socrates affiliates the soul's vision of relief with hope and thus with pleasure; the absence of such a hope with pain. With this, Socrates begins a long passage of the discourse aiming to establish that pleasures and pains can be true or false. As we are capable of true and false opinions, so we are capable of the anticipations of pleasures and pains – which anticipations are themselves pleasures and pains of the soul – that are connected with true and false opinions. The opinions that lodge in our souls like words and images have their source in memory and perception, and in the feelings (*pathēmata*) (39a), thus sharing an origin with the pleasures and pains of the soul alone. Perhaps because they exhibit a shared being by virtue of their common becoming, pleasure of the soul is vulnerable to the falseness of opinion, and where the vulnerability appears most clearly is in the visions of the future that false opinion holds up to the contemplation of the soul, misleading it into the pleasure of anticipation of that which is either wicked or nothing at all.

Addressing the reason that some men are shown true images and are thus inspired with true hopes or pleasures, Socrates finds the explanation in the friendship of the gods for the just, pious, and good man. We may thus trust that the opinions and the hopes and the anticipations of pleasure of the just, pious, and good are all true, specifically the hopes that they have for the pleasures that await them in heaven. But Socrates has shown nothing by way of a demonstration of any of these teachings on the helpfulness of the gods. The opinion that our right opinions are gifts of the gods to the pious must eventually be understood in its relation with the doings of Socrates, who before our eyes is himself endowing Protarchus and perhaps others with a correction of their hedonistic opinions and thus helping to save them from false pleasures and pains.

Socrates now proposes that the only badness of pleasures lies in their falseness, a conclusion to which he has been pushed by the near reduction of pleasure to opinion, of course in the soul. As one might say, if the soul's mind were only wisdom, then the opinionative underside of wisdom would not exist to falsify pleasure. Protarchus is not prepared for the radical intertwining of pleasure and knowledge, and protests that wickedness must have something to do with the badness of pleasures. Socrates agrees that they might take the point up at a later time, but he dismisses it for the present in favor of an argument showing that the soul compares the magnitudes of expected pleasures and pains, projecting its recollections of past states of body under the influence of the deceptions introduced by remoteness in time, as the eye is deceived by distance in space. Thus truth and falseness can attach to pleasures and pains without infection from opinion but through another failing of the mind, namely, miscalculation. It has by now been made clear that a life of pleasure is necessarily in some large measure a kind of life of the mind, understanding by mind not wisdom alone but the other powers of truth and untruth that must be included in an animate intelligence. How might one understand the issue between "the life of pleasure" and "the life of mind" if the two are inseparable?

Still not content, Socrates sees a way into greater falseness of pleasure and pain than has yet come to light. He would like to know what follows from the admitted fact that pain and pleasure have their origins in the disruptions and restorations of our natural somatic state: he asks, what if neither corruption nor restoration were taking place, dismissing Protarchus's objection that that would be impossible and eliciting the conclusion that there would then be neither pleasure nor pain. Thus, a condition for absence of both pleasure and pain would be the cessation of motion in the body. Socrates makes reference to the wise men whose saying is that everything is always in flux upward or downward, a dictum that would seem to obviate any rest from pleasure or pain. But Socrates reminds Protarchus that there are changes within our bodies, of which growth is the prime example, that are below the level of our consciousness – an argument reminiscent of the earlier one that distinguished the bodily motions that find their way to the soul and those that die out within the body. The proponents of the physics of universal flux cannot convert their insight about the motion of body throughout the whole into a truth about pleasure and pain, thus into a truth about human life or its goodness.

Having noticed the wise men who give life only the two possibilities of pleasure and pain, refuge from both problematic, he pursues his purpose of demonstrating that life has three possibilities: pleasure, pain, and neither. In order to proceed, he must confront the theorists who reduce the true possibilities to only one, namely pain. Pleasure, they teach, is merely the absence of pain. These are men who are said to be cunning in matters of nature, and also particularly hostile to Philebus, that is, to hedonism. Their position is a curious one, for while they deny that pleasure is anything, they are repelled by it through some natural disgust, and they hate its power. Socrates considers them to be mistaken in their theory but on the right track in their morality. The wise men of flux upheld a physics of motion that Socrates does not refute, but they drew an untenable, unedifying moral conclusion from it, while the present misohedonists begin with an edifying moral instinct that will prove, under Socrates' guidance, to be inconsistent with physiology. Socrates' project will, at best and to the extent possible, articulate the facts of nature and the facts of the human good.

Describing the misohedonists as comrades-in-arms, Socrates proposes to Protarchus that they track the allies' disgust with pleasure all the way to its origins in the definition of the nature of a class of things, in particular, pleasure. This proves to mean locating anything, and thus pleasure, in the thing's most concentrated form, which in the case of pleasure is in the body in reaction against or relief of the most concentrated pain. A man's worst moments are his times of most intense bodily disorder, say in feverish illness. If the most intense pleasure is pleasure itself, and pleasure itself arises out of pain itself, then the misohedonists' point seems to have been demonstrated:

pleasure is nothing but the relief from or the absence of bodily pain in disease.

Socrates does not criticize the apparent nonsense in speaking of the "greatest" and "most intense," or the origin, of something whose nonexistence is to be proved. He will explain much later (51a) that he has wished only to make use of the misohedonists while making his argument that some pleasures are illusory and unreal, and others exist not purely but in mixture with pains. Since Socrates had already proved in his own name and without affecting to discover the reasonings of his "allies" that pleasure resulted from the correction of a decay from the natural norm, it is hard to see what he thinks his argument gains from the witness of these extremists whose merit is a moral predilection. From this point (45d) forward to 51a, Socrates' argument will consist of a correction of the misohedonist view that pleasure is simply non-pain of the body.

Socrates begins the striking anatomy of pleasure that follows with a showing that some pleasures are mixed in that they are in both body and soul and some in that they are also mixed with pain, while some lodge in and are of only body or soul. Because of the peculiar mixing together of pleasure and pain at the same time, as in the pain of an itch which lies deep in the body and the pleasure of the scratching which relieves only the surface, it is possible for the same mixture to appear to its host as pleasure or pain. Socrates carries this theme forward through the investigation of the pleasures and pains of the body and also of the body and the soul together, as in the case discussed earlier in which the body is in one state and the soul anticipates the opposite state, providing a pleasant antithesis to the actual distress. Socrates explains that he will now say what he did not say when the latter case was first discussed, namely, that in the utter enormousness of the frequency of occasions when body and soul diverge in these directions, there is only one mixture of pain and pleasure. More pointedly than ever, Socrates argues an ontology that seems to defy logic: mutual contradictories can exist simultaneously, at least in an animate being, and their coexistence is called a One. Is unity a name for plurality of opposites, as if Being were a coin with One on the one side and Strife on the other, everything always being in motion upward or downward, advancing toward order or decaying from it?

Socrates proceeds to the pains and pleasures of the soul by itself, showing in a tour de force of psychology how the pains of anger and other passions combine with the pleasures of the same, arguing in an extended passage that men take pleasure in the ridiculous lapses from self-knowledge of their friends while at the same time enduring the pains of envy. He brings this exposition to its climax in a summary of the argument: in threnodies of mourning as in tragedies, not only on the stage but in all the tragedy and comedy of life, pain and pleasure are mixed together at once, as also in myriad other things (50b).

Having anatomized the mixtures of pleasure and pain in body, soul, and body and soul together, Socrates finds it natural and somehow necessary to consider the unmixed pleasures. He begins by repeating his disagreement with those who deny that pleasure is anything more real than cessation of pain, true as it might be that many pleasures – as he has shown – do have that character. Asked what are true pleasures, Socrates replies that they are those connected with the beautiful colors, shapes, odors, and sounds, delightful when perceived but not missed or yearned for painfully when they are absent. He explains that the shapes that he has in mind are not the shapes of animals or paintings, that is, not the shapes of the natural things or the artifacts that mimic them, but the geometric ones, in perceptible manifestation and not as objects of contemplation; indeed, manifested in products of the woodworker's art. He emphasizes the innate, everlasting beauty of such things, which is the source of the unmixed pleasure that they give. After the pleasures of the sense of smell and sound, Socrates adds the pleasures of knowledge if they do not originate in hunger for knowledge or in the pains of such a hunger. From this we understand that the philosophic life, driven by conscious wonder and earnest yearning for the knowledge that relieves the distress of confusion, is not a life of unmixed pleasure but rather resembles human existence altogether in its composition of tragedy and comedy. In a brief exchange (52ab), Socrates and Protarchus make it clear that the feelings of pleasure and pain that they have been discussing are the natural and spontaneous ones, not those that arise out of thought or reasoning about things. The pure pleasures of sensible beauty are free gifts to us from nature; the pleasures of philosophizing are neither pure nor natural; the loss of knowledge is not the accompaniment of a disarrangement that causes pain and that calls out for the restoration that brings pleasure. Nature does not sound an alarm to alert us to the loss of knowledge as a good; as merely natural beings, we would sink painlessly into the stupor of senility or diseased obliviousness. Socrates' proof that there are pleasures that are unmixed with pain serves to refute the misohedonists' contention that pleasure is only a release from pain, but it has gone further in implicating the question of philosophic inquiry. We would be satisfied with our grasp of his meaning if he had not closed this part of his argument with the remark that the pure pleasures of knowledge belong not at all to the many but only to exceedingly few. What can he mean except that to a very few human beings it is given to know without desire or painful effort, as if truth were simply and directly to appear to them as a beautiful odor or sound might present itself, but having the character of an effortless insight into the noetic beauties of the world? It could not plausibly be said that the natural world is a great machine inclined to the realization of the multitude of mankind's purest pleasure; almost the reverse.

Now (52c) Socrates makes a remark that ostensibly summarizes and in fact breaks into the argument. He says, with much reservation, that, having moderately well discriminated the pure pleasures and those fairly correctly called the impure, they may go on to add that the turbulent pleasures (say those that come with scratching an intense itch) are unmeasured while the opposite kind are measured. The former, in body and soul, are of the class of the infinite, the latter of the measured. We have been brought back to the quadripartition of the first part of the dialogue, but the return is jarring because it contradicts flatly the repeated and uncompromising assertions (27e, 31a) that all pleasure is in the class of the unlimited. Protarchus accepts the new position without objection. It would appear that the introduction of the distinction between mixed and unmixed or pure and impure has had a decisive influence on the characterization of pleasure as either finite or infinite: not pleasure as such but the kind of pleasure determines whether it is finite or measured. According to the authoritative quadripartition, everything whatsoever is infinite or finite or a mixture of the two compounded by Cause: mixture means mixture of finite and infinite. As the investigation of pleasure was driven forward by the argument that pleasure is only surcease from pain, pleasure came to be portrayed as very often mixed with pain, and the leading distinction that emerged was between the mixed and the pure pleasures, the former being indeed a relief from pain even if by anticipation rather than surcease, the latter pure primarily in being unmixed with anything other than themselves, accompanying the unsought perception of purely beautiful things, enjoyed with a tranquil satisfaction. The pure pleasures in this last sense are pure in the sense of "good," as calm, serene, controlled – in brief, moderate or measured – and they recommend themselves self-evidently as good with respect to a human being's happiness. The application of finite to infinite in general is in the interest of the order of the cosmos and all its constituents, including in that order if not simply meaning by it the articulation of matter in ways that guard the world from being populated by monsters. As the argument draws closer to the final definition of good, the analysis of pleasure must be cast under headings that are appropriate to the definition of the conditions of human happiness or the good for man. The pure pleasures must have a place in contributing to human good; their very purity or freedom from admixture with pain is the basis or condition for their moderateness or freedom from frenzy and ecstasy alike. Socrates had long since pronounced that it would not be necessary to investigate the kinds of pleasure for the task of determining whether pleasure or wisdom was second best after their combination. It now appears that the unity of pleasure is radically and decisively fractured. To be replaced by a duality or a double duality: mixed and pure, unmeasured and measured. The "unity" of pleasure is compelled to give way, or to be superseded, in the interest of the project for understanding the human good. Alternatively, man's good would be unattainable by him if pleasure were effectually a unity. It is of the greatest importance to mankind that pleasure is not a one.

Now Socrates moves (52d) toward the definition of the human good by assimilating to each other the true and the pure, and then describing the pure form first of pleasure and then of wisdom. As the purest white is also the truest and most beautiful white, so the purest pleasure and the purest knowledge are the truest of their kind, and thus belong to good – and so we might imagine the analysis to run quickly to its conclusion. But Socrates injects into the argument the thought that pleasure participates in Becoming, not in Being, by which he presumably means that one is necessarily, by virtue of what pleasure is, approaching it, passing through it, or leaving it behind. Of such things he says they are always for the sake of something else, as a means is for the sake of an end: Becoming is directed toward Being, and what has the status of an end has also the character of good. Thus pleasure does not belong to the good.

It is hard to understand how this depreciation of pleasure, even or especially in pleasure's purest form, does not carry knowledge or thinking down with it too, for the purest pleasure is precisely that which accompanies the presence of those unsolicited insights or knowledge gained without any admixture of painful desire for it. Moreover, such knowledge itself certainly comes into being and, as we saw, can pass away. It belongs fully as much to the realm of becoming as does the disparaged pleasure that it engenders, but its failure to qualify as an end is not only suppressed by the argument but is tacitly contradicted when Socrates presents the life of purest thought as most choiceworthy – the life of Being and Good. For the moment, we cannot do better than to notice that if the purest pleasure falls short of Good because pleasure belongs to Becoming rather than Being, then the purest knowledge or thought must be able to survive the same test if thought is to prove to be good. Before going on to subject mind and knowledge to the test, Socrates argues the folly of the hedonism that would make pleasure so unqualifiedly good as to make the man who feels pleasure the good man, ignoring such virtues as courage and moderation. We are left to wonder whether the wise man as such is courageous and moderate and in all ways virtuous, or even whether he would need to be in order to be thought good by this criterion.

Socrates discovers that there are sciences that are useful and others that are purely theoretical, as there is an arithmetic and a geometry for carpentry and then there is also the philosophical mathematics which recognizes only identical entities (presumably points, lines, and numbers rather than how many men or horses in two armies). It is given to Protarchus to conclude from this that the most precise arts are the ones that arise in connection with the eager effort (*hormē*) of the really philosophic, who presumably generate the most precise, hence presumably the purest knowledge. But it proceeds from their *hormē* and hence is not an unsolicited insight but produces a pleasure in them preceded by a desire, a lack, a pain. Perhaps it is for this reason that Socrates now nominates the dialectic power as not to be judged behind any other.

Dismissing Protarchus's argument that Gorgias would regard rhetoric as most powerful and best, Socrates insists on associating good with truth and purity rather than usefulness or advantage. If the present line of reasoning were to be pursued, the good for man would be disturbingly disjoint from man's practical advantage and thus perhaps even his survival. Having prepared for the mutual affiliation of dialectic, knowledge, and truth, Socrates is in a position to disparage those arts and their practitioners who exist in the realm of opinion, "and even if they think themselves to be investigating something of nature, know that all through their lives they investigate the things of this cosmos – how they come into being, how they are acted upon and what they do" (58a–59a). Thus we are exposed to a mighty distinction between nature and cosmos, the former being the realm of the objects of contemplation, the latter being the world of cause and effect, of what we now, in accord with Kant, call the world of the laws of nature. It is in this cosmos, this orderly world of experience, that all things are in a state of coming to be and passing away, of ubiquitous flux and thus of ungraspability. Therefore it can be said that the purest knowledge is of the eternal, changeless, and unmixed things – or of their nearest congeners – and this belongs with wisdom and mind. The search for the purest knowledge has ended: it is knowledge of the pure.

Immediately (59e), Socrates assigns to himself and Protarchus the character of *demiourgoi* or artisans whose task is to produce a mixture of wisdom (*phronēsis*) and pleasure. He appears to be demonstrating in act that the dialectically achieved knowledge about the purest pleasure and the purest, most useless knowledge is itself useful for the humanly advantageous purpose of combining the pure into a mixture. Repeating the issue, which is whether pleasure or knowledge comes closer to the good, and repeating also that the good is that which leaves no need unsatisfied, Socrates repeats at last that neither the life of mind without pleasure nor of pleasure without mind would suffice for any man; thus neither wisdom nor pleasure is the good. Their purpose must now be to discover Good, which they know must be sought in or as a mixture. If Good is a mixture, it belongs to the class of the impure, the things that are touched with Becoming and are passed by by Being – the things that cannot be grasped because they are forever changing. Of course what Socrates the *demiourgos* will confect here as good life will exist neither in the realm of nature, where the eternal and pure have their being, nor in the mere cosmos, where rhetoric and politics would be required to gain it an actuality among men, who might in any case be unequipped to live it.

Having gained again the admission that neither pleasure alone nor mind alone constitutes the good or the good life, Socrates begins the final ascent toward the true good for man (61). We know from the beginning that the good life – which is so indistinguishable from the good that we fall easily into the habit of thinking that good has meaning only in reference to human existence

– depends for its coming to be on good mixing, whatever that might prove to mean. Although some kinds of knowledge are truer and higher than others because they pertain to the beings that most truly are, they are insufficient to life, and to them must be added the humbler knowledges that belong to the human sphere, even though they are tinged with falseness; and also music and every other kind of knowledge. Of the pleasures, the pure and true must be accompanied by the necessary ones, presumably because there would be no human kind if it did not perpetuate itself through seeking the pleasure that is preceded by longing. The admissible pleasures are the ones that comport with what we can divine to be the idea of the good by nature in man and the whole.

These things granted, with all their implication for the qualified good of the good for man and for all, Socrates calls next for the inclusion of truth (64b) in the mélange that has already been required to admit something of the false. Hardly any formula of edification could be more routine and thus more empty of particular meaning than the bare imprecation of the truth. Socrates lifts his call for the truth above inanity by describing truth as indispensable to the becoming and the existence of what comes to be and exists. We might not know what truth is, but we know that it is necessary for becoming and existing. What is soon to follow will reveal what is necessary for becoming and existing, and in so revealing will shed light on truth, and on good and beauty. Before that, though, Socrates declares that their present discourse seems to him to have wrought, figuratively, an incorporeal cosmos that will rule nobly an animate body: the fabricated idea of this world of coming into being, existing, and dissolving – the rational principle or truth of this phenomenal world. This expression of Socrates', which rounds off a major portion of the dialogue, should be considered alongside the earlier passage (59a) in which cosmos was disparaged by comparison with nature, cosmos being this world of becoming and of being acted upon and of making, indeed the realm of the arts and knowledges that are of practical benefit to human beings, contrasted explicitly with the realm and faculty of truth, said to be appropriated to eternal things, unmixed things. The argument is drifting toward the adaptation of truth to eternity in the cosmos as distinguished from eternity simply. What this means more concretely will appear in what follows.

Socrates opens the final section of the dialogue by suggesting that he and Protarchus are now before the gates of the good itself (64c). To facilitate their passage within, he proposes the decisive question: what that is in or of "the mixture" (presumably always the mixture of all wisdom and some pleasures, but now with the late addition of "truth") seems to be most venerable and most emphatically the cause of its being universally liked. The answer comes forth: measure and proportion are indispensable to the being of the ingredients and of their combination. But as we have recently learned, truth is necessary for the being and becoming of what is and exists. We may therefore say provisionally that truth is the measure and proportion of combinations: right amount, and right amount in relation to other amount, i.e., at best, commensurability. So far as the cosmos is the sum of all becomings and durations, a compound of compounds, its truth and cause is measure. But to measure is joined proportion, the other name for which is commensurability. Commensurability or proportion is the relation between two measured or finite amounts both of which are measurable by the same measure. But, as in the relation between the circumference and radius of a circle or the perimeter and diagonal of a square, there exist irrationalities or incommensurabilities that testify to a limit that binds the truth itself, a limit that indicated perhaps "why" the things in the cosmos do not endure forever: the truth of the cosmos is a mixture of reason and unreason.

From his declaration that measure and proportion are indispensable to things and their mixtures Socrates now (64e) draws a consequence: since measure and proportion are everywhere assimilated to beauty and virtue, the power of good may be said to have fled for refuge in the nature of the beautiful. It is as if the good is being hunted from one apparently safe place to another, each conception of it proving insecure in turn, the latest being the identification of good as beauty and thus as measure and proportion. Whatever else has been made clear, it has now been revealed that we are in pursuit of the good.

To this point, Socrates has drawn both truth and beauty into the sphere of measure and proportion. He says now (65a), "If we cannot catch the good with or in one idea, let us take it with three, beauty, proportion, and truth, saying that these considered as one might most correctly, of all the things in the mixture, be regarded as cause, and through these as good, it has become so too." Apparently, the Idea of Good is a triplex made one, and the common ground to which the three are reducible is measure or proportion. The Idea of Good, itself a mixture, must be subject to the rule that its central ingredient, i.e. measure or proportion, is dominant in its own constitution. Only measure and proportion, three considered one or made one by having a single Idea stamped on them by us (p. 145 above), lie within the Idea of Good as an ingredient of it and also lie within it in the qualified sense in which cause is "in" or "of" the mixture to make it and its components endure as components and as composite.

Reverting now (65b) to the original dyad of pleasure and wisdom as "the mixture" superior to each of its components, and reverting also to the old question whether wisdom or pleasure stands closer to the good that neither of them by itself can claim to be, Socrates proceeds to compare each of them in turn with each element of the composite that is the test or standard, which is beauty, truth, and measure. In doing so, he will without explanation again restore (65c) the lately added and removed "truth" to mind (*nous*) and pleasure as the goods to be tested, thus producing the puzzling situation in which truth would have to be compared with itself since it is put in both the test and the thing to be tested. As will be seen, though, Socrates in act does finally drop "truth" from among the goods to be tested (mind or wisdom, and pleasure) with no more explanation than accompanied its recent insertions. Rapidly he "shows" that wisdom or mind, the two being used interchangeably, is much closer than pleasure to truth, measure, and beauty, each in turn. Now he has completed his demonstrations and is ready to pronounce the good.

As is to be expected, he passes from the thing to be tested to the thing by which it is to be tested in seeking the highest or first among the goods. The first choice of eternal nature is measure and what belongs to it, and the second is proportion and what belongs to it, which is beauty, perfection (*to teleon*), and sufficiency – all modes of proportion. Third, after the threefold criterion that has been reduced to a dyad by the subsumption of beauty under proportion, comes mind and wisdom (*nous* and *phronēsis*). Acknowledging this, one will not deviate far from the truth, he says, thus introducing truth in its own name in a manner that could be called casual or incidental, as if, however exalted it may be, it did not have a distinct or self-subsistent being. Today we would say of it, to convey that meaning, that it is not a thing. It remains unmentioned in the fourth rank of good, which consists of sciences, arts, and right opinions – things of the soul that resemble good more than pleasure does; i.e., resemble measure and proportion more than pleasure does. By insisting, through the explicit application of the ordinal numbers in the ranking, on the duality of the chief criterion of good, namely, measure and proportion, Plato/Socrates calls attention to what I have referred to as a demotion of the One and, simultaneously, of the irreducibility to each other of measure and proportion or commensurability. As number or measure dominated the infinite in combining with it to form Cause, so now incommensurability asserts a silent influence in keeping measure and commensurability apart. Certainly, not all things that are "kept apart" are as such "incommensurable" with each other; but what are we to think of two such as *metron* and *summetron*, together forming good, troubling the unity of good with their intransigent duality?

Finally, in the fifth place, the pure pleasures unvexed with pain are ranked in relation to good: finally but yet not quite finally, for Socrates refers to the sixth judgment of their discourse, with which it will cease. What is that judgment? If it exists, it is to be found in the short passage that precedes the end of the dialogue, a passage that Socrates introduces as a third presentation of the argument. He reminds of the view that pleasure is the good and of his own judgment that mind is better but that something else might be superior to both, and that mind would be closer than pleasure to that third. With particular emphasis he reminds of the ineligibility of both mind and pleasure to be deemed "the good" because each is not self-subsistent, sufficient, complete. These three attributes are the ones named in the immediately preceding (66b) elaboration of the second highest good or component of good: proportion, beauty, completeness or perfection, and sufficiency. This was from the very beginning the decisive criterion of good, sine qua non, known as such by Socrates and applied by him equally against *nous* and *hēdonē*. It appears that the sixth judgment is the one that determines the second criterion of good to be also first. As if to help us to see the direction of the argument, Socrates is made to refer to the sufficiency of the reasoning by which wisdom and pleasure were proved to be insufficient: not enough, falling short in amount, number, or measure. Proportion points to measure and measure points to proportion. They exist in relation to each other like the twin bodies of a binary star, a one in two and two in one. If geometry is the science that encompasses measure and proportion, one might agree with the judgment that the diligent study of geometry is an appropriate preparation for inquiring after Good.

Socrates closes with a remark that depends for its force on the dissimilarity or disproportion between man and all other animal life. Though every other living thing were to rank pleasure as the good itself, still it would be true that for man another good is better. Precisely while saying this, he speaks of the multitude of mankind whose judgment is the same as that of the beasts, opposite to what comes forth from the muse of philosophy. The true incommensurability of man and beast is revealed in or through philosophy, at exactly the same moment that mankind itself is revealed as composed of parts separated by a profound incommensurability or irrationality. The end of the dialogue returns to and perfects the beginning.

9
The Whole as Setting for Man: On Plato's *Timaeus*

Plato's *Timaeus* brings together Socrates and three of the four people who had requested, and received, on the preceding day, an account by him of his views on the polity. The review that Socrates gives "today" of the account that he gave "yesterday" presents the barest sketch of a portion of the *Republic*: division of labor resulting in a warrior class that is good to friends and harmful to enemies (acting on a definition of justice proposed and rejected in the *Republic*); gymnastic and music education for such guardians; their renunciation of wealth in favor of community and virtue; masculinization of women and their admission to all activities in the city; dissolution of the family; a eugenic arrangement, falsely put forth as a lottery, by which the authorities will procure the mating of good with their kind and bad with theirs, and the continuing promotion and demotion of citizens between the classes of good and bad (evidently made necessary by the predictable failure of the predictive eugenic device). Notably missing from the review as such, and perhaps therefore also from the account being recapitulated, is any thematic reference to the philosopher-king, that is, to the sine qua non of good polity, namely, the conjunction of reason and power that supposedly would guarantee effectual good in the polis as it would do also in the cosmos as a whole under god. How far it might do so is hinted vaguely in the passage (19e) in which Socrates, alluding to the men who would be at the same time philosophers and statesmen, doubts that Sophists could rise to the subject of those men's doings in verbal and literal polemics.

The *Timaeus*, which will prove to be about the constitution of the whole, is thus a sequel to the *Republic* in the triple sense that the bulk of *Timaeus* follows directly a sketch of a sketch of the *Republic*, the action of *Timaeus* follows the action of the *Republic* as the lesser Panathenaea follows the Bendideia, and the argument of *Timaeus* is set in motion, if somewhat indirectly, by Socrates' desire to see the good polis, presumably that of the *Republic*, in action, which proves to mean in strife. The good polis is situated in a whole from which strife cannot be banished, as will appear; the good polis must necessarily contemplate and be fit for war, if only because for some reason there must always be defective cities. From Socrates' desire to see the good polis in action flows not awkwardly the question, What is the nature of the Whole in which man, his good, and his politics are situated? How hospitable to man, his good, and his politics is that Whole?

Socrates' desire to be told about "our" city in contention is to be gratified in a complicated way. After he has disqualified Sophists for the task, on the ground that they are rootless wanderers, cityless and thus without the interest from which comprehension could grow, and has rejected also the poets, whose gift for imitation leaves them helpless when the task is to speak of what they have not experienced, Socrates turns to his companions, Critias, Hermocrates, and Timaeus, neither Sophists nor poets, who should prove equal to the request. They proceed through the recounting by Critias of a palaeology of Athens that had originated with Egyptian priests and descended by way of Solon to one Critias's ancestors and thus to Critias himself. At the heart of the tale is an apparent confusion: When Socrates inquired about "our" city, he meant the good city of his sketch, but Critias's tale will refer to primordial Athens, of course also "our" city, to which will be attributed much that earns praise by resemblance to "our" city of the sketch. Critias's tale will blur the distinction between the good polity that could be considered simply good and the polity of a polis that might have been the best to have been experienced by men, and thus perhaps the best possible.

Critias begins the history of the tale he is about to tell with an encomium of Solon, the apparent conductor of the story into Greece from Egypt. Solon, the wisest of the seven sages, is described as an accomplished poet who might have become an outstanding one if he had not turned to statesmanship, or rather legislation, in the service of Athens at a time when the city had fallen into corruption. We are given to understand that Solon returned to Athens carrying with him an image of the ancient city in its excellence. Nothing within what is written in the dialogue reveals whether or how far that image guided or could have guided Solon's legislation, or whether Solon's poetic gift might have encroached on his ability to project what he had never experienced and so could not imitate. The praise of Athens implicit in its palaeological identification with the good city seems to be diluted by the invasion of the city's recent historical legislator by a poetical genius.

The thematic response to Socrates' request for a discourse on the good polis in action begins with the recounting by Critias of Solon's story. This occurs in a passage (21e–26e) in which Critias adumbrates the account of the good city in action that, according to the plan, would be presented fully in *Critias,* to be followed by a discourse of Hermocrates *(Crit.* 108) on a related subject not specified. Critias proceeds to relate that Solon, traveling in Egypt, learned that the Egyptians possessed written records of their history reaching back eight thousand years, and a knowledge that Athens was a thousand years older than that. It was that palaeo-Athens whose extraordinary virtue came to a peak in the war that Athens won for Greece, defeating the hordes from western Atlantis and saving all in the East from subjection. The Athenians' ignorance of their noble origins is explained by the incidence of natural disasters that obliterated entire generations, inducing an amnesia that the literacy they lacked could have averted. In *Phaedrus* (274c ff.), Socrates is elaborate on the price paid by mankind for the Egyptian gift of letters, but Egypt here gets back some of its own by showing the Athenians that they do not know themselves, as they might have done in the face of a devastating cosmos, because they could not set themselves down in writing. Plato's obvious inversion of East and West, and replacement of Persia with Atlantis reminds the Athenians that their written record is mirror as well as ikon. The Socratic depreciation of writing might be unqualifiedly defensible in a world to which overwhelming natural calamities were unknown; but the Socratic world is a cosmos of brutal blindness to the difference between nobility and barbarism, Athens and Atlantis. The full meaning of the blatant substitution of Atlantis for Persia in this tale will not become clearer until in the *Critias* itself the genuine merits of Atlantis are disclosed – wealth and power temperately used, splendor combined with mild institutions and no lack of military prowess – until a decay set in that we know from the *Republic* inevitably afflicts and brings down the best of regimes that the mind can discover. It is notable that *Critias* contains a much more extensive description of Atlantis than of palaeo-Athens, and in fact never more than reaches the theme of palaeo-Athens in action at war. The intention of *Timaeus-Critias-"Hermocrates"* is silently interred.

At any rate, an important element of what the Egyptian priests imparted to Solon was the *precis* of the Egyptian constitution, offered as the reproduction of the palaeo-Athenian polity, itself the supposed regime of the good city. Cited first is the caste system of division of labor: segregation of priests, artisans, herdsmen, hunters, farmers, and warriors, which latter were singular in using shields and spears under the tutelage of Athena. Further, as for "wisdom" the law provides for the investigation of the cosmos with a view to discovering all the ways in which the divine beings bear on human things, up to divination and medicine. Seen in a certain light, the "wisdom" of the Egyptians and of the palaeo-Athenians was identical in its principle to modern natural science, aiming, as both do, at the relief of the human condition through the extortion of the secrets of the visible world for the sake of disarming and exploiting the cosmic forces. The "wisdom" that they conjoined with the power had the character of *epistēmē,* not *sophia,* for their minds were burdened with a sense that throughout the visible world there blew a wind that bore the seeds of their destruction. Athena, war-loving and philosophic, out of her care for them planted the Athenians in a well-tempered climate suited to bring forth the wisest of men. The philosophy of Athena herself seems to have consisted of effectual knowledge of cosmic causes and their human bearing.

Now Critias presents a perfunctory sketch of the war of the Atlantans and the palaeo-Athenians (24e–25d) in which nothing circumstantial is said about the action, but the merit of the Athenians and the historic importance of their victory are lauded. In ways that are almost obtrusive, Plato will suppress the description of the good city in action throughout the supposititious *Timaeus-Critias-"Hermocrates."* Whereas in the *Republic* (466e ff.) Socrates describes the manner of the good city's war-making as evident, so much so that he appeared on the point of passing over it in favor of the kingship of philosophy yet he then proceeds to discuss it in detail, here in *Timaeus* his chief or ostensible interest is in the manner of the good city's war-making and the subject does not arise either here or in the sequel. One wonders whether the good city in its state of action, that is to say at war, must by the nature of things shed its goodness, which is its justice, because to make war means and can only mean to do good to friends and allies and to harm enemies. To escape the force of this stricture by appealing to the conception that it is just to give the unprovoked aggressor what he deserves, or even to reciprocate whatever the other has imposed upon one, is only to flee to yet another of the definitions of justice that Socrates had exploded early in the *Republic,* readmitting them (442e) by exposing them as vulgar reflections of true justice, which is a rulership by alliance made "possible" by the willingness of unwisdom to be governed by mind. If the justice of the good city is to be saved by an invocation of the formula that justice is doing one's own singular deed, but the good city in its peculiar act is at war, then even without foreknowledge of what is to follow in *Timaeus*, one may be prompted to wonder about the human situation, about the inescapable imperfection of our organs of social life, and eventually about the blindly destructive cosmos, capable of appearing as the monstrous overwhelming or as the cleansing instrument of *nous* and good, nature or god, or perhaps both if they should be seen as one and the same. That the *Republic* should be "followed" by *Timaeus*, the grand cosmology, thus seems right, as it also seems right that the "problem" of the cosmos should be brought to sight through humanity as seen through the prism of political life where justice or good has its equivocal problematic existence.

Critias has now given a preview of the story of the Atlantans and the palaeo-Athenians, promising to tell the story in full, in due time, if Socrates will accept it as tantamount to a discourse on his good city in action. Socrates consenting, Critias announces the plan of the discussion that is to follow. First, for no reason that is stated, the eminent astronomer Timaeus will speak to begin with, on the coming into being of the cosmos and then finally on the generation of man *(anthrōpōn physin).* Critias will proceed with the human part of the account, assimilating the available human beings to the palaeo-Athenians and those in turn to the citizens of the good city. Critias pointedly omits Hermocrates from the plan, leaving it to Socrates to reintroduce

Hermocrates as a prospective speaker early in *Critias,* thereby furnishing the occasion for a somewhat sharp exchange between Critias and Hermocrates who speak in insinuations about each other's courage. That of Hermocrates is never tested.

The discourse of Timaeus occupies almost the whole of the dialogue. It begins with a proemium that is preceded by Socrates' injunction to Timaeus that he call on the gods, as is customary, before beginning. Timaeus complies rather perfunctorily, revealing in the first speech of the subsequent dialogue, *Critias*, that the god to whom he prays is the one created long ago in deed and just now (in *Timaeus*) by us in speech, i.e., the cosmos itself, as it exists in its apparent inaccessibility to our perfect understanding and as it exists in the likely construction of it with which we are to content ourselves.

Timaeus begins his discourse by distinguishing the Being from the Becoming things, correlating the former with Knowledge gained through thinking and reason and the latter with Opinion gained through sense perception without reason. Whatever Becomes does so necessarily as the effect of a cause. As Timaeus proceeds, he translates, for the immediate purpose only, cause into maker or artificer *(demiourgos),* contrasting the maker who contemplates an external model, always the same, and the maker whose envisioned paradigm is itself something that came into being (and thus was and will be other than it is). Of course, what is fashioned after an eternal paradigm must necessarily be beautiful (*kalon*), that made after a produced one, not so. Timaeus is speaking the language of Socratic orthodoxy, which is why we are especially interested in the locution (28a) that refers to the artificer's producing the "idea and capability" (*idea kai dynamis*) of his object. The translation of *idea* as form or shape (Schleiermacher says Gestalt) is not satisfactory in view of other passages (cf. *Philebus* 25a; *Statesman* 258c) in which Plato speaks of ideas as being made or brought into being by men, in the teeth of the most widely accepted view of Platonic philosophy as insisting on the Ideas as the eternal and intelligible archetypes. It would seem that, whatever might be the eternal paradigm of the whole that is copied by god, that paradigm does not have the name of Idea.

The cosmos is a perceptible, and it therefore came into being and is among the things accessible to opinion and must be the effect of the operation of some cause. Timaeus speaks of the difficulty of discovering the maker and father of this whole, adding that it would be impossible to speak to "all" about him even if he were discovered. Yet Timaeus is able to go on to offer as an evidence on this crucial point that it is clear to "all" that the artificer was contemplating an eternal paradigm in making this whole, for it is the most beautiful of the things that have come into being and its maker is the best of causes. The visible world or cosmos is subject to perception and opinion but the paradigm of which it is the merely temporal copy is knowable and always Same. Timaeus now makes it clear that the subject of his discourse will be the visible whole, the copy and not the archetype, and therefore that what he will have to say will itself have the character, which is to say the lack of clarity, of certainty and of intelligibility, belonging to a copy rather than having the quality of demonstrative truth. Throughout the body of his extended statement, Timaeus will maintain what he has prepared in this his proemium, that his account of the whole is only likely, as befits a likeness, and should be judged with the understanding that human beings can do no better. In view of the utter improbability or implausibility of much of what Timaeus will cover with the word *eikos* or some form of it, it is best to understand by it, through its translation as "likely," a likeness to the truth as a myth or even a benign falsehood that may be a verisimilitude. In the last words he utters in *Timaeus*, Socrates concurs in the burden of Timaeus's proemium, offering no comment on the plain implication that the necessarily good Father and Maker of all did not open up to man the greatest boon that human beings could enjoy, which is certain knowledge of the eternal being that is the truth of their existence.

It is on the point of the goodness of god that Timaeus begins (29d) his immense lecture on the whole. Timaeus affirms the goodness of god, presenting as the instance of goodness his absolute freedom from envy of any thing of any kind. All should be as good as possible, that is, as much like himself as possible. We need not suppose that goodness means only freedom from envy, and indeed what follows immediately makes such a supposition impossible, but we cannot exclude it from the characteristics implanted in his works by the good maker who seeks to make his products like himself as far as possible. If men were made without envy, by how much would contention and the likelihood of conflict be reduced? We do not know, any more than we know what the action of the good polis would consist of, or whether the polis would come to be, if envy did not exist among men. At any rate, Timaeus adduces the authority of the wise men *(andrōn phronimōn)* for the assertion that the governing principle of generation and of the cosmos is this of the goodness of the maker and his desire that everything resemble him in goodness as far as possible. But could a mere human being *know* this sovereign truth about a being who is not a copy of anything but is both the artificer from paradigms and also, evidently, himself the self-imitating paradigm of freedom from envy, and of good in any other sense as well? Timaeus speaks cautiously, twice (29a and 30a) appealing to the criterion of the rightly suitable, *themis,* in justifying his attribution of goodness to the making and desiring of god. His discourse is in fact a hymn to the goodness of the god and his work, reaching a climax in the argument that, a rational entity being superior to an irrational one, the cosmos must have reason, thus a soul, and must therefore be a living thing, an animal. This, says Timaeus, is what ought to be said *(dei legein)* according to the likely account (30b).

In the short passage that follows, Timaeus attempts to justify that paradoxical characterization of the cosmos as an animal by describing the paradigmatic animal of which the cosmic animal is a copy. Instead of a description of the archetypal animal, Timaeus recites the formal property of the absolute intelligible animal *(noēton zōon)* as being simply what includes within itself all the particular intelligible animals, as the cosmos contains all the particular visible animals. Shortly, Timaeus will enlarge on this sparse disclosure and in so doing will suggest that the cosmos, the animal of animals, must be scrutinized with limitless attention if the difference between it and a machine is to be detected (cf. 77b).

Now Timaeus wonders whether the heaven is one or many or infinitely many and decides that it must be one, for it is the animal that includes all the intelligible animals and must therefore be the ultimate singular of that kind. It is notable that Timaeus approaches the question of the unicity of the cosmos through the quality of the whole as a living thing. Turning to the generated, bodily cosmos, he explains its visibility and its palpability through its composition of fire and earth respectively, thus obliging himself to explain the union of two unlikes. This he does by recourse to proportion, and more specifically to the mean proportional. For reasons mathematical, the three-dimensional cosmos must consist of four elements, thus introducing water and air, in order to satisfy a condition arising out of the nature of proportion, and it is that proportionality among the elements that makes a one out of the many that they are. It goes without saying that to speak of proportionality among fire, earth, air and water is to treat them as quantities, which Timaeus will do elaborately in a trigonometry that is to follow, for which he prepares by describing the cosmic animal as including all the shapes *(schēmata)* there are while it itself is a sphere (33b). We can only wonder how a perfect sphere could contain perfectly the rectilinear figures which will be the matter of Timaeus's eventual trigonometry, as we might hope that he will let us see how proportionality, the uniter of the unlike, binds together body and soul without reducing soul to quantity. The question will soon be addressed in some fashion.

Now (33b–34a) Timaeus provides the details of the appearance of the cosmic animal, the great living globe. It has no eyes or ears, for there is nothing outside itself to be seen or heard, nothing with which to breathe or eat or excrete for all air is within it and all matter is simply recycled within it. Its sufferings and its doings originate as they must within itself. For hands and feet it could have no use. Its only motion is the rotation imparted to it by god. The cosmic animal is self-contained in every respect in which a recognizable animal is not, and it is utterly helpless, namely, with regard to locomotion, in an important respect in which recognizable animals are self-dependent. What could save this description of the animal of animals from the imputation of cosmic perversity would be the presence within it of a soul that accords decisively with that of some recognizable animal. To the description of the cosmic animal's soul Timaeus now fortunately turns (34b).

We learn first that the soul, whatever it proves to be, existed before the body. Since it will soon be called by the word Idea, we might suppose that it is the pre-existing reason, rationality, or truth that finds a manifest perceptible reality in matter. What follows will be a lesson in the nature and meaning of such a relation of rationality and embodiment.

The soul of the cosmos is a compound constructed of the Indivisible/Always-the-Same and the Corporeal/Generated/Divisible, together with a third that is a mean between the first two. We know nothing whatever about the nature of a composite of two mutually exclusive contradictories such as divisible and indivisible. If it were "somewhat divisible" it would be simply divisible. Timaeus allows that it is difficult to mix such immiscibles as other and same, but explains the result as the effect of the force applied by god. Whatever the difficulties that hinder mixing the immiscible, the reason for positing such a mixture becomes evident when Timaeus describes the distribution of the improbable mixture itself into portions: He had to provide for the division of Indivisible/Same into quantities marked by eternal being, eternal order, and endless mutability. As he now makes clear, his mind is fixed on number and proportion or ratio. The sequel will show that his mind conceives the cosmos as the visible that embodies the rational *qua* mathematical. It is given to Timaeus the astronomer to describe the soul of the cosmic animal as the rationality or mindedness that governs the motion of the great cosmic beings. He will eventually (47b) speak of the revolutions of reason *(tou nou periodous),* as he now (36e–37a) speaks of the soul's participating *(metechousa)* in reasoning and harmony, leaving us to weigh the import of what he has presented since he showed that the motion of the cosmic animal's body was simply imparted to it, its doing as a whole entity being only an endless rotation. Now we know that the soul that suffuses that body is the rationality of mathematics, a passive or embedded reason rather than thinking: again, a quality imparted to it. Nothing that Timaeus has said contributes, except by mere asseveration, to our belief that the cosmos is a living, that is, a self-moving and thinking being, except by inference from a definition of life that we are expected to deduce from the asseveration. If life is no more than the execution of imparted motions and the possession of a rational principle that is in fact the mathematical formula that describes those motions, then the cosmos is a living thing with a soul that is indeed bonded to a body as a body and its state of motion or rest are inseparably bonded. In a passage of striking boldness (40a,b), Timaeus, while speaking of the divine luminosities in the sky, will identify their uniform motion in one place with their thinking always the same things about the same things.

When Timaeus finishes his verbal construction of the cosmic orrery

(36d), he considers himself to have finished, *eo ipso* the verbal construction of the soul. He has told of the soul's composition out of the natures of Same, Other and Being *(ousia),* the ingredients apportioned and kept together by the unfailing adhesive, proportion. Now (37a) Timaeus sets out to explain how soul works to produce opinions and knowledge, proceeding to declare that, without noise or sound, when soul seizes upon something whose substance *(ousia)* is distributed or is indivisible, the soul is moved throughout itself and declares *(legei)* the truth about what it has encountered, generating true opinion about the empirical and Other, and knowledge about the rational and Same. He gives the reader every reason to conclude that soul receives and conveys its intimations by way of motions and without words; and he ends by denying that what entertains opinion and knowledge is anything but soul. This after he has used the same word, *ousia,* to mean substance *qua* Being and substance *qua* thing-that-is, leaving the reader to wonder how or whether he distinguishes them.

And god saw what he had wrought, and he was pleased, but he saw before him the task of making the cosmos, the conjoined body and soul, even more like the paradigmatic eternal animal, within the constraint that nothing made could be eternal. Thus the generating father took it in mind to make "a movable image of eternity" *(eikō kinēton tina aiōnos)* (37d), a simulacrum of the eternal resting One in the temporal that moves according to number, the visible Many. Time and Heaven are coeval, which seems to compel us to conclude that Eternity preceded Time, that Eternity "was" before the god made the Heavens and brought into being the motions that divide Time into days and months and years. But Timaeus denies immediately that one could say that Eternity "preceded" Temporality, just as one must not say of Eternity that it was or will be, only that it is. Time cannot be a portion of Eternity because the eternal is precisely One and Indivisible, which is "why" it is also simply Being itself: Eternity and Being converge in IS. If the Eternal could speak, it would say (and one must defeat the temptation to say, "It would *always* say") "I am," never "I shall be," but of course there is no way to conceive of the Eternal's speaking, for speech implies before and after in utterance.

Timaeus's account of the eternal and the temporal obliges us to interpret his declaration that the latter is the image of the former when the latter is the contradiction of the former. A movable image of that the essence of which is to be inaccessible to the concept of motion is more than merely paradoxical. It has the character of an idol, the image of the unimaginable, than which it is hard to conceive of anything more false or more misleading. But Timaeus goes no further than to allege that the temporal is the image of the eternal "as far as possible" (38b). What is the intention behind the divine ordering of the visible so that it might suggest the invisible, the temporal to point toward the eternal? We are told (39b) that god lit the heavens with the sun so that the animals who were capable of it might participate in number, through astronomy – what one might call the gift of the heavens. We are given to believe that god formed the heavens to be a light to the understanding of men, to set them in fact on the road to philosophy (cf. 47a,b).

Now god must fulfill the cosmos by installing in it not only those animals which are the heavenly gods, mostly of fire, the luminaries of day and night, but also those corresponding to the remaining three ideas of animal life – that which moves through the air, that of the water, and the kind with feet that go on land. Marveling at the intricacy of the heavens, Timaeus observes that the enormous complexity of the divine movements aloft presents itself to those who cannot calculate in the forms of signs and terrors. The very heavens that god constructed to be a visible image of the intelligible paradigm become, across the grain of his desire, the ground of fear and superstition. Could god have made men proof against unreason? Before we are given the answer to that question, Timaeus notices in a brief passage (40d–41a) the Olympian gods, the popular gods of the city, leaving no doubt that his speaking of them in the same breath with those frightened men who cannot see divinity in the heavenly arithmetic is purposeful. He pours his sarcasm on the poets, who claim a special relationship with the gods they confect, giving out what they make it appear was revealed to them by kinsmen. Whether this speech gave pleasure to Critias we have no way of knowing. It is followed immediately by Timaeus's distinguishing the gods whose motions are evident and those that reveal themselves only so far as they elect to do so, thus making clear his own understanding of the mode of god's communication with mankind. Timaeus's speech is a likely likeness of truth, as god's visible world is a likeness of eternity. Timaeus teaches that the Timeless and unmoving is pictured in the motion inseparable from the nature of the organs of Time. There is apparently no way to reach truth, i.e., being, except through the mediation of its imperfect likeness or incorporation. Arithmetic itself has to come to sight, literally, on the suggestion of the luminous bodies in the heavens; but is there anything aloft that makes sensible the arithmetic and harmonic means by which intervals and their innumerable subdivisions are brought into order by the active mind of man? If mankind is to any degree free from the hand of god, it would seem to be through possessing the power of calculation, by use of which the universe ceases to be, in itself, in principle, mysterious, unintelligible, and therefore frightening. By these reflections, we can help ourselves to understand Timaeus's animadversions on the poets, who seem to be doing something not completely different from Timaeus's own act: with their Ge and Uranus, their Kronos, Zeus and Hera, they were making an account or likeness of the same phenomena of Heaven and Earth, and the same birth of Time, that struck the eye and then the reflection of Timaeus. Is not Timaeus's speech a cosmologic poem in prose? Is it not a poem because it is a myth, as he himself calls it (59c,

68d, 69b)? We would only be compelled to look for the difference between them. Timaeus's account differs from that of the poets in that his god and gods are incapable of misanthropy, and thus cannot be thought of as fearsome. Not Timaeus and not any other man could deny the occurrence of natural catastrophes capable of destroying some or even all human and other life on earth, but for Timaeus there is nothing malign and therefore nothing frightful in the reason of the whole, which is mathematics. Timaeus has discovered the god who is free from misanthropy, who so far as possible brings only good to man, and whose beneficence does not consist in a mere harmlessness arising out of irrelevance to human happiness, for god is the ground of philosophy.

This is not to say that the life of man is without penalties of a divine origin. Timaeus composes a tale (41a–d) of a conclave of the gods, convoked by god himself whose purpose is to charge them with the making of man and all the other animals that are not divine. Timaeus's god delegates the birth of man to beings who themselves came into being, for if he himself were to be the generator of subordinate animals they would have to be immortal. He explains to his addressees, the "gods of gods," that although they themselves came into being, they will not pass away, for only he could bring about their dissolution and he would not be guilty of putting asunder what he had joined together, thereby explaining too why he may not generate man. Yet there must be mortal animals, for the perfection of the whole demands that the perfect animal include every possible kind of living thing. Timaeus's god calls for the generation of animals who must be mortal "lest they be equal to the gods," but the tale makes it unmistakably clear that the interest being served is the completion of the visible manifestation of the intelligible whole rather than the aloofness of god. The burden of god's speech to the gods is his refusal to be the culpable cause of any ill that might befall man, including the rebirth in an inferior form that will follow man's foreseeable wickedness as its punishment. The gods whom he charges with the management of man are not fallen stars but exactly those luminaries to whom he engages for an undisturbed existence. Timaeus has contrived a god the father to whom creation could look with affection and respect, unspoiled with fear but who demands no testimonies of gratitude or subservience and whose laws are written in their subjects' composition where reasons for transgression may of necessity lodge but temptation thereto would be irrational.

Now Timaeus begins his description of the interplay of the ceaseless flux of matter that is the somatic ground of animal life and the revolutions of the soul that is joined to the body. Between 42e and 46c, he elaborates a dynamic mechanics to account for nutrition and perception, all in terms of motion and, self-evidently, of what is capable of motion. In the short but weighty passage 46c7–e6, Timaeus relegates these causes in terms of flux of body to the class of secondary or subordinate causes, speaking of them as being among those that god makes use of "to serve him for perfecting as far as possible the idea of the most good." Here Timaeus disparages the mere physicists or corporealists for failing to understand that not body but only soul can think. Distinguishing the causes belonging to mindful nature *(emphronos physis)* and those belonging to the motion that arises out of mindless necessity, he admonishes the lovers of mind and knowledge to regard the former first and then the latter. Timaeus has distinguished nature and the visible world, and the respective studiers of the two realms, as Socrates does in *Philebus* (59a) where he differentiates nature and cosmos and their investigators explicitly. It is to be noted particularly that Plato puts the disparagement of the mere scientist in the mouth of a professional astronomer who evidently had no need to abjure the cosmos in order to reach the philosophic insight into nature. Since everything said is being said in the presence of Socrates, the reader is prompted to wonder whether the latter's silence is the acknowledgment of a merited rebuke of the turn from science he claims to have had to make for the sake of wisdom *(Phaedo* 96 ff.) or is his tacit admission of concurrence in a remark that expresses his own profoundest belief from the beginning.

In fact enlarging on this thought, which grew out of his mechanical explanation of the power of sight, Timaeus asserts that the thing of greatest worth contributed by our vision, and so intended by god, is that it opens up to us the spectacle of the whole, number and "the nature of the all," and thus philosophy, of which he says that there can be no greater good for a mortal. Perhaps strangely, Timaeus can go on to refer to the good which we should say that greatest good itself promotes, namely, our own emulation of the serene and orderly reason of the heavenly geometry. Philosophy, the investigation of the inner nature of the outer cosmos, is the means to the perfection of human life, for it is the means by which that soul that is shared by all and by man may be brought, within man, to the same tranquil perfection of revolution that governs throughout heaven. Similarly, hearing is given to us with a view to the reception of music, thus to harmony and the enhancement of the orderly revolutions of the soul within. It is hard to conceive of a universe not grotesquely different in appearance from the one familiar to us in which the whole would be more benignly hospitable to man, to his tranquility and his perfection, or the god of the world more kindly affected to us. We must therefore make the necessary effort to remind ourselves that Timaeus's tale is being told in response to Socrates' request for an account of the good city in action, meaning in a state of contention or war.

We are assisted in that effort by Timaeus's announcement (47E) of a change in the direction of his speech. Hitherto he has concentrated in the main (he alludes to a brief exception, which might be 40d–41a, on the poets) on the workings of mind; now he will speak on the things that come about through necessity. He must do so because the generation of this cosmos was by way of a mixture of mind and necessity, a dyad that must forever dominate the whole. In order to investigate necessity, Timaeus must consider the nature of fire, water, earth and air as those ingredients, always misunderstood as Primordial in their perceived character, were before the coming into being of Heaven. If Timaeus is speaking accurately, he is affirming the existence of the elements in some absolutely archaic form before the beginning of time, or before there was before, "during" unimaginable eternity. Whatever that form might prove to be, we know certainly that the elements in their verity cannot be likened to syllables or irreducibles. Timaeus knows that in essaying to describe the truth of the effectual universe, he must include the influence of the orbital (48b) cause as well as the eternal static, and that his project for analyzing the so-called elements is the signal for a re-commencement of the account of the whole. At the outset of what he repeatedly asserts will be only the likeliest of such accounts, he invokes the protection of god the protector (of travelers? 48d).

The second account of the whole begins (48e) with a revision of the schema of forms *(eidē)* that Timaeus has relied on hitherto. Besides the forms of Paradigm and Imitation, a third must be brought out which will be the medium in which all Becoming takes place. The study of fire and its congeners is the necessary beginning of the explanation of the requisite third fundamental.

The beginning of Timaeus's new account reveals immediately his rejection and the basis of his rejection of the popular understanding of the status of the four supposed elementary materials. By processes of rarefaction and condensation, the so-called elements are transformed into one another (54b–c, earth alone will be shown as remaining uncommuted): what is now water condensing into stones and earth or becoming air through rarefaction, air in turn becoming fire that condenses into air that turns into moisture which again solidifies as earth and stones. The standing elements are replaced by a ceaseless flux. The issue now becomes, what that is not in flux supports that fluctuation that Timaeus sees as he deepens the investigation into the heart of that in which Becoming is "the truly subsistent by nature" (52b). The first, negative answer is, it is not the familiar elements, for each of these is already formed as a kind of something whereas what is to be sought as the absolutely underlying must be receptive of all forms, itself precisely and therefore possessing none.

Timaeus's new account of the whole begins as a project for discovering the most general categories of all things. These prove to be three in number: the thing itself; the perceptible of the thing itself; and that in which all things are that are. Timaeus "knows" that there is such a thing as, for example, unchanging fire itself because he "knows" that Knowing *(nous)* differs from True Opinion and it follows that each must have its proper object, the object of *nous* being the very form or *eidos* of fire itself. This ungenerated, unalterable, unreceptive, impenetrable, immiscible, imperceptible (definable apparently in privatives except for "intelligible") corresponds with what we expect to recognize as the Idea of Fire, the answer to the question what is fire. Next, there is what everyone perceives as fire and calls by the same name as the first, but that comes into existence and passes out of it always in some location *(topos),* always moving, accessible to what Timaeus calls opinion *(doxa).* Third, there is everlasting Place, which comes to our mind through a confused inference that we draw from the fact that everything we perceive sensibly exists in some location. Because every copy of paradigmatic being is somewhere, we falsely suppose that the all-inclusive, absolutely enfolding and thus somehow supporting is space, in some otherwise unoccupied portion of which each existent finds its locus. But Timaeus, in his depreciation of this instinctive or pre-scientific conception of space, implies that the encompassing, that in which we and all things live and move and have our being, is more than the receptive as the merely void would be receptive; it is the actively receptive that enters into the existence of every entity. Timaeus had intimated its nature provisionally where he said that fire is the local ignification of the everlasting Place, as water is its hydrification (51b, 52d). Besides Being and Becoming, the paradigmatic whence and the perceptible engendered, there is the underlying Wherein that stands as the matrix of the elements as of all the manifest flux, a participating medium, ubiquitous as aether but endlessly protean in its potentiality for materializing as objects of perception.

It is the very plethora of potentialities that it contains that gives this Third Fundamental, the Suckling Nurse of the Generated (52d), its efficacy in shaping the whole while serving as its host. According to Timaeus's story, Place is full of potentialities which exist in a state of tension with one another and thus in a paradoxical condition of productive activity. The activity produced by the friction, as we might say, of dissimilar potentialities is explained by Timaeus's construction that posits motion as the result of the presence of heterogeneity, or Other. He attributes motion, a shaking or being shaken *(seisthai)* (52e), to the all-embracing and all-receptive Place, a motion that appears to be an example, perhaps the only example, of the doing of a self-moved or unmoved mover. It is notable that the movement within Place is self-evidently not movement from place to place and also that it is not the effect of an intelligent, purposive intention but is the mechanical result of "mere conditions," say of the necessity that heterogeneity – less irenically called strife by the predecessors of Socrates – generate motion.

There is one feature of Timaeus's account that should be noted especially, namely, his insistence (50d–e) that the recipient of forms *(morphas)* have no form of its own, just as the sculptor's clay must be kneaded into perfect smoothness, at the same time, as we have just seen, that the heterogeneity of potentialities within it be so real as to have the power to generate motion. To put the issue otherwise, the great recipient of forms, if capable of motion and of being moved, and as we shall see of transmitting motion, must be material, but be simultaneously in one sense only the possibility of being formed yet in another sense already contain the forms of heterogeneity within. It would seem that the form contained within must be of such a nature as not to violate the condition that Place as a whole be perfectly unformed. What Timaeus alleges is not incompatible with the presence within Place of the eternally existent possibilities of all things that can come to be – possibilities which qua archetypal and eternal are indistinguishable from the Ideas.

Any such speculation would have to be compatible with Timaeus's notion that movement results from the relation of the potentialities within Place, indicating that he conceives those potencies or powers *(dynameis)* as being literally energetic, as if the very existence of Other means tension or strife, for good or ill without any inclination of strife itself toward good or evil. At any rate, the action of the potencies so agitates the entirety of Place that Place in turn displaces the forms, sending all flying, at the same time sorting out the four elements in their rudimentary conditions so that each consorted with its own kind before the whole was made up out of them. Now Timaeus proceeds to the crucial description of the construction by god of the four elements, constituted as shapes *(schēma)* by forms and numbers *(eidē* and *arithmoi).* What follows (53c ff.) is the detailed trigonometry by which Timaeus rationalizes atomism, thus curing it of the mindlessness that would render it unacceptable to a thinker who could not represent the whole without good, somehow understood, as present at the beginning. Thus Timaeus sets out to describe the nature of the smallest particles of the four elements, presenting it through a tale of their first production. Since they are solids, their bulk must be bounded by planes. He does not consider the possibility of spherical atoms, which would have the merit of mimicking the perfect whole but which, of course, could not abut one another except at points of tangency, leaving interstices void of elementary matter. Timaeus's physics rejects the hypothesis of void not only through the construct of Place but through the undefended assertion of the rectilinearity of the plane surfaces bounding the smallest particles (subject to the reservation that finite rectilinear figures could not, as the curvilinear also could not perfectly fill a sphere) which he refrains from calling atoms, i.e., uncuttables, because, as we know and as we shall soon be told in a corrected version, the small particles are eminently frangible and largely commutable from element to element.

Rectilinear plane figures are composites of triangles, and all triangles can be conceived as composed of right triangles, isosceles and scalene. Timaeus now (53e–54a) adopts Beauty as the criterion of the excellence of the entities he must discuss, Beauty somehow standing in place of or as in fact being Good, and he declares the scalene right triangle to be the most beautiful thing out of which to construct the beautiful elements, for it is the immediate component (when doubled) of the equilateral triangle. Timaeus says in passing (53e) that his reasoning will disclose, if it succeeds, the truth not only about the generation of the elements but also about the mean proportional *(ana logon en meso),* i.e., the expression a:b = b:c, which happens to be the formula for the relation of the segments of the Divided Line. What is the truth about the mean proportional, and how can it be related to the isosceles right triangle? Perhaps as follows: The so-called Pythagorean theorem indicates that the relation between the hypotenuse and the legs of the isosceles right triangle involves an incalculable square root, what the Greeks called, as we still call, an irrational number. The proportion between the leg and the hypotenuse of an isosceles right triangle is as illusory or anomalous as the relation between the diameter and the circumference of a circle, notwithstanding that the quantities being related are perfectly finite. The relation of mean proportionality cannot be applied to the sides of an isosceles right triangle without maintaining the absurdity that the square on the hypotenuse is equal to (rather than twice, cf. *Meno)* the area of the square formed by the legs as sides; but the intrusion of the irrational $\sqrt{2}$ in the arithmetic of the isosceles right triangle points to the parallel fact that affects the mean proportional as it necessarily incorporates the power of 2: the irrational is in principle inescapable by the perfection and beauty of number. The irrational lies at the heart of the beauty of the most beautiful and most constitutive of forms. It might be worth mentioning further that the Greek word for the potentialities whose tension resulted in the basic, fruitful agitation of Place is *dynamis*, the word for an exponential power.

Timaeus develops (54c ff.) in detail the construction of the smallest particles of the four elements, fire, air, and water out of scalene right triangles and earth out of the isosceles, the latter element constituted as a cube each of whose six sides is formed of four isosceles triangles. We are not told why the square, the side of the cube, is shown to be constructed of isosceles rather than scalene right triangles, which can be done easily. To have done so would have gained the advantage in elegance of reducing earth to the same mathematical element, the scalene right triangle, as the rest of the cosmos. Timaeus appears for some reason to make earth exceptional when he constructs it of a triangle that unites the equality of two of its sides with the irrationality in the dimension of the third. However this may be, Timaeus stops to make explicit that the primary scalene triangle has a hypotenuse twice the length of the shorter leg, and that the remaining side must therefore be equal to or some multiple of the square root of three, of course irrational. Out of such anomalous material the entire visible universe is to be constructed, afflicted by $\sqrt{2}$ and $\sqrt{3}$. Timaeus remarks as if casually (55a) that the encompassing sphere of the whole will consist of equal and like parts, declining to consider that rectilinear solids cannot fill a sphere but could at most be conceived as approaching infinitely such a repletion, on the assumption of the infinite divisibility of the included particles, a concept similar to that on the basis of which √2 and √3 might be discussed as proper numbers. Concluding his account of the ground of the four elements in four polyhedrons, Timaeus remarks in passing that a fifth polyhedron remained, which god used up for depicting the whole in life *(diazōgraphōn)* (55c). We are not told whether this means that a fifth polyhedron is the substrate of a soul-stuff, nor does Timaeus clarify his remark in any other way.

Timaeus is confident that the proportions of the agglomerations of the invisible particles and the motions of the visible bodies are all accomplished by god in accord with the nature of necessity and harmonious proportion (*ana logon)* (56c), proportion, as we remind ourselves, being the cosmic adhesive. We receive the impression that the proportionality or rationality and harmony of the composites is not destroyed by the irrationality that we have seen to be lodged in the absolutely primary elements of the elements. Stated differently, the metaphysical, mathematical, or theoretical irrationality of the incalculable √2 and √3 do not seem to cause a failure of cohesion and order in the empirical cosmos. Are we entitled to surmise that the world appears to Timaeus as an order, proportion, or harmony at whose birth disproportion or unreason collaborated? What follows immediately might be construed to favor that surmise, for it consists of Timaeus's tale of the war of the elements – how earth is broken down by fire, air or water, not to the point of the corruption of the four-square minuscules, which are not earth but proto-earth, but sufficiently to lose the character of proper earth until by *chance* they meet again (*xyntykhonta*); and how the particles of water, fire, and air engage one another in a polemic chemistry conducted on a field of battle where victory and defeat (56e–57c) result in the splitting and recombination of the molecules and consequent commutation of elements (earth excepted). Timaeus explains these happenings by recurring to the trigonometry of the primary forms with their angularities of greater and less acuteness, adding now to the properties of the small particles the alternative of submissiveness in defeat, with loss of identity as a result, and combative resistance to domination, resulting in lonely exile or defeat and assimilation. Timaeus has composed an epic of war that could claim to describe a combat whose duration, scope, and consequences exceed those of the war between the Greeks and the Trojans as the latter exceed those of the war between the frogs and the mice. Plato has made Timaeus the rational poet of the everlasting epic of the rational and the irrational, of peace and war.

There is ceaseless restlessness throughout the whole, brought on by the action of the cosmic sphere's centripetal compulsion which seeks to fill every emptiness, and thus promotes the war of the particles as they encounter, fracture and reconstitute themselves. Necessary for the origination of motion is dissimilarity or Other, without which there is no distinction of mover and moved, and also there is the primal impulse that has its source in the sphere's irresistible compulsion to minimize its volume. In his present account of the sphere's struggle against every vestige of void within it, Timaeus does not of course consider the ubiquity of Place as synonymous with the a priori exclusion of void from the sphere of the whole.

At this point, it might be in order to observe that Timaeus's first major argument, the one that culminated in the entity of Place, was dominated by the goodness of god who suffused the whole with reason and ordered the heavens to display themselves and their secret arithmetic to man for the advancement of philosophy. Since the recommencement, Timaeus has scarcely noticed god but has confined himself to the elaboration of a mathematical physics that purports to account for the ground of all matter and the origin of motion. The transition from the doing of god the mindful sower of soul to the power of necessary truth that marked the new beginning will be sustained as Timaeus passes from his account of what is perceptible to his account of perception (62c ff.) and therewith of the causes of the perceptibility of the perceptible.

Fire acts on our body by virtue of the geometry of its particles, which are sharp, small, acutely angled and in rapid motion, thus apt for penetrating, dividing and cutting our flesh. Timaeus seems to be aware of no need to bridge the huge gap between the interaction of particles and the sensation of warmth beyond the suggestion that the word for heat is related etymologically to the word for chopping up. Even if the etymological speculation be not fanciful, it would bespeak nothing more useful than a tautology or a prescientific hunch.

As Timaeus goes on to account for "cold," he refers to the expected phenomena of motion, compression and density, but adds the observation that whatever is driven together or compressed contrary to nature will fight according to nature to remove itself from its affliction. Of course the unnatural compression that underlies the shivering of the uncomfortable man might have been produced by his exposure to sleet, which is as natural as is his compression and discomfort. The natural sleet and the natural mechanics of the man's particles are in the paradoxical relation of opposing influences whose strife is indistinguishable from their harmony. The boundary between agitation and serenity begins to become indistinct. Timaeus's discourse on the nature of heavy and light (62c) continues in a similar vein. Heavy and light seem to have to be understood by reference to above and below, heavy meaning no more than seeking below and light the opposite; but Timaeus reminds that the whole is a sphere composed of particles whose motion is governed by the centripetal thrust inherent in the sphere itself, tantamount to abhorrence of void. The aggressive angularity of the particles does the rest, and Timaeus has thus shown how there is no absolute above and below, only inner and outer. He has replaced, for the philosophic mind, the naive image of a cosmic equatorial plane with a rational schema of center and periphery. In general, the principle of Timaeus's physics is not gravity, attraction, or "love" but compression, struggle, or "war" that produces the effectual simulacrum of *philia* forcing like to associate with like by sorting the particles according to their size and geometry.

Timaeus must explain pleasure and pain (64a). Suffice it to say that he does so in terms of the motion of particles, the sensations of pain or pleasure depending on the resistance to their displacement or lack of it on the part of the various particles. In passing, he refers the pleasures and pains associated with fillings and emptyings in the body to "the mortal of the soul" (65a) which can hardly be incorporeal. His account of the senses of taste and smell runs in the familiar mechanical channel, but his explanation of hearing produces the surprising assertion that the motion of the audible that comes from without terminates at the liver. Ridicule would be premature in view of the eventual identification of the liver as the organ of divination (71–72). His account of vision and the perception of colors turns on the interaction of the fire emanating from us and the fire that encounters that optic stream from without. Timaeus refers to his explanation as a likely myth (68d) (cf. 59c – "the idea of the likely myth": idea as *plausible construct*).

Having drawn this part of his tale to its conclusion, Timaeus declares that his discourse has so far dealt in the things that are born of necessity, which the Demiourgos took and used in generating the autarkic, most perfect god. The Demiourgos is the architect of the good in everything that was to come into being. Thus, two kinds of causes are to be distinguished, the necessary and the divine, and it is the divine that must be inquired after in order to gain a happy life so far as our nature permits. The inquiry into the necessary is for the sake of the divine, for it is impossible to reach the latter without going through the former. With this statement, Timaeus purges himself of the imputation of being a vulgar mechanist. Equally, there is no approach to philosophy except through knowledge of the polemic reason that lies in the heart of the perfect god cosmos.

Timaeus now (69b) proposes another re-commencement in order to complete his myth. He repeats briefly the tale of god's infusing the original disorder with commensurability *(symmetria)* within and among the parts so that, however possible, they should be in a state of proportion and commensurability *(analoga, symmetra)*. We are in a position to take seriously the qualification "however possible" that Timaeus attaches to those terms of mathematics. Dwelling on god's delegation to his progeny of the task of constructing the mortal things within the one cosmic animal he had made, the tale relates how the lesser gods encased the immortal soul in a body in which they enclosed also a mortal soul that Timaeus describes as the seat of pleasure the tempter to wickedness, pain the evictor of good, rashness and fear the advisers in folly, spiritedness obdurate before dissuasion, and hope the seducer, all mixed together with irrational sensation and headlong lust. They did this out of necessity – so much we are told and no more, although our minds are drawn back to the worm of irrationality and incommensurability lodged in the core of the apple of ineluctable mathematical reason. We know without being told that that necessity was superior in power to everything that could be called by the name of god, and that the highest god had power only to keep his hands clean by deputizing others to execute the demand of necessity that man be made punishable before he merited punishment, the bitterest *hysteron proteron* to mar the work of a philanthropic god – or the most consoling myth to illuminate the mind of a philanthropic man.

Making the best of an imperfect situation, the inferior gods take pains to keep the mortal soul away from the immortal as well as they can, seating the latter in the head, the former in the trunk, further dividing the trunk with a diaphragm so that the better passions, courage and spiritedness, might be nearer to reason and abler to collaborate with it in restraining the base desires. Timaeus has begun his anatomical psychology on the premise of the tripartition of the soul that is familiar as a principle of the Platonic Socratic doctrine. We can only surmise, helped by Socrates' silence, how much of Timaeus's discourse is gratifying to Socrates. Timaeus goes on to describe the organs of the body according to the ways in which their purely mechanical functioning serves, as well as possible, the hegemony of reason over the passions lodged in those organs. Thus the lungs cool and protect the heart, put in place for that purpose by the provident gods who, as Timaeus says, planted there "the idea of the lungs" (70c). Soon (71a) he will say that god, not the gods, contrived "the idea of the liver" and installed it in its place. Unchecked by Socrates, Timaeus refers easily to the idea of lungs and liver, without any such hesitations as perplexed young Socrates over whether there could be ideas of the hair, nails, and mud *(Parmemides* 130c–d). Installing an idea appears to mean fashioning a concrete body that has a function for which the body is adapted. In the present case, the idea of the liver is set in its place so that the mirror-like organ might reflect the monitory thoughts of the mind as frightening images to overawe the organs below the diaphragm. Timaeus produces an extraordinary account of the interaction of mind and liver, showing in detail the corporeal states of the organ as effects of a particular state of the mind, and the psychic equivalent of each of those states of the organ in what might be seen as an exact parallel of soul and body. The astonishing doctrine of the liver comes to a head in Timaeus's disclosure of the liver's function in divination. The liver, participating not in reason and wisdom *(logos, phronēsis),* lies asleep at night in a tranquil state of equanimity and performs its divination. Timaeus surprises by failing to offer a single hint of an explanation of dreams as consequences of fevers or chills, hunger or satiety or any other condition of the body. What he stresses instead is the functioning of this important contributor to our psychic life in the absence of any reasoning within it whatsoever. Dreaming, or divination, arises in us exactly when the mind is either dormant or distracted by disease or "enthusiasm," some invasion by god – at any rate not in command of itself. Since Timaeus distinguishes dreams and waking visions, we gather that dreams belong to the dormancy of the mind and waking visions to its distraction and enthusiasm. In either case, the true interpreter of divination or the true prophet is that man who is in full possession of his mind, for the frantic and possessed, considered by the vulgar to be prophetic, would only compound the unreason inherent in the enthusiasm. Every intelligent man, in a state of vigilance, is his own prophet, the construer of his visions and voices. What Timaeus calls divination or prophecy is given to us in mitigation of our baseness, not of our ignorance; it is an instrument of conscience, not of revelation, as we in our time might say, and as such as Spinoza would find reasons to reaffirm. For Timaeus, the mortal soul is a party to the struggle of good against necessary badness, a struggle that is an episode of what appears as a cosmic polemic, evidence of which we have already seen.

With a remark about the function of the spleen as the cleanser of the liver Timaeus concludes his discourse on the mortal and immortal soul (72d), and proceeds to the discussion of the rest of the body, more exactly, of the coming to be of the rest of the body, "in the same fashion," by which he apparently means explaining the form of an organ as instrumental to a moral good for man. The first explanation of Timaeus's that we will encounter is of the belly.

The central fact is the spectacular length of the intestines. For this Timaeus has a characteristic rationalization: because of our grossness, we would surely go to excess in eating and drinking if the intestines, by their great length, did not retain food and drink inordinately and thus delay the sensation of depletion that would be the signal for further gourmandizing. Even the body is enlisted in the moral combat against itself. Timaeus's inference of morphology from moral teleology is as evident here as in any of the other manifold places in which it presents itself as epiphany.

In an extraordinary passage (73a–75d), Timaeus recounts the generation of the bones and flesh and other such bodily matter, but especially of the "marrow" which plays a crucial part in the constitution of living material. We are told that god reverted to the pristine triangles, selecting the best of them and recombining them as the most precise specimens of the four elements. Out of these he made marrow, the all-seed for every mortal kind. This marrow is said by Timaeus to be the medium or substance in which soul is bound to body, that is, in which life itself comes to be. God divided the life-stuff into portions that he shaped in conformity with the kind of soul each was to embody. The portion that was somehow to contain the divine soul or mind was formed as a sphere (as was said before [44d]) in the first story of the cosmogony. That the brain bears only vague resemblance to a sphere is a fact that may be passed over in the interest of the intended meaning of the passage, which seems to be that the morphology of the visible and generated organ is inseparable from its psychic nature, excellence, and function. This marrow in which body and soul are united is distributed in various shapes and then encased in suitable bones, rigid and jointed, along with the apparatus of connecting tissue and flesh that make up the body as we know it – all presented as for the sake of the protection of the seed within, i.e., the marrow. The bones most be-souled *(empsychotata),* most inclusive of soul, are least covered with flesh; those with least soul, with most and densest flesh: the gathering of flesh about the head would have made the mind oblivious, unreceptive to the signals from without, as if those latter were emanations resembling missiles obliged to penetrate matter by parting it with force.

Now (75a–b) Timaeus reveals a deep-lying tension in the nature of things: the necessity that accompanies our existence has produced a disjunction between what conduces to activity of the spirit and what, through abundance and density of flesh, conduces to protection of the corporeal medium of that activity. The lungs do not suffocate the heart that they protect, but a mass of flesh and bone about the brain-marrow would stultify the mind within it. Our makers, having deliberated, chose intelligence for us rather than longevity. That they decided as they did was perhaps to be expected; that the choice was forced upon them, or that the whole is so constructed that the good of intelligence is by its nature exclusive of the good of (indefinite) existence is sobering and astonishing. However the antithesis is to be explained, we see it borne out in the fragility of the good city of the *Republic;* and we see its thought affirmed in the Garden of Eden.

Yet Plato sees what might be the exception to this rule that tends to prove it. The mouth serves the end of necessity by admitting nourishment, and of the most good by expelling speech, the instrument of mind. It can serve the two otherwise conflicting ends by violating the principle, said to be nature's own, that each function is performed best by that agent whose only function it is. This dictum is the basis for the division of labor that inspired the structure of the best polis, in which the coincidence of mind and power, of intelligence and force, of reason and coercion, in the person of the philosopher-king represents the same violation of the principle of division of labor, of disjunction of necessity and good, as comes to sight in the physiology of the mouth. The natural principle of division of labor, necessary for the achievement of the good, seems to rest on the conflict between the conditions of durability or existence and the conditions of intelligence or mind or, to fall in with Timaeus's assimilation to each other of mind and Being, then of Being itself. We have been well prepared for a disjunction between existence in time and the timeless being of unalterable mind, but it is surprising to find that what we may have been prepared for was not the mere disjunction but the active opposition between the temporal and the eternal. At the same time, but in the contrary direction, the supposed antinomy of the body on the one hand and both soul and idea on the other seems to be compromised in the physiology that encompasses the implanting of the idea of the lungs and the idea of the liver as well as the animization of the marrow and the motility of the soul. While nothing should induce us to forget the majestic orderliness of the motions in heaven, we are reminded that the order or intelligibility within those motions is supplied by reason in the form of a mathematics dominated by proportion but vexed with the incommensurabilities of the irrational numbers.

Timaeus explains the genesis of skin and hair (76), and then comes to account for the presence of the nails. He purports to describe the synthesis of sinew, skin and bone that eventuates in nail, and then takes the occasion to remind of the difference between the co-causes or subordinate causes that brought the thing into being and the superlatively causal intelligence *(aitiōtatē dianoia)* (76d) that intended its existence with a view to what was to come. What our makers foresaw was the descent from man of all the other animals beginning with woman, many to be in need of something harder than mere flesh at the tips of their extremities. What Timaeus is adumbrating here is the tale of the punishment of evil-doers by demotion, after death and by reincarnation, through the ranks of the lower forms of life. Woman is indeed derived from man, not to be his companion but to be his fate; but of this we shall learn more when it becomes Timaeus's theme.

Still to be explained is the genesis of man's nourishment. Timaeus will not undertake to explain the preservation of life in man through nutrition without remarking, with an apparent casualness that belies the gravity of the remark, that man's life consists, by necessity, of fire and the breathed air *(pneuma)* (77a). This bold affiliation of life to the two most rarefied material elements will be amplified (80d) when Timaeus maintains that fire reduces the aliment to particles of usable size and then rises with them after the ascending breath itself, in a collaboration of blood and breath that is in our day too understood to occur, if with a different bearing. In any event, what feeds us must resemble us sufficiently but not excessively. Accordingly, the gods made a mixture of the human nature with certain other "ideas and sensibilities" *(ideais, aisthēsesi)* (77a) to form the vegetable kind. "Everything whatsoever that participates in life may justly and most rightly be called a living being," (77b) the latter term *(zoon)* being the word also for animal. Aristotle *(de Anima,* 414a,b) will speak of the vegetative soul as present in those living things that are without thought or locomotion. He will not make the astonishing assertion that they know sensation, pleasure and pain, and desire, which Timaeus affirms in an access of dogmatic consistency with what he has described as characteristic of man's lower belly. What characterizes, and impoverishes, the soul of the lower belly, shared with the souls of the vegetable "living things," is the incapacity for the internal motion that is the condition for a mental life as also for local motion. Timaeus does not retreat from the association of the functions of life with the motion of matter. The detailed account of the physiology of nutrition that follows is itself preceded by what appears to be a description of the circulatory system, a description that rationalizes the bilateral symmetry of the "veins" and their turning about the head as being in the service of revealing the sensations from both sides of the body to the whole body. His anatomy of nutrition and respiration is of interest to us for the vigor with which it is made consistent with the universal principles of mechanical necessity i.e., motion of body and plenitude of matter, i.e., absence of void. The life of the cosmos and of all the lesser living things belonging to it is dominated by the contiguity of irreducible particles of matter that absolutely fill the whole and that are characterized by motion traceable to the trigonometry that becomes phenomenal through the linked media of heat and cold, and rarefaction and condensation. From the remoteness of the heavens to the ventral recesses, the whole is one and explainable as one, enabling Timaeus to offer to elucidate (80a) therapeutic cupping, swallowing, the motion of bodies through the air, and the character of sound, including the pleasure given to the wise by their perceptions of the sounds that mimic the divine harmony in mortal motion. Many other wonders are rendered intelligible by the power of the insight that there is no void, no running down of motion through its dissipation into an emptiness. We are not forbidden to speak of nothing, but it is clear that we can do no more than say its empty name. Having grasped this and also the ineluctability of the impulse by which like is obtruded upon like, the thinker will recognize in every part of the cosmos the replica of the whole, lest we have forgotten it. Timaeus refers (81b–d) to the polemic trigonometry that is at the root of the irenic attraction of like and like. The triangles of the body become exhausted in their ceaseless combat with the external, and they become incapable of attacking the alimentary material with a view to co-opting it to the animal. The inner triangles can no longer defeat but are defeated by the exoteric world. This is senescence, and when the triangles have lost their efficacy, or as one might say their spiritedness, the soul departs pleasantly because naturally: the essence of death in our cosmos is not rest but defeat by an externality that always lurks for attack.

The foregoing conception of uneventful death is carried forward and confirmed in the immediate sequel, a long and detailed passage on morbidity (81e–86a). What might be called basic disease occurs in the presence of excess, deficiency, or displacement of quantities of the four elements in the body, or the alteration of them to form unsuitable variants – perhaps isotopes – which disrupt a physical equilibrium that is maintained in the body only so long as like is added to or taken away from like and the proportions of the whole are unchanged. Like to like and the stability of proportion are a formula for the reconciliation of ceaseless motion and unbroken rest. The massive existence of disease testifies to the power of the forces whose tendency is to oppose that reconciliation. Timaeus's advance to the second order of disease indicates something of the character of those forces. There is a natural direction for the generation of the derivative materials of the body from the primary four elements: marrow, bone, flesh, and sinew, as well as blood to begin with. Then, with the incidence of disease, instead of flesh and sinew being formed from blood, for example, flesh degenerates and reverts to the veins, attacking the blood. Enmity and war are the terms used by Timaeus to characterize the relations among the components of body that have departed from the order of their natural revolutions (83a). In sum, when blood is replenished not from its natural nourishment but by a reflux toward itself of its own product, the application of "opposite" to like is contrary to the laws of nature *(para tous tēs physeōs nomous)* (83e). The great standard of nature is an order whose principle of like to like is called, in an exceedingly rare use of the expression, the laws of nature; the standard is not called an Idea, the eternal unchangeable which is the true being of every becoming. It is hard to conceive the efficacy or constitution of a successful foe of the Idea; but disease compels Timaeus to conjure the successful enemy of the laws of nature. He discovers a blind necessity, call it the irresistible cosmos, in which strife and the irrational coexist in enduring tension with reason and good personified as a god. We are presented with the spectacle of the principle of like to like, which is a *philia,* in perpetual struggle with a principle of hostility. Since the struggle of concord with discord is a struggle, it appears evident that the dominance of strife is assured not by its victory but by the mere fact of everlasting engagement.

Timaeus proceeds from the pathology of reversals of the natural order of construction to the body to what he calls the third kind of disease, traceable to disorders of the internal air, phlegm, and bile, in each case brought on by a blockage in the system of circulation that is such a massive phenomenon of vitality. Should the fiery bile press its attack overwhelmingly, it would reach to the marrow itself and destroy by heat the bonds that fasten the soul to the body – a manner of speech that cannot be presupposed unconditionally to be purely figurative.

Suitably enough, Timaeus passes on to the diseases of the soul that arise out of the state of the body (86b). He has in view such mental disorders as madness (*mania*) and stupidity *(amathia),* insisting that whatever partakes of these is sickness, immediately identifying the excess of pleasure and pain as being of that kind and as the greatest of the diseases of the soul. He traces the venereal frenzy to a superabundance of semen which is in turn produced by a porosity of the bones. (He does not discuss nymphomania.) He leaves no doubt that the wicked are not so voluntarily and that to blame them is not right. In this striking disquisition, Timaeus has found means of arriving at the conclusion that no man is voluntarily wicked. Wickedness is indeed inseparable from a failing of mind – a proposition akin to the Socratic formula that virtue is knowledge – but the wickedness and ignorance or stupidity in the soul have their causes in defect of the body and its nurture *(trophē)* (86e). The unbroken silence of Socrates in the face of this confirmation of his doctrine that no one is wicked voluntarily leaves the question of his reaction to such confirmation open to speculation.

Timaeus elaborates his referral of the vices to states of the body by relating the states of the body to the movements *(phora)* of the soul, in apparent appeal to a principle of the parallel of body and soul if not the reduction of the latter to the former. Completing his pathology of the soul, he asserts that the evils of political regimes and of the things spoken in public and private, not counteracted by any education, comprise a second cause of men's wickedness, involuntary just as was the diseased state of the body. The true malefactors are the ones who make men wicked, not their corrupted victims. And whom, we may ask, could he regard as more culpable than the veritable corrupters of youth. He closes by recommending to each that he flee from evil and pursue its opposite, but only after he, Timaeus, has drawn man and his soul into the closest proximity to the cosmos and its governance by necessity.

As a physician of body and mind, he accepts the burden of proposing remedies as well as providing pathology and diagnosis (87c). The principle of restoration to health is, understandably, the same as the principle of the maintenance of health, namely, symmetry and proportion between body and soul. Symmetry or commensurability and proportion between incommensurables would be unintelligible except as a figurative suggestion not meant for close inspection. But Timaeus is at some length in prescribing for the combination of both body and soul that we call living being, doing so in terms that make clear the seriousness of his belief that vice and disease, virtue and health, are states belonging to a whole in which body and soul are locked in a relation of reciprocating motions – such a doctrine as seemed novel to Thomas Hobbes when he proposed it. A powerful soul shakes the body for good or ill, and a domineering body joined with a mind that is small and weak will be home to a gross human being, stupid, forgetful and ignorant. Lest body and soul fall into disproportion, they should both be cultivated to strength, and the means for achieving such symmetry are gymnastic and music. This evocation of the *Republic* brings sharply to view the difference between the repression of the demands of the body that is characteristic of the *Republic* and the prominence of the body's influence in its copartnership in motility with the soul that is asserted in the *Timaeus,* as if the latter dialogue is itself in a relation of corrective counterpoise with the work to which it is the sequel.

Music and gymnastic are presented by Timaeus as forms of exercise, modes of inducing motion in soul and body so that both may imitate as far as possible the *eidos* or form of the Whole itself, which is in ceaseless motion; for only in motion can the hostile influences, also motions, be kept at bay or overcome and like be allowed to consort with like for the preservation of health. The physic of reciprocal automation on the part of body and soul together constitutes the true or best regimen for the composite animal, the basis of a life most according to reason (89d). It is notable that, in the passage of the *Republic* (444) that may be considered parallel to Timaeus's discussion of health and virtue, there is no reference to motion, although there is repeated reference to nature and to natural hierarchy. The *Republic* dwells on hegemony (of the best), Timaeus stresses reciprocity between higher and lower, the two differing from one another as hierarchy differs from equilibrium. As will appear presently, Timaeus has almost completed the account that will constitute his project for bringing heaven down to earth with his moral kinetics.

Now Timaeus turns to the condition of the guiding soul itself, a subject that he will treat only cursorily. Recurring to his account of the three parts of the soul as located in the head, chest, and abdomen, Timaeus simply adapts to this configuration the doctrine of balanced. proportional motions and (which must invigilate the drowsy reader) of the superiority of motion to rest, that he has already amply elaborated in his physic of the body and of the composite of body and soul.

Having shown the origin of man, Timaeus prepares for the conclusion of his discourse by describing the generation of the rest of the animal kind, and in so doing reveals that his account refers literally to "man," that is, the male human being. In a tale that, like so many before, he characterizes as likely *(eikotos),* he will assert that men who were cowards and who lived unjustly were reborn as women. The gods made the anatomical modifications necessary to bisexual reproduction, and in this way women and the whole female kind came to be. Surely we learn more from this about the meaning of "likely" than about the genesis of the female sex. That this tale conveys a moral judgment presented as the spirit of an event or course of events in the cosmos is a truth that is not a mere likeness of the truth, although the content of this story has the appearance of an unashamed burlesque. What is indeed likely is that Plato has employed a modality of myth, in which gods play a part by courtesy while the effective causes are those of the material cosmos – a civic poetry complementary with that alluded to in the *Republic* (607a). The burden of the myth, "plausible" if the reader is amiably credulous, is that the cosmos collaborates in the moral judgments and distinctions of higher and lower, although it itself knows no simple up and down.

But male human beings decay not only into females but also, if they are of a flighty, atmospheric mind, "meteorologists" who reason about what is aloft simply from the evidence of their eyes, into birds, denizens of the element suitable to their soul. These must be the cosmologists, as distinguished from physicists, of *Philebus* 59a. The plodding men who never look up, who know nothing of philosophy or the nature of the heavens but live the life of the chest become the beasts who tread the earth with hands and heads pulled earthwards, pulled closer and closer to earth in proportion to the degree of their kinship to base earth until, in the extreme, they become the legless that squirm on the earth itself. The utterly stupid and wicked are sent to inhabit the waters, completing the tale whose moral seems to be, like to like throughout the cosmos, the soul itself obeying the universal order whose character is best represented in the kinetic of the four elements. This "verisimilitude" with which Timaeus closes his discourse is cunning and comprehensive in its portrayal of the generation of living things within the whole as a degeneration. It leaves unexplained and incomprehensible the alleged reverse movement from, for example, the mollusks of the ocean floor to a life of higher reason. Would the reversal of the direction of rotation of the universe, and the resumption of direct divine rule of the world *(Statesman* 273) be the condition of progress among the living things, and primarily among men? There may be no simple "down" in the visible whole, but as the *Republic* testifies in its way through the easy decay of the good city, and as *Timaeus* testifies in its way in its terminal myth, there appears to be an effectual "down" in the moral and political life of man. How then explain philosophy? Philosophy seems to be that gift for converting the struggle of good and evil, or of upward and downward, of folly and reason, into reason itself by the unending contemplation of the whole theater of that struggle, in confidence that the whole is somewhat, if inertly, inclined to good by permitting that unending contemplation.

Timaeus takes leave of his completed task by rapturously describing the cosmos as the visible living being that envelopes the mortal and immortal ones – a perceptible god in the likeness of the intelligible, greatest, best, and most beautiful, most perfect in its becoming, this one heaven, unique of its kind.

10
On Ancients and Moderns

To speak of ancients and moderns is inevitably to invoke history: there was an ancient epoch and there is a modern epoch. Time has passed, by which we are more than likely to mean that *a* time has passed. To speak of ancients and moderns without further clarification is also to leave in doubt whether the question concerns the ways of life of ancient people and modern people (what it was like to belong to the generality of mankind "then" as distinguished from now) or whether the determining question is what appears to be a simply scholarly one: ancient thought set beside modern thought. Finally, it has been true for centuries that merely to say the words "ancients and moderns" is to summon the image of a quarrel. One's first tendency is to regard the existence of the quarrel as self-evident. Upon slight reflection one tends to dismiss the "quarrel" as an obvious anachronism and thus a self-evident impossibility: how can there be a quarrel between parties only one of whom is alive to participate in the contest? It would be more precise to speak simply of the rejection of the ancients by the moderns. Upon further reflection it appears that there is indeed a way in which the quarrel might exist and be of utmost seriousness, namely, if the moderns rejected the understandings of the ancients on subjects that the ancients knew to be problematic and which they themselves had already debated. In such a case, the moderns would appear as late entrants in a debate or quarrel the issues in which had been defined by the ancients. In any event, it would be unwise to prejudge the extent of the moderns' rejection of (quarrel with, if necessary) the ancient wisdoms. I believe that the juxtaposition of ancients and moderns will reveal, not surprisingly, such a considerable agreement regarding the identity of the highest questions that the observer of the spectacle will be convinced that there is such a thing as philosophy – not only philosophies or "western" philosophy or periodized philosophies but the apparently timeless contemplation of the timeless. This inference of an enormous homogeneity will have to be extracted from a complex heterogeneity, typified but far from exhausted by the disjunction implicit in the distinction Socratic-preSocratic. If the quarrel between ancients and moderns can be in some way composed by appeal to "philosophy," can the disjunction between the thought of Socrates and his predecessors be immune to the same considerations of composition? I will try to show that it is not, without in any way depreciating the great differences between the understandings of the modern philosophers and the ancient, nor between those of the pre-Socratics and of the preeminent classics. Further, I will attempt to relate those differences in thought to the differences in the conditions of life, as well as we can envision them, between the multitude of denizens of antiquity and modernity.

It must be obvious that the foregoing is a grievously incomplete statement of how the account stands between antiquity and modernity. Certainly there is an antiquity that is not Greek, as we would remember if we stopped to remind ourselves of what exactly the moderns passed under review when they examined their moral and intellectual patrimony and "rejected antiquity." Fully one half of Hobbes's *Leviathan* is exegetical or ostensibly exegetical. Descartes addressed the doctors of the Sorbonne on questions belonging to their province of theology. Spinoza could not enter on moral and political philosophy without traversing the same difficult territory. Locke was noticed with concern by clerical contemporaries. Rousseau proposed a civil religion that had to diverge from the scriptural. The list could be extended. We must conclude that our understanding of modernity could be corrupted from the outset by a massive misunderstanding of the "antiquity" that modernity rejected; and the distortion of "antiquity" as if it comprehended only its rational or only its revealed element would be precisely the misunderstanding that could produce that corruption.

We are now in a position to set out our schema of inquiry. The Platonic/Socratic philosophy is regarded as marking an epoch, presenting the image of profane antiquity as consisting of a darkling primordial episode and an enlightening reformation. The advent of scriptural dispensations presents a more complicated version of the same general paradigm: there was a benighted primordial conception of the divine, displaced by the enlightening reformation that revealed the absolute unity of the god that cannot be represented in any visible form. To this illumination was added a testimony that includes the teaching, "In the beginning was the Logos, and the Logos was with God, and the Logos was God," a thought that resonates astoundingly with the declarations of ancient pagans of the age before Socrates. I will argue that the manifold that we so imprecisely call "antiquity," when our intention is to juxtapose antiquity and modernity, had as its common purpose to explain the whole, meaning by "explain" to find the First within it and to learn the genus of the First: whether it is irreducible corporeal substance or the intelligible that in some accessible or inaccessible way inhabits the whole as its innermost truth or being. And further, I will argue for the presence in the minds of the thinkers in every age, of the everlasting wonder about how the human being lives in a cosmos whose innermost truth is the truth that man's utmost efforts, unaided or assisted, bring to light: do we dwell in a world that is to us as our father's house or is the whole an immeasurable ocean of riches and afflictions that are assigned to us by the blind and deaf one who gives and takes away according to our aptitude rather than our righteousness?

We begin our tour of antiquity with a glance at the archaic men whose preoccupation with the First expressed itself in theogony and cosmogony. It is of less concern to us that some of them located the First in night and others in air or some other particular irreducible than that they personified that First by giving it a name and by deeming it divine. Should that ancient act on the part of the poets and the shadowy Orphics move us to speculate whether it belongs to humanity to regard the First as defining what deserves to be called god? But the First is also the irreducible, what cannot be described by reference to anything else that is "more primary." That irreducible may be the "Highest," that from which all things flow: but irreducible itself evokes also the Lowest, the out-of-which all things are composed. In contemplating the minds of those archaic men, we have the singular opportunity to observe human beings at the work of making their god or gods, which is only to say manifesting their understanding of what it is that deserves the name of god, or deploying their imagination, that faculty for reconstructing experience, to the same end. The quest for the absolutely primary is apparently the theozetetic deed, the quest for what deserves to be god, a quest that seems inseparable from the essence of the human condition. It will surely be found among the doings of such moderns as Descartes and Spinoza, to take two preeminent examples. What is by no means certain is that all those who are in pursuit of the primary know or think themselves to be in quest of what deserves to be called god. Perhaps the divine is primary; but is the primary divine? We receive an early intimation of a difference between antiquity and modernity when we notice that our contemporaries have been schooled to detach the search for the first from a search for the highest. If the preSocratics did nothing else for us, they would have put us in their debt for compelling us to wonder whether the endeavor to penetrate our natural surrounding directs us necessarily to seek a "divine" that includes an excess beyond the "primary" or whether the "primary," whatever it proves to be, can have nothing added to it and is "divine," if the term must be used, simply and precisely because there is nothing that can be added to it: not willing, not hearing, not speaking, and above all not caring.

Homer and Hesiod and the other remote ancients indeed sought to explain to themselves their natural environment, inquiring into its Primal, whether Night or Chaos (perhaps meaning "chasmic," as in the division of the waters above from the waters beneath) or something else, with which we need not be concerned any further than to note that they put their minds to the First of all. It is obvious that they thought not only of the absolute Before but also of the absolute Thereafter. We are told about the teaching of the archaic figure, Musaeus, to the effect that the just will revel forever in drunken gluttony while the wicked will be condemned to perpetual fruitless toil or worse. From all this we know a great deal about the wisdom of preSocratic antiquity. It encompassed the First, the divine, the irreducible, the just, and the life of the soul in a dimension of the whole that is not part of our natural experience: they found it either impossible or inadvisable to explain their natural experience wholly within their experience. Their intellectual effort might be characterized as a seeking for a truth, that is to say an intelligible, the necessity of whose existence became plausible to them within a world of experience whose character it is to point "beyond" to experience that could not be had within this world of nature. In brief, they "knew" of trans-empirical truth, and they "knew," by way of their "knowledge" of the immortal soul, that the human being lived in a universe in which cognizance was taken of the difference between good and evil as practiced on earth. When we say that they "knew" of these things, we are speaking somewhat incautiously, for we do not know how far the sayers of these things believed them and how far they uttered them for merely practical reasons. Soon we will be in a position to make a plausible judgment on this question, at least with respect to some of Socrates' predecessors. To all of this should be added the insight attributed to the Orphic ancients that the whole is pervaded by Necessity and Inevitability (*anagkē*, *adrasteia*), which is at the very least consistent with the notion, indispensable to any possible understanding, that the whole is a scene of ineluctable cause and effect.

As we continue to try to define "Antiquity" for ourselves, we pass from the dim region of the archaic poets into the area populated by the writers known to us through the fragments and reports of their work preserved by commentators and doxographers. We encounter Anaximander immediately. His contributions to cartography do not concern us, but his physics does intensely. He is reported (Diels-Kranz 12Al, after Diogenes Laertius II 1) to have discovered that the most underlying or irreducible is not any of the hitherto named elements such as air and water but rather something called the Infinite, Indefinite, or Undefined (*apeiron*), that which is presumably "more primary" than anything to which a form or a distinctness from anything else could be attributed. There is the primal substance, there is eternal motion, and there is a most pregnant doctrine of coming into being and passing away. According to Anaximander (Diels-Kranz 12A9 after Simplicius, with special reference to the status of elements), each thing that comes into being does so through the destruction of something else, and for this annihilation each new thing must eventually pay with its own dissolution in order to make way for another entity burdened by its birth with a debt that it can repay only with its death. Like all things, we arise from the dust to which we must return. This is what comes to sight as the justice of the cosmic order. Anaximander could serve as a type of the natural philosopher in that his paradigm of justice encompasses a scheme of punishment that is complete within the limits of the natural world alone, requiring no reference to a state of the immortal soul in a world hereafter. His conception, as it is known to us, is asymmetrical, taking cognizance of offense and punishment but not of goodness and reward. In any case, Anaximander makes it clear that a doctrine of universal flux not only can but may easily be infused with a moral concept, such as that justice means equal and exact "paying back," and especially the paying back of being for being, life for life, in a natural setting of endless becoming, preservation and destruction. This, the law of retaliation, might even be called the law of nature. For future reference, we may note here the rejection by Socrates, early in the *Republic*, of the proposed definition of justice as "paying back." Would it be fanciful to invoke another ancient rejection of the law of retaliation, the one that sought to replace "an eye for an eye" with "turn the other cheek," as we struggle to define the "antiquity" that "modernity" confronted? Whatever may be problematic about it as a definition of justice, Anaximander's Rule has the merit of identifying an unchanging that is deeper than the transient palpable and that embodies universal right.

Among the predecessors of Socrates, the preParmenidean Eleatic Xenophanes is one who commands a certain attention. Now looked at askance as a theologian, and suspected as a poet, he denounced the manufacture of gods in the image of man, recoiled from the baseness of deities so coarsely generated, and insisted that god is one, for all is one and one is god. In his *Metaphysics* (986b21),[1] Aristotle says of Xenophanes that he made nothing clear (*outhen diesaphēnisen*). Possessing so little of Xenophanes' writing, we are inclined to try to understand rather than to judge of the justice of Aristotle's severe criticism: on its face, it seems to mean that Xenophanes simply presented his insights as wisdoms, unsupported by demonstrations, as a poet or myth-maker would. Trusting Aristotle in this, we nevertheless retain Xenophanes in our regard for his vision of a one divine that is altogether different from and higher than everything in the empirical manifold. Clearly present to his mind is the notion that will find expression in all the subsequent ages, that is part of Platonic Socratism, and that for all we know was anticipated by his own predecessors, namely, that the popular religion is a form of blasphemy. Heraclitus will give reason to think that the popular religion *must* be a form of blasphemy.

Heraclitus, like many of his age, saw all things as in flux and saw the flux equally as itself supervened by what was not in flux, namely by what he called *logos*: "Hearkening not to me but to the *logos*, it is wise to agree that all things are one" (Diels-Kranz Fragment 50. *Ouk emou alla tou logou akousantas homologein sophon estin hen panta einai*, after Hippolytus). The one that is all things is called god by Heraclitus: "God is day night winter sum-

1 See G.S. Kirk and J.E. Raven, *The Pre-Socratic Philosophers* (Cambridge University Press, 1980).

mer war peace . . ." (Diels-Kranz Fragment 67) in an apparent annihilation of contradiction that is known to have aroused Aristotle and that we might be inclined to see as a viewing of all things under the species of eternity. Heraclitus had the reputation in antiquity of being a rebarbative eccentric – a caustic, riddling recluse whose misanthropic rejection of mankind was a legend in his own time. What is there about his understanding that could have led to such a violent disenchantment with and withdrawal from the social and political existence of man? The most general answer is that he had learned to mistrust and presumably then to despise the judgment of men, who were on the whole incapable of seeing into the truth of all things; for "the nature of things is wont to conceal itself" (Diels-Kranz Fragment 123. "*physis kryptesthai philei*," after Themistius) and mankind is disposed to ignore the universal in favor of the particular and each to judge according to his own dim lights. One of the most striking sentences reported of him runs, "To" (or perhaps better, "In") "god, all things are beautiful, good, and just but men take some to be unjust and some just" (Diels-Kranz Fragment 102, after Porphyry). Heraclitus may not have been the first to be struck by the curious fact that the *logos* of the whole is absolutely pervasive yet mankind, immersed in and existing by that truth, is largely impervious to it. As he perceived the *logos* of god the all-comprehending, he presented an image so forbidding and so paradoxical that it is not to be wondered at that the mankind he hoped to enlighten spurned him and thus earned his reciprocated rejection. For he taught that war is universal and justice is conflict, and that all things come about by conflict and necessity (Diels-Kranz Fragment 80, after Origen/ Celsius), thus harking back to Anaximander's doctrine that each owes its being to the death of something else, and justice is achieved through the ceaseless exchange of death for life. Heraclitus's world is without the consolation of a knowing god: "Neither any gods nor men made this cosmos, for it was always and always will be – everliving fire kindling in measure and quenching in measure" (Diels-Kranz Fragment 30, after Clement). Heraclitus's vision was of a whole that is first in being and divine by virtue of its utter totality. All things within it came to be and remain in existence by and through a tension, call it conflict or "war," that produced a world rather than a chaos because a power supervened over the contradictions and made them fruitful. That power was called *Logos*. It should equally well be called measure or proportion, *Metra*. The two Greek words are rendered kin through their common reference to reckoning. The innermost truth of the whole is to be sought and found in the equilibrium of pressures that imposes limits on the capacity of each striving thing to overpower the resistance to its expansion. Within the whole, all things are commensurate, thus *metra* and *logos* can ordain a cosmos. In this understanding Empedocles too will concur, envisioning a *logos* that is the proportion that reconciles inescapable Love and Strife, the two that are as basic to the world as the four elements. The preSocratic thinkers were of course not naive reductionists who left no room in the cosmos for dual or other manifolds that cannot be transcended.

We see dimly how Heraclitus stands in relation to Socrates: Heraclitus recognized well that there is philosophy and there is the ordinary understanding of men, and because the generality would not and could not be led up to the light, he renounced their society and their way of life and speech, bitterly and intemperately. He was the immoderate priest of measure, who saw no limit to the hegemony of commensurability in the cosmos and who at the same time abused the political or ordinary condition of man because the sacred *logos* was neglected within it. He does not seem to have considered that the recalcitrant ignorance of men, which is at the root of his esotericism (only to them that have shall be given), is an aspect of the *logos* of his one god. What political conclusion he drew from all this is faintly indicated to us in his dictum, "The people must fight for the law (*nomos*) as for the city wall" (Diels-Kranz Fragment 44, after Diogenes Laertius II ix 2). He sounds like one of the early discoverers of the wisdom of Hobbes, those men who did not trust the intervention of nature to provide the pattern of a good human life but who regarded the bulkhead of law or convention as the defensive wall that man must draw about himself in a world in which the natural rule is the simple exchange of life for life. Heraclitus may be thought to have seen the respectable face of conventionalism.

As for Socrates, we see him standing by without expressing objections while Timaeus unfolded a universal scheme in which proportion does indeed constitute the Good, but in a cosmos at whose heart lie entities like *pi* and the inescapable square roots of two and three, the spectral reminders of the irrational in the core of the whole. Socrates' withdrawal from the political mankind that withdrew from him was itself measured: ironical, and without the disenchantment that cannot arise except as the epilogue to an illusion. His vast concessions to the indispensability of political contrivances, institutions that not only do not flow from nature but violate it, are brought forth with pious reverence for *physis*, much as Aristotle would do in proclaiming the city to be a natural growth while acknowledging that the actual cities are more or less monstrous deviants. Socrates appears to have found a way to hold the balance between the conflicting elements of partial truth and thus to have given the world its first example of high philosophy. Who is to say how accurately the difference between Heraclitus and Socrates is measured by so petty a quantity as their respective reputations for freakish eccentricity, which is the popular judgment on an eminence's moderation? In any event, one may decently guess that Heraclitus deserves a place of honor among the preSocratics who stirred the issues that became Socrates' concern.

We should take some notice of Pythagoras, not so much because of his renowned confidence in the mathematical reason of the whole as because of his vision of the relation between the wise and the unenlightened and between philosophy and kingship, subjects whose bearing on the status of Socratism is obvious. Pythagoras, known to us only by report, was the hegemon of a full-fledged cult complete with ranks of initiation into the mysteries, with rules of strictest secrecy, and with tenets that, when perceived in their epigrammatic nakedness, astound with their crankiness. For example: "Stir not the fire with iron"; "Putting on your shoes, start with the right foot; washing your feet, with the left"; "Never step over a cross-bar"; "Do not sit on a quart measure"; "Spit upon the trimmings of your hair and finger nails";[2] and many others. There is much room here for the exercise of apologetic hermeneutics, of which some is on the record, but the impression of cultivated mystification is hard to avoid. Were these singular oddments a pabulum for novices or were they intended to be digested by the initiate? We do not know; but we do know that Pythagoras was not only the sachem of a cult but also a mathematician of some sort and a ruler, said to be a successful one, of a city, namely, Croton. The clue to his importance is to be found, I believe, in his character as mathematician. Though famous for his eponymous proposition, the profoundest preoccupation of his following was arithmetical rather than geometrical. Through Aristotle's many references to him and his school it may readily be seen that Pythagoras had a vision of the whole as having an absolutely intelligible core: to the empirical world there corresponds a numerical structure of truth so deep and so pervasive that the very concept of "perfect," conceived arithmetically,[3] must be understood as applicable equally to morality and physics, to the human and the nonhuman world alike. In this perspective, it matters little that the Pythagorean dicta smack of superstition at its darkest. In their errant way, the Pythagoreans "knew" that the contraries that Heraclitus also held to compose the world are overridden by the unifying truth of number.

How are we to reconcile the notorious secrecy and cultishness of the Pythagorean movement, its confidence in the single mathematical truth of the human and non-human world, and the propensity to rule in the city? The plausible answer is that Pythagoras aspired to bring the implicit order of the whole into concrete manifestation on the plane of politics, but with an apparent intention to restrict the decisive knowledge to an elite that he could control, either to monopolize the arcana of power or to protect the truth from the perils of

2 Iamblichus in Diels-Kranz, following Kirk and Raven, *op cit.*

3 Ten, the perfect number, is the sum of the first four integers, which, qua point, line, triangle, and pyramid respectively, are primary entities. Four is itself of divine weight. It seems strange that a mathematician who knew, although he certainly did not originate, the "Pythagorean theorem" should have retained his numerological optimism in the face of the irrational numbers that the theorem brings to mind.

exposure. The critique of the Pythagorean project is sufficiently indicated in two passages of Aristotle's.[4] Aristotle writes, "Pythagoras first attempted to discuss virtue (*aretē*) but not in the right way; for by reducing the virtues to numbers he made his study of them inappropriate; for justice is not a square number." And "The Pythagoreans had before this treated of a few things, whose definitions they connected with numbers – e.g. the opportune, the just, or marriage. But it was reasonable in him [presumably Socrates] that he inquired into the 'what is.'" From these remarks, if not from the *Nicomachean Ethics*, we can gather that Aristotle considered justice to be beyond a formulaic definition, such as could be the material of a handbook for governors. Further, considering only the unsympathetic allusion to the reduction of marriage to arithmetic, it is easy to see the basis for such a satire on Pythagorean science as is implicit in the fiasco of the "nuptial number" that Plato offers for the improvement of mankind. If we continue to search for the image of antiquity as that image is filled in by the disjunction preSocratic-Socratic, a suggestion comes to mind in this shape: Heraclitus abjured the political society of his congeners and Pythagoras embraced it, each in confidence that he had seen into the truth of the whole. Socrates stood between them, having found a way to live within and without the city and having discovered a mode of parlance that was reticent without being perversely enigmatic or redolent of shibboleth. With no illusions about bringing the heavenly order down to earth, he never abandoned the earthly order on the ground that it refused the transcendent. Can we prevent ourselves from being reminded of another ancient, Moses, whose task it was to go up and then to descend bearing to earth the heavenly legislation for ordering the best regime?

Parmenides was another of the preSocratic legislating sages of Greece. It will always be matter for wonder that the men of that bent who meddled with the politics and consorted with the governors of cities – Solon, Pythagoras, Parmenides, Plato and Aristotle themselves – lived out their lives, while Socrates perished at the hands of the city from whose affairs he took pains to remain distant – except that his fellow-citizens were shrewd enough to sense the expansive rule that lay latent in his meagerly attended conversations, and also perceptive enough to intuit as contempt what he put forward as a cautious preference for a private life.

Parmenides expressed himself in poetry that is notoriously hard to interpret, thus making himself available to those few who go by the path of truth and being rather than to those others who traverse the way of non-being and opinion, as he has it, or becoming and mere perception. He taught the unicity of the whole out of time, one indivisible and motionless Being that is the truth

4 *Magna Moralia* 1182a11 (Diels-Kranz 1.452) and *Metaphysics* 1078b21 (Diels-Kranz ibid.) usefully brought together by Kirk and Raven, *op cit.*

within the swirl of mere experience. He is conducted to his wisdom by the daughters of the sun who lead him into light and who intercede with Justice herself (*dikē*) for his admission to the place that is entered through the gates of night and day (Diels-Kranz 1.228 Fragment 1). It appears that Parmenides received his great illumination as an instruction from the "daughters of the sun," by which we may understand those luminaries of the firmament who have introduced men to the *logos* of the universe in every age. It is Justice who guards the access to truth, a notion that would remain dark to us if not for the clarification implicit in Parmenides' verse to the effect that Justice would not so relax her rule as to permit anything of Being to become or to vanish (Diels-Kranz 1.234 Fragment 8). No doubt cognizant of Anaximander's Rule of Universal Exchange in a whole wherein flux would otherwise threaten to impose lawlessness, Parmenides takes his stand and shows Justice as drawing the line at any exchange between Being and Becoming. Nothing can come from nothing, nor can there be any true annihilation within the whole whose absolute unity struck Parmenides so forcefully. If we ask how Parmenides' insight differed from Anaximander's, for example, it is Plato who provides a strong intimation in the dialogue named for Parmenides. There, by contriving the confrontation between Socrates and Parmenides, the subject being the status of the Ideas, Plato lets it be seen that Parmenides held the doctrine of the unity of the whole in its most extreme form: only One is, the only Being that there is is the Being of One, and that truth is the sovereign Truth of the whole. Anaximander is struck by the scheme of "justice" that guarantees the perpetuity of the whole by imposing within it the law of strict and equal compensation of existence for existence. Parmenides is struck by the scheme of "justice" that forbids any commerce between Being and the meaningless, unintelligible non-being. Anaximander's doctrine is driven by physics, Parmenides' by metaphysics. Plato's *Parmenides* reveals that the Socratic doctrine of the Ideas, which is the Socratic orthodoxy on the subject of the One that inhabits the Many, is less radical than the Unity theory of Parmenides in the obvious sense that for Socrates there are many Ones, though exactly how many such there are is unclear to Socrates, at least in his youth. Can they all be reduced to a grand exhaustive One, and if so, what would be its name? Plato's *Timaeus* concludes with a climactic definition of Good that reveals Good to be a composite held together by proportion. If proportion is prior to good, but proportion is compelled forever to live side by side with the irrational *pi* in the inner recess of the whole, then the unity of the primordial principle of the whole is an equivocation: proportion and the incommensurable are held together in a world-producing conjunction that must be governed by proportion, or the power that makes the world would fail: but "proportion" is the name given to what reconciles itself with its opposite. We hear echoes of Heraclitus and Empedocles; but are we hearing them in the voice of Socrates? Not literally, for it is Timaeus the astronomer who leads the cosmogonic discourse to its polemic-irenic conclusion. If we are to draw on Plato's *Timaeus* for help in assessing the relation between Socrates and any others, then we must recall that the *Timaeus* begins with a Socratic discourse about politics (a summary of parts of the *Republic*) that includes the thought that the city is performing its most characteristic deed when it is at war. It would appear that the polemic premise of the Socratic mandate that sets the dialogue in motion agrees broadly with the equivocal composition between proportion and its contrary with which the dialogue ends. While saying this, it must be kept in mind once more that any concurrence of Socrates in the arguments of Timaeus is only tacit: he never so much as murmurs a reservation. We may conclude, therefore, that Socrates held to a less radical doctrine of One and Many than that of Parmenides and more emphatic than that of the school that taught that All is War. Again, Socrates appears as a man of the middle. It would be unjust and unwise to leave this aspect of the issue that separates Socrates and Parmenides with this silent awarding of the palm to Socrates as the more moderate thinker because something more serious even than moderation itself might be at stake. Parmenides was in pursuit of the absolute all-uniting One that is beyond time, that must be and that the mind cannot distinguish from unsurpassable Being, different from every thing that exists in mere thinghood or partiality. Parmenides was in pursuit of the First and Highest, which is that which is fit to be called god. Why should he not be honored above the man who cannot transcend Proportion – unless Proportion is a name for the absolute unsurpassable intelligible serenity, the timeless *logos* by virtue of which there is a Whole, that noetic immovable that is First and Highest and is fit to be called god. Why doubt the gravity of the dialogue between Parmenides and Socrates?

Can one deduce from all of this anything about the human or political meaning of Parmenides' thought? Perhaps this: Parmenides left no doubt that he saw mankind as divided between those who follow the path of truth and those who go the way of opinion – a view in no way remarkable or original. There is indeed a cosmic order and justice; but how does it make its way into human life? If Parmenides' participation is to be taken as a serious act and not a mere expression of ambition (as to which we cannot be certain), then we may suppose that he considered the rule of a philosopher, one such as himself, to be at least effective in if not simply indispensable to enlightening the darkened place that is the ordinary habitation of mankind. Parmenides differs from Socrates in the obvious way that Socrates did not rule or seek to rule. But Socrates admitted that a good man could wish to rule if only to avoid being ruled by men who are worse than himself, as those who ruled him in Athens must surely have seemed to him. Why may we not assign this reason for Parmenides' assumption of power? And why may we not equally assume that Socrates abstained from rule because it was beyond his grasp? Our speculations along these lines are bound to be inconclusive. Would our attempt to distinguish the conceptions of justice held by the two men be less so? Parmenides apparently subscribed to the received definition of justice as *quid pro quo*, with the far-reaching and deeply meditated restriction that there can be no exchange between Being and not being. Socrates, rejecting this definition in so many words, proclaimed justice to be keeping or keeping to one's own or to oneself. But this, as the basis of division of labor, points inescapably to exchange at the same time that it points to the philosopher's appropriating to himself sole and unlimited power, a possession and a burden for which only he is fit. Is the opposition between Parmenides and Socrates a metaphysical one without practical consequences, except on the plane of biographical accident? Socrates claimed to have abandoned the study of the non-human things and to have given most of his life's attention to the study of mankind and its condition. Parmenides, for all that we know of him directly, appears to have done the reverse. Yet it is Parmenides who ruled a city and Socrates who recoiled from politics. Are we forced back on so slender a support as the conjecture that Socrates would have accepted nothing less than the absolute power of his supposititious philosopher-king, knowing that its occasion is as probable as is the success of a "nuptial number" or any other scheme of dogmatic rationalism; while Parmenides was willing to accept such rule as his subjects would proffer and at their pleasure, thus evincing a pragmatism that betokens anything but intransigent rationalist dogmatism. If we could satisfy ourselves that Socrates, the more single-mindedly he devoted himself to the study of the human things, the more he was confirmed in the conviction that unreason is as embedded in them as it is alongside the rationality of the Whole, we would know that his alleged simplistic rationalism, and hence optimism, is a vulgarization of his thought. So long as this issue remains in unclarity, the line between Socrates and this most weighty of his predecessors will remain to that extent ill-defined, as will the radical originality of Socrates; but what stands out clearly enough is that the question of the rule of philosophy directs us to the deepest questions regarding the place of man in the Whole – the character of the Whole as a home for man and, therewith and necessarily, the existence, meaning and character of god or gods.

A word should be said about what might appear as the marginal consideration of how Socrates and his predecessors expressed themselves. Parmenides, as an eminent example, wrote poetry. Poetry at its best and most serious, that is to say as it is in and for itself, can claim to be the inner truth of what it touches: the articulation of sheer and immediate insight unimpeded by the drag of ratiocination and thus having access to the inmost recesses at the threshold of which reason encounters plausibilities as often as necessities and thus is frustrated by doubts and alternatives. In its tortuous locution poetry imitates, and so doing pays its respects to the sanctity of, the veil that obscures the innermost, at the same time draping intuition in the raiment of beauty. The Socratic criticism of poetry on political grounds fades into banality before the radical criticism of it that is implicit in Socrates' abstention from poetry as a means of philosophic utterance. In his deed, Socrates demonstrated the gulf that separated him from Parmenides: Socrates asked while Parmenides told. By his interrogation, Socrates did not merely play the part of the stimulator of other men's minds, or of the corrector of their errors in the most forceful way. He also, perhaps primarily, was denying that it is by immediate intuition that mankind enters the secret places of the Whole and that it is by assertoric declaration in a baritone idiom which elevates itself above daily speech that mankind announces Truth to itself. Socrates the asker of questions was the one who claimed for himself the wisdom of knowing what and that he did not know. In finding the middle ground between surrender to the enormousness of the province of curiosity and the confidence that that province can be measured conclusively by an intuitive eye, Socrates may have invented philosophy.[5] For future reference, it may be said that he never abandoned doubt.

From this rapid overview of Socrates' patrimony, two names may not be omitted: Protagoras and Gorgias. Protagoras is famous for the sentence, "Of all things man is the measure – of the things that are that they are and of the things that are not that they are not." If he had said only that man is the measure of all things, he could be taken to have meant that there is no justice or virtue or even pleasure except as men define those things. While he could possibly have been a radical conventionalist regarding justice and the like, it is very much more likely that Protagoras had it in mind that to discriminate between what is and what is not, or to investigate and determine being and becoming, is a human task, the responsibility of human wisdom. When coupled with his denial that he knows about the being and character of gods or that perhaps anyone can know about them, he confirms that knowledge of whatever can claim to be primordial, perhaps Being itself, is simply human knowledge. His pantheon would resemble Olympus in no way if the First and Highest were Being itself. How he stands in relation to Socrates is perhaps best indicated by the way in which Plato begins and ends the dialogue that bears Protagoras's name. The two disagree at first in that Protagoras asserts and Socrates denies that virtue is teachable, while they disagree at last because they have exchanged positions. As it appears, if one of them is right, the other must be wrong. Why? In Plato's *Theaetetus*, Protagoras is made responsible for the view that knowledge is perception, and thus by implication that all is flux. If human knowledge is necessarily reducible to perception, then there can be no true knowledge of Being without recourse to some knowledge that transcends, or enables man to transcend, the flux that is what is known by *aisthe-*

5 Zeno did not discover dialectic, as is sometimes alleged; he practiced, and perhaps discovered, demonstrative or eristic questioning.

sis, perception. Only if Protagoras can know of that transcendent can he claim to be the measure of the being of the things that are; and then, perhaps in the view of Socrates, his disclaimer of knowledge of god would be a self-misunderstanding – unless it were an irony. Which it is is very hard to say.

Of Gorgias relatively much survives, but for our purpose little needs to be noticed. He had an inordinate confidence in the power of speech. One might call him the rhetorical parallel to Hippodamas, who also had an unmeasured faith in the suitability of schematic "reason" to practical politics. Gorgias's confidence in the power of speech extended to the belief that he, or perhaps man "in principle," could prove the most outrageous proposition, such as that nothing exists. This extreme doctrine, which attracts at first with its implication that persuasion is more powerful than coercion, proves obnoxious to the criticism that everything it adds to reasoning it takes away from Reason: it brazenly boasts of man's power to make the lesser argument the greater. Not because its claim outreaches its power but because the claim itself threatens any confidence in wisdom as well as in justice, the pretension of Gorgias and his fellows was unacceptable to Socrates. That in the end he was tarred with the brush dipped in pitch of the rhetoricians' preparation only testifies to the prudence that lay beneath Socrates' rejection of any claim that speech has unlimited power. As the intemperate "rationalists" implicated him and philosophy in their visible atheism, so the overreaching rhetoricians implicated him and philosophy in their arrogant sophistry. In his civic downfall can be read much of the ground of Socrates' posture in relation to his predecessors.

We come at last to the sophist Antiphon. One extended quotation from his surviving work will suffice to make the necessary point:

> Justice, then, is not to transgress that which is the law of the city in which one is a citizen. A man can therefore best conduct himself in harmony with justice if when in the company of witnesses he upholds the laws, and when alone without witnesses he upholds the edicts of nature. For the edicts of the laws are imposed artificially, but those of nature are compulsory. And the edicts of the laws are arrived at by consent, not by natural growth, whereas those of nature are not a matter of consent. So, if the man who transgresses the legal code evades those who have agreed to these edicts, he avoids both disgrace and penalty; otherwise not. But if a man violates against possibility any of the laws which are implanted in nature, even if he evades all men's detection, the ill is no less, and even if all see, it is no greater. For he is not hurt on account of an opinion, but because of truth. The examination of these things is in general for this reason, that the majority of just acts according to law are prescribed contrary to nature.[6]

6 This and the following passage are taken from Kathleen Freeman, *Ancilla to the Pre-Socratic Philosophers* (Harvard University Press, 1957), p. 147.

The wisdom of Antiphon may be completed for our purpose with his observation: "But life belongs to nature, and death too, and life for them is derived from advantages, and death from disadvantages. And the advantages laid down by the law are chains upon nature, but those laid down by nature are free." What Antiphon has made perfectly clear to any who would come after him is that the appeal to nature as the supreme moral authority is as heavy with danger in one way as the appeal to convention is in another. Antiphon corrects the wisdom of Anaximander, who saw in nature the unforgiving morality of a life for a life. Antiphon transforms this insight with the discovery that the life lived according to nature is the life of freedom, civil existence is a form of bondage, and the law of the city is no more authoritative than mere opinion, that much disparaged alternative to knowledge, which in the present case consists of matter that could be fatal to orderly life. Antiphon bequeathed to his successors this unwelcome antithesis: life lived freely according to the crystal truth of nature (as it would be lived by the blood-stained ancestor of Gyges) as against life lived in constraint under the rule of prohibitions and prescriptions that emanate from mere men, but men whose natural instinct teaches them, if nothing else does, that wisdom and truth lie in obeying the natural call to advantage. If the natural truth of advantage is sovereign in nature and in civil society alike (because justice is only the advantage of the stronger), is not the project for peaceful and noble human life doomed by the power of the natural Whole in which our existence is inescapably enclosed? Would our last best hope consist in a self-induced confidence that speech conquers almost all, and can make an enclave of decency for us in a universe which reveals its truth at night – unspeakable darkness to which light is the exception and daytime a passing relief? This may in fact be our human situation. Then we would await the speaker who would detoxify nature, declaring its superiority to every artifact in power to bestow good on man, while at the same time displaying conventional civil society at its purest and describing it as grounded in nature: the political philosophy of the best regime. Were such a project to be described as turning the neutrality of nature against itself for the purposes of mankind, the description would appear to fit the schemes of Descartes and Hobbes, as well as those of the artificers of the Olympians who took notice of man. But if political philosophy could be said to be the reconciliation of man to his cosmos on terms that ennoble his life to the extent possible, on premises that do not transcend reason alone, then Socrates can be said to have concocted political philosophy out of the abundance of his inheritance from those we call pre-Socratics, and to have done so in a way that distinguished him from his modern successors by his having kept man's nobility always in sight as his star and compass.

It is well to make explicit what Socrates did not do. He did not discover the disjunction of one and many, of a phenomenal flux and an intelligible immobile, of a whole cosmos and its inner *logos*, of body and soul, of rational and irrational, of a few and a many, of opinion and knowledge, of nature and convention, of guarded and unguarded speech. Others before him saw that the Whole could not be reduced to some simple that was free from duality. He did not discover the goodness of a private life, nor the teaching of an immortality and of a reward and punishment hereafter; nor did he discover the scandal of the vulgar pantheon or of an unworthy supernaturalism, or the question whether the whole is ruled by some principle of good and if so what that principle or justice might be. He was not the first to scrutinize the poets with a critical eye.

What then did he do? How did he enlighten his age? I believe that in creating political philosophy, according to the suggestion put forth above, Socrates proved to be the man who provided the most moderate and at the same time the most elevating resolution of the question, How is man situated in the Whole? His disjunction of the philosopher and the *polis* in his act is accompanied by his conjunction of the philosopher and the *polis* in his speech. Do his act and his speech cancel each other by contradiction or do they combine to teach a lesson? I believe that in their combination they embody the substance of the first of the profane Enlightenments of the western world. By an Enlightenment I mean a radical ingathering, scrutiny, revision and reorganization of the moral and intellectual patrimony, with the specific intention of bringing mankind closer to a life dominated by the truth of man's positive relation to reason. The act and the speech of Socrates teach that highest reason, wisdom, or philosophy is ruling yet nowhere rules. There is a worm of unreason that inhabits the core of the overpoweringly rational whole, as we might have surmised by giving due weight to the invasion of the body of mathematics itself by the intractable *pi*. Proportion itself, or commensurability, has its limits; and whatever this may portend for the fate of the cosmic whole, its bearing on the perfect adjustment to each other in political society of the varieties of human soul is clear for all to see who do not blind themselves.

How does the Socratic Enlightenment address itself to the demoralization latent in the dissemination of such doctrine? The practical task of Socrates is defined by the two aspects of his insight: the reason of the Whole and the unreason in the Whole. In the *Statesman*, Socrates is made by Plato to concur by implication of silence in the definition of statesmanship as an art of inspiriting and restraining, according to the need of the ruled. In the *Theaetetus*, Socrates performs an exercise repeated elsewhere, with a success dependent on the docibility of his interlocutor, by which he encourages his fellow-inquirer to take heart and never give up in the struggle to probe into the being of the things, an inspiration called forth by his having reduced his companion to paralyzed confusion and a reminder never to lose sight of what remains problematic or mysterious. Surely there are things that Socrates knew well that he knew; but one of them was what and that he did not know. His achievement may therefore be called an Enlightenment of restrained practical expectations, driven forward by an unquenchable purpose to keep his congeners mindful of the best and the highest of which they are capable. With a view to later developments, the Socratic achievement might be called also an Enlightenment of residual doubt.

It is remarkable that the Socrates we know is much more an anthropologian and a psychologian than a theologian. When he discloses, at the end of his life, that he had long since given up as unpromising the study of the nonhuman for inquiry into the human world, he appears either to have surrendered to a discouragement that deflected his philosophizing ever after or for whatever other reason to have decided to abstain from inquiry into the beings aloft. Again with a view to later developments, we may observe that the Socratic Enlightenment had a human orientation but could afford to leave largely obscure the degree to which it was circumventing the received conception of deity. In its zetetic mode, the Socratic Enlightenment stood out against the assertoric imposition of immediate insight, and against the poetic revelation of gods that were at the same time embarrassingly natural in their impulses and marvelously unconstrained by the limitations of nature in gratifying them.

We remind ourselves easily at this point that there was a sacred as well as a profane antiquity to which the modern Enlightenment addressed itself, and that there was in that area an evolution that might well be described as an enlightenment, indeed as the absolute illumination of mankind through Revelation. The only way to characterize the scriptural Enlightenment briefly is to describe it as the immediate revelation of the self-identified First and Highest as the absolute One, the utmost principle of the universe, communicant with man but utterly inconceivable by him, absolutely righteous, solely hegemonic, legislative for mankind and thus careful that the goodness of the whole be actively present in the existence of men, invulnerable to the constraint of His natural creation, and retaining forever a measure of His inscrutability, thus guaranteeing that the universe will always be a mystery. Although a mystery, it may not lawfully be an object of investigation but only of inquiry into the further clauses of the law. The scriptural Enlightenment relieved mankind of the degraded belief that the First and Highest is accessible to the eye and thus can be rendered in any image, though it remained accessible to the ear, thus accommodating the righteous *logos* of the whole to the taming of mankind. The scriptural Enlightenment presented the paradigm of the perfect order that would be installed among men if they had not been made, for reasons to remain dubitable, subject to corruption. In ways very different from those trodden by Socrates, the oldest scriptural Enlightenment measured out the wisdom of a whole at whose center lay a perfection whose reason must remain forever veiled to the human mind and whose goodness must remain forever an inimitable aspiration. The subsequent scriptural Enlightenment vastly enlarged the promise of an approximation of the human condition to the cosmic, closing the distance between heaven and earth by showing the birth and death of God, and displaying his return to life as the good to be available to the simplest of men. In the end, the intimacy of the divine and cosmic with the human and terrestrial will be sealed by the millennial rule of men by divinity on earth. In the meantime, the ultimate triumph of the humblest is vouchsafed through their subservience to the commandment of love, enforced with the fullest insistence of divinity exactly because only the power that exceeds nature can make the demand that (fallen) nature refuses. The Christian Enlightenment is in its own way the great outcry against nature, that devastating disappointment to a humanity that craves a more nurturing domestication in the universe.

When we speak of antiquity and modernity, and of the reaction of modernity to and against antiquity, we should have in mind so far as possible what the giants of the modern Enlightenment themselves contemplated when they opened a retrospective eye. It is not impossible for us to reconstruct that vision. When Machiavelli looked back, he saw a profane antiquity that expected much of nature and a sacred antiquity that accepted little from it. By this I mean that he misunderstood the crucial pagans as projectors of so-called imaginary republics that were intended as paradigms of concrete civil societies, whereas in fact it was a work of the Socratic Enlightenment to stand between those who proclaimed a simply perfect cosmic natural order that can be translated into the human condition and those who saw the natural order as fully illustrated by the jungle. On the other hand, Machiavelli understood well the theology that perceived the glory of God as resting on the disparagement of God's natural creation: not only must man be molded athwart and elevated above his nature but, in the same spirit, nature as a whole cannot be understood as defining the possible. The highest excellence is a defiance of nature, as the highest truth is displayed in miraculous contradiction of natural causation. If a Renaissance of antiquity was the cradle of modernity, then it should be said that the Renaissance conflated the Christian antiquity that it knew and the profane antiquity that it had not studied diligently, perhaps because it easily accepted the Christian appropriation of pagan philosophy to be its servant. Modernity was generated out of a profound insight and an extensive misconception.

Hobbes will maintain and Spinoza will confirm that there can be nothing in Scripture that is contrary to reason if Scripture is an emanation from a worthy god. Thus there grew up an immense rational exegesis to which Descartes and Locke also contributed. That exegesis had the broad purpose to eliminate the contradiction of nature by revelation, in effect to reassert the worthiness of the natural Whole to be considered as infused with the *logos* of what deserves to be called god. If Descartes himself, in the *Meditations*, had not used the expression First and Highest, apparently to mean by it the innermost truth of the whole, we might be reluctant to introduce it into the account of modernity's own quest for what I have called that which deserves to be called god. In the case of Hobbes, it is made clear that the true improvement of the human condition depends on transmitting to the plane of mankind's everyday existence the decisive knowledge concerning nature. That knowledge might be put summarily as follows: man's well-being does indeed require an overcoming of nature, not by means that are above but by means that are within nature. Since the time of the Hebrews, men had been encouraged if not constrained to look for the ultimate causes of things outside of nature. Thus they made for themselves a world in which the demonstration to one another of their most cherished beliefs failed, they were returned to the archaic mode of discourse, which was assetoric, and the verification of verities was inevitably left to fire and the sword – all in a world in which the dictate of nature itself only too manifestly favored war over peace. Until the true status of man within nature was sufficiently understood by sovereign and subject alike, there would be no peace, no enlargement of the mind and thus no increase of comfort to the body. In Hobbes's particular view, the chief obstacle to the advancement of reason was grounded more in the sacred than in the profane antiquity, although he had to blame Aristotle for encouraging the Scholastics to multiply substances where there were only accidents. Hobbes complained further of Aristotle that he promoted popular government by preaching down tyranny and preaching up a natural standard of right for every mischief-maker to appeal to against the always threatened bulwark of sovereignty that holds nature at bay. Perhaps there is justice in the odium in which Hobbes, an architect of emancipation, is held by partisans of freedom, as retribution for his portrayal of Aristotle as a resource for demagogues. With more justice, Hobbes took his place among the modern writers who denounced the Aristotelian and Scholastic enlargement of nature beyond positive bounds to include the famous formal and final causes, Aristotle himself going to the absurd extreme of declaring the natural sociality of man, in the face of the most obtrusive evidence. Exploding these causes was to strike a blow against that exaggeration of nature's philanthropy that moderns insisted on finding in profane antiquity. The blow glanced to wound also the theologians and other believers who could find in every gift of nature a testimony to the solicitude of nature's author. It must be said that the simplicism of the interpretation put by the modern Enlightenment on the pagan antiquity becomes as visible in Hobbes's conception of Aristotle as trusting nature to civilize man as it did in Machiavelli's sarcasms directed against old projectors of visionary republics.

The seminal contributions of Descartes to the birth of modernity and the modern Enlightenment may be seen as flowing from a single philosophic aspiration, which was to achieve certainty of knowledge for the good of man. The achievement of certainty is a locution whose negative equivalent is the removal of doubt. Descartes conceived that doubting everything was the precondition for doubting nothing. His demonstration of the existence of God and of the deathless soul was of course rooted in doubt, however decently dissembled. As his labor draws to its close on the Sixth Day of his *Meditations*, it is evident that he has indeed proved the existence of the First and Highest: the truth and *logos* of the Whole, revealed in mathematics. Descartes can say with an undivided mind that In the beginning was the *logos* and the *logos* was with God and the *logos* was God, and, so saying, he can understand himself to be the prophet of the true religion whose communicants are proof against the blasphemies of idolatry and every form of superstition. The liberation of man from disease, toil, confusion, and the tyrannies of zeal is the promise that lies within the book of the unfolding of nature. No one could have believed more wholeheartedly than Descartes that if mankind knows the truth, it will make them free. Since Descartes gave it as his judgment that intelligence is perfectly distributed, for everyone is satisfied with his share, it may be taken for granted that Descartes had only limited confidence in any project for enlightenment in the sense of a penetration of every mind by the truths of highest philosophy.

The philosophers of the modern Enlightenment saw their predecessors of the ancient profane Enlightenment as trusting inordinately in a nature they did not have the means to understand; and their predecessors of the ancient sacred Enlightenment as trusting inordinately in a supernature that no human being might ever understand. The modern Enlightenment can claim to have found the method for removing doubt about the natural whole by redrawing its boundaries to exclude the dubitable; but it did not, nor does it think it did, thereby render the whole of our universal setting exhaustible by science: modernity repeats in its own mode the wisdom of Socrates, which was to know that he did not know.

When Kant insisted on purifying virtue beyond every consideration of consequent good, he estranged our goodness from our nature as radically as did the theologians of man's fall, although as a self-understood prophet of the true religion that is open to reason alone. So doing, he gave us yet another reason to wonder whether the full history of modernity must not contain a discussion of the question, How much of the modern Enlightenment in an unwitting rediscovery of timeless possibilities, much as we earlier found ourselves moved to ask how much of the Socratic Enlightenment was an ingathering of the preSocratic wisdom. In one respect, however, we may be confident in the originality of the modern Enlightenment's orientation: it was possessed by a spasm of optimism for the fate of man for which there is no profane precedent. The more that it tightened man's hold on nature, the more it loosened the hold of nature on man, with the promise not of a millennial but of an imminent victory over the natural satan. The historical plasticity of the human nature formulated by Rousseau found its way easily into the Socialism that promised freedom from want, from coercion, from false belief, from unreason whether institutional or domestic, public or private. In view of how the modern Enlightenment matured, it is worth recalling that modernity opened with the disparagement of visionary republics. Machiavelli's call to man to take control of his fate was heeded so enthusiastically that it became the inspiration for a vision that reveals itself now as phantasmagoria.

What then to make of Hegel's formulation of a dialectic in which the decisive contradictions are perfectly "overcome" or mediated? Is the new dialectic at once the transcendence of the Socratic Enlightenment and also an apparent correction of the modern Enlightenment's resignation to an irremovable Dubitable? It may be left an open question whether Hegel's radicalization of the modern Enlightenment's rationalism is the perfection of that Enlightenment or whether, by grounding that consummation in the biography of human consciousness, it historicized the human repository of Being itself. If the latter, then Hegel would deserve to be thought of as an early if not the first post-Enlightenment modernist, if not the first "post-modernist."

Can anything be said about the way of life of the innumerable millions who have lived within or alongside those ancient and modern struggles to understand or come to terms with the whole that enclosed them? The ancient Hebrews must have lived in fear of God, the harshness of exile testifying to the disfavor of a father from whom they could only hope some resumption of his blessing when he sent them his anointed to rule them again in a godly way. Christians were confirmed in that hope because God had fulfilled part of his promise before their eyes; for the rest, they must bear their lot in patience imitating Christ by suffering the world according to the example shown to them by Christ on the cross. The pagan multitudes lived we know not how. Was it in the shadow of Olympians, beings who somehow were the forces of nature but also flourished as anthropoids, thus bridging the gap between man and the natural All? Perhaps we are limited to the speculation that their lives were bounded by their poetry, their laws, and their labor. About them we may ask the grand question that, when answered, tells much about life in any human epoch: What was the characteristic mystery that beset them? What in their daily existence passed their understanding? Their laws were clear to them and their labor was only too self-revealing. What was there to puzzle them but nature itself – stupendous seismic calamity, the rotation of heaven, the birth of animals. For all the enlightenment of the sages of Greece, and for that matter of Egypt and elsewhere, the wonderment of ancient men must have turned on the mysteries of their natural environment. This is no longer true. In the age dominated by the modern Enlightenment, the mysteries that are closest to us, that literally surround us, are not those of nature but of art. So profoundly mysterious to us are they that their mysteriousness to us is concealed from us. In order to work and in order to have respite from work, we are compelled to manipulate what we cannot understand. How many among us literally know what we are doing when we activate any of the countless tools and conveniences that dominate our existence? Very few. It is a paradox of the Enlightenment that it planted us in impenetrable quotidian darkness of artifact while relieving us of the sense that nature was the true mystery. If this was the price that had to be paid for the political liberation that is one of the jewels in the crown of modernity, it may well have been worth paying.

We are entitled to wonder whether it belongs to the human condition that something be mysterious to mankind, and the difference between one epoch and another lies in the identity of the mystery. But in asking this, we find ourselves involuntarily thrown back upon the wisdom of the Socratic Enlightenment: we human beings are led to know ourselves, with and without reference to our historical setting, by recognizing what it is that we do not know.

11
The End of History in the Open-Ended Age? The Life Expectancy of Self-Evident Truth

Whether history has ended is a question subordinate to several other questions: Is history a thing? If it is a certain something, of what kind is it? Is it of the kind capable of having an end? What could be the meaning of "end" as applied to such a thing as history? And does "Now" have the character that would satisfy the definition of "end" to mean "nothing thereafter," for that would presuppose the extinction of the world, which is not contemplated. It follows therefore that What is history? is really subordinate to the question What must history be if it is to fall within the class of things having an end, whatever that word proves to mean, without presupposing the annihilation of everything? Now we have progressed far enough to see that we need one word that means "end as last one of all" and another that means "end in another sense that we have not yet been able to define." Let us use "terminable" for the former and "perfectible" for the latter.

If at least one thing, namely, the Whole, is not terminable, then history cannot be absolutely comprehensive but must be a part of something larger. It would be a finite part of the infinite Whole. Some things would fall within history and some would not. But before knowing what kind of "thing" history is, we can scarcely know what it includes or pertains to, what kind or kinds of things it *can* include. The mutual dependence or "coprimacy" of the fundamental questions need not paralyze the inquiry, but it will compel us to make a beginning that is arbitrary. Let us begin with ends.

Whatever other meanings may attach themselves to the word "end," there is one meaning that no other can exclude or replace: an end is a "toward which," in time or space or being. That a thing has a "toward which" is a sign that it is either terminable or perfectible or both. "Toward" implies movement or change. Bodies move toward a place where they are not but where in some sense they ought to be. Young plants and animals "develop." Minds "grow." Why is there such a thing as a "toward which," and how far is it affected by "ought"? We know that a body on a slope moves down, it has a "toward which" imposed on it by a truth inherent in matter. Living things develop in obedience to a truth imposed on them by obscure necessities. Minds grow to some extent in spite of themselves. It is clear that the "ought" that goes with "toward which," in the examples that have come to mind, is an ought of necessity, not of freedom, choice, or good. The necessity is of the nature of truths. Truth is necessity, necessity is truth – thus far. So an end is a place or a state in which something subject to change must find itself by reason of truth.

Where is that truth or necessity? We will not know whether, in speaking of the "where" of truth, we must continue to flounder in the language of metaphor until we know whether a truth is a something that can be "somewhere." In the meantime, we will ask whether the truth that dictates its end to a thing is within the thing or external to it. Where is the principle of gravitational attraction, and where are the truths of genetics which govern the development of living things? We are inclined to say that the truths are incorporated in the individuals that they govern, but this is to beg the question, because what we would like to know is exactly whether there is a truth that "is" (using "is" as the verb that corresponds with "being") independently of its "incorporation." But what would be the mode of being of something – truth – that "is" without any existence in which to express itself, so to speak; for the being or end of the truth of gravitation seems to be to induce certain states in bodies. Can – indeed, must – a truth have an end, a toward which or consummation? Or is its being its only consummation, its perfection and its satisfaction? In the latter case, we human beings would have to ask ourselves how we could become aware of a truth that need not and does not manifest itself in an existent? Our only answer would have to be provisional: by our power of ratiocination, we come to conclusions whose existence lies in the logic that dictates their absolute necessity. We prove the necessity of their government of things by the necessity of their own being as demonstrated to ourselves by ourselves, we having informed ourselves that there is a question to be answered because we have taken note of existent things whose behavior puzzles us: from the existent things to the necessity governing them, which is the truths, then back to the existent things. But this exactly avoids the question whether there is truth, and if so whether we human beings could be aware of it, if it were absolutely and in every way detached from empirical, existent manifestation. What is a truth that is not "about" something capable of coming within experience, not restricting experience to sense perception but in any sense however wide? This is not the place to rehearse the Socratic doctrine of Ideas or the Kantian critique of pure reason, but rather to return to the problem of a possible end of history, making use of whatever aids we have gained along the way. To justify the foregoing as helping us toward our goal, it should be said that the proposition "history can end" implies that there is a truth in the world of experience.

Before leaving this area of troubling questions, all of them attached to the thesis that history can end, one further formulation of our problem should be considered. If there is an inner truth in the whole, is it of such a nature that it *must* come forth, or rather that it *might* come forth and be manifest, or even that it absolutely *cannot* come forth as empirical? Otherwise put, is there a *logos* that is immanent in and thus inseparable from the material in which it must utter itself; is the *logos* such as to be brought to actuality only if aided by fortuitous chance; or is the *logos* of such a nature as exactly, by virtue of its nature, to be in a state of opposition to the material in which it would utter itself, as would be the case if blind and stupid matter were an insuperable frustration to reason? Will there be an apodictic demonstration that one of these describes the condition of truth in the whole? The very question whether there can be such a demonstration is likely to remain in contention indefinitely. But until such enigmas are replaced by conclusions, history itself will not be brought to a conclusion, for history, which is human history, is lived in the mind as well as in the city. The attainment of admirable politics is a true marvel, but it does not exhaust human experience.

Suppose now, to resume, that there is no truth, certainly no truth accessible to us human beings that is not incorporated, that is, that is not in principle manifest or brought to our mind by a thing or things that exist. (Let us set aside the truth of the moral law, which may or may not be known to us with certainty and without experience as a ground.) Suppose conversely that there is nothing that comes within our experiences which is not the expression of a truth that has the force of governing necessity by which it controls what we have experienced. What must we suppose next in order to give a ground to the thought that history has an end, apart from whether the end is at hand? We would have to suppose that history is one thing like every manifest thing; that it is not only or essentially the conglomerate of occurrences but that it is itself an occurrence; that although it encompasses things or parts, and so belongs to the class of wholes and not parts, it behaves like a part in the relevant respect, namely, that it is under the influence of a necessity that is a truth by its having to progress toward its perfection rather than eternally to be in possession of it; that there is not one order of explanation, truth, or being for Whole and another for Part, but one order for both, meaning thereby that "toward which" is intelligible when applied to a true whole just as it is when applied to a true part. Can "toward which" bear a meaning that is applicable to the Whole and also to a part? What can change mean with respect to the literal Whole, if not simply rearrangement of its parts? It could mean much more: the growing disclosure of the interior truth of that Whole, an act that is either the actualization of the truth of the Whole at the initiative of the Whole – the supposition of Revelation – or the growing presence of that truth in the minds of the only intelligent beings capable of knowing it, namely, man. Then the unequivocal end of the Whole, its perfection, would be the completion of its self-disclosure and the perfection of the intelligence of the intelligent being.

Perhaps we have gone far enough to venture a definition of the end of history and its conditions. The conglomeration of human experiences, itself having the character of a perfectible entity, has been propelled by a truth, which is the necessity of its being, to a consummation that expresses that necessary truth in its totality. The attainment of the absolute human "toward which" is the end of history.

In order for that consummation to be veritable, it must be known as a consummation to the being whose perfection is asserted in and through the fulfillment of truth in him, that is, the completion of his understanding. His understanding of what? First and foremost, of himself, which means of his human condition; but it is absolutely impossible to understand his human condition without understanding his position within the Whole of which the human is only a part. The exhaustion of knowledge of the human is impossible without exhaustion of knowledge of the Whole, for without the latter we do not know conclusively how important we are, or where we stand in relation to the Whole that conditions us, that is, in the end, our condition. The limit on our knowledge of the Whole is, in another guise, the limit of our knowledge of ourselves, as will be clear to anyone who wishes absolute knowledge of the fate of the soul. In brief, for human history to end, we must have conclusive knowledge of the Whole; but the only settled knowledge of the Whole that has ever come to the mind of man is the knowledge that what we face when we confront the Whole are alternatives, not resolutions. The human contemplation of the Whole is the history of the human contemplation of the Whole, a history without end. Revelation provides not a refutation but a confirmation of this thought, for what Revelation reveals is the inscrutable God. Neither reason nor revelation discloses to man fully and without residue of mystery whether or why the truth of the Whole is a power rather than an object, an efficient rather than a formal cause. Without such knowledge, every supposition that the end is accomplished is veiled in uncertainty because the ground of the end lies in doubt.

But why may it not be argued that man is indeed in possession of the absolute knowledge that is the condition for the completion of his history, for he possesses the knowledge that ultimate knowledge is knowledge of the intractability of the alternatives – say, for convenience, reason and revelation, or ancient and modern philosophy. Suppose in brief that to know the reason that lies in one's doubt is to replace the doubt with the decisive wisdom. Let us accept that argument and suppress the question whether nothing new can come hereafter to the mind of man. How can we move from the speculative absolutization of knowledge, which is the knowledge that absolute knowledge is knowledge of intractable alternatives, to the conclusion that constitutional democracy is the best regime – and let there be no doubt that the end-of-history thesis is a modern transform of the ancient best-regime thesis. Is there any need to say more than that the end-of-history thesis is essentially modern, that is, that it itself belongs to one branch of the intractable alternatives and that its universality or absoluteness is ipso facto destroyed? There is indeed a need to say considerably more, for its "essential modernity" may be its strongest defense rather than its fatal weakness, its demonstration of progress. If, as is obvious, it connects a disclosure of truth-within-the-Whole and the passing of time, it may be vindicated by its very insight, of which it is its own decisive evidence. By what then might it be overthrown, its premises being defended by their abstractness, if not by the falsification of its concrete conclusion, which is that a certain political order is the best regime?

Our task is twofold: first, to bring to light the premise of the end-of-history thesis that the truth within the Whole is a cosmic conspiracy for the good of man, a power that disciplines the enormous reticulation of causes and effects to cooperate in the achievement of the human state of rational freedom, thus apparently implying that everything that has hitherto represented itself as a free act of man was an unselfconscious movement on the part of a figure in a clockwork – there has been no freedom until "now." And second, that the regime of constitutional democracy, of rational freedom, is so incontrovertibly the best political order that the truth of the Whole, in causing it to materialize, becomes visible as a force for accomplishing the predestined consummation of man's life in society.

The first part of our task has been addressed in the foregoing sketch of a critique of the end-of-history thesis as a metaphysic of politics. It remains to attempt a critique of the thesis as a political philosophy of the best regime which identifies liberal constitutional democracy as that very regime. Fortunately, it will not prove necessary for the present critical purpose to describe the best political order, but necessary only to consider the arguments that trouble the identification of our own as that apex of social evolution.

Support for the special distinction of the liberal regime should not be drawn from recent events in the communist world, partly for the trivial reason that these events are sure to be followed by others that are unforeseeable, partly for the reason that the turn from socialism is a turn of *faute de mieux* with an economic rather than a moral meaning, and partly for the reason that the intelligible as such is not confirmed in its truth by the empirical but is simply made visible to us thereby; it is rather the empirical that is explained by the intelligible, for intelligible implies exactly an appeal beyond the empirical.

That the turn from socialism might move in retrograde or other vagrant directions is only too obvious. That the turn would not have occurred at all if socialism had generated prosperity is at least as likely. That socialism is incapable of generating prosperity is no more likely, but so far as it is credible it seems, but only briefly, to accord with the end-of-history thesis *qua* political theory. For history, rather than imposing capitalism as the scourge for which socialism was to be the remedy, appears to have ordained socialism as the failure destined to precede liberal capitalism in order to attest the truth and goodness of the latter. How curious, if the socialist regime whose only speculative support lay in the end-of-history thesis were to be consumed for the strengthening of that fickle theory, which now sets its seal not on the removal but on the robustness of the institutions that promote rivalries within society. The theory of history and the socialist regime that served each other as support and corroboration have parted ways because the theory has changed its mind about what is to be understood as progress.

The Soviet leader has admonished the West not to gloat. His advice is sound for a number of reasons, not all of which are merely political and some of which come to view when we look, for this invidious purpose, at our own innermost composition.

We begin with the thousand-times rehearsed birth of modern liberalism out of the philosophy of the sixteenth and seventeenth centuries, with additional impulses contributed in the eighteenth century. Unable any longer to share in the prevailing belief that the Whole is informed by a truth that exerts itself on our behalf in exchange for man's abasing himself before it, the bold spirits began a revision of the inner spring of the world. In fact, they reinvented nature, with famous effects on human life through technology and political science. The greatest power in the universe proved to be not man's master but his slave. To know this was the beginning of wisdom. But the emancipation, the empowerment, and the enlightenment came at a singular price: man had to give himself over to nature as completely as, theretofore, he had been required to give himself over to his erstwhile master. That this was a new bondage came eventually to be seen, first when it became clear that man supine in nature was a frightened wretch, and later when the plenitude of accommodation to nature, could man be capable of it, was interpreted as the loss of freedom and therewith morality on the part of an automaton. Modern liberalism, whose claim to be the best regime we are now testing, was born out of the philosophic struggle to order man's relation to nature in such a way as to avoid any confrontation with it as our master while extracting every service from it as our servant. It would be a fatal mistake to consider those services to be limited to technology. As important are the enormous practical benefits conferred through the cunning of nature, by whose agency our freedom is sustained and our prosperity enhanced as by an invisible hand. Mastery of nature is as profoundly dependent on obedience to it as was ever the case between man and master in the Age of Faith; only in those days the sovereign laid down a moral law while at present the imperial order is that of cause and effect.

In the light of its genesis, how may we describe our liberal regime with a view to judging its eligibility to be known as best of all and apex of history? It is the regime of freedom and reason. It is the regime of reason because it acknowledges no power superior to that which joins cause to its natural and naturally knowable effect. Knowledge is the knowledge of that conjunction. Wisdom is the prudence that exploits that knowledge. Freedom is the actualization of wisdom in private and public practice. Modern liberal society is framed in freedom, and thus in reason.

How has liberal life in fact unfolded? It would be impossible to answer that question without taking note that the liberal societies have existed like cells with a penetrable wall. Human communities have long proved to be permeable by alien influence, but the liberal societies are unique in incorporating their permeability in their definition. They cannot do otherwise while remaining faithful to their commitment to freedom. If there is a tension between liberal dedication to freedom and liberal openness to whatever threatens it, the perfect resolution of that tension has yet to be found. Fortunately, perfect resolutions are not necessary in practice, but they are indispensable to a theoretical showing that the object is an epitome of reason, where contradiction is intolerable.

The freedom that is the pride of liberal constitutionalism is well understood as both limited and confirmed through autonomous acts that are, as autonomous, testimonies to freedom. These free acts of self-restraint take place on the plane of government and law by the mediation of representatives, but they cannot take place on that plane only. For the true perfection of the freedom of the liberal society, its individual members should be disposed to will what is worthy to be willed as that is made known to them by reason itself. In borrowing the language of Hegel in order to round out the notions of Rousseau, we engage in an exaggeration that helps to reconnect freedom and reason: if there is something fatuous about demanding that each member of the liberal society will the rationally attested willworthy, in what more moderate sense is the demand met that freedom and reason pervade the ultimate community? The petty reason of individuals who participate in affairs and the myopic volition that collaborates with their shrewdness must surely be overridden by a Reason and a Will that dignify the best political order by raising it to levels of which its denizens are unaware. Granting the power of the benign *logos* with its invisible hand, it follows that the true reason and freedom that endow the lives of the beneficiaries of liberal life are as remote from the knowledge of those human beings as if the latter were drones toiling in a commune of bees. Where reason lit the active mind of every citizen and disclosed to him the truth that ennobles him in defining his freedom and guiding his will, the regime that truly perfects history would be in place. Is there no education, no concert of art, religion, and ordinary schooling, that could equip the members of liberal society to recognize their own dignity? The higher and lower culture of the West would by itself be enough to suggest a discouraging answer. The actualities of freedom in liberal society have not accorded with the idealities of reason contemplated by the end-of-history thesis. Too many influences that the thesis can dismiss as merely adventitious or marginal, historical in the humble sense, such as the migrations of peoples, the developments of technology, the discovery and dissemination of substances that console and accelerate demoralization, all these and more – irresistible by liberal society, partly because it is in principle permeable by everything from without and partly because it understands its freedoms in a way that makes it vulnerable to everything within – all seem to mock the allegation that we are at the peak to which man is predestined by cosmic truth.

We might be in danger of imposing an unrealistic and unnecessary condition on the end-of-history thesis, which after all does not itself use the language of "best regime." Why should not the ultimate political society be the best possible rather than the best simply? Because attributing the power of governing history to a force that *must* stop short of procuring the best is to conjure a contraption whose oddities accuse it of makeshift. Truth moves through the world with a benign purpose using nature as its instrument. Then it encounters nature in the form of human nature, and the very truth itself finds its beneficence halted at the point of second-best for humanity. How might one verify this affirmation of an obdurate nature in revolt? When we encounter the inborn contumacy of man in Scripture, it appears as the mysterious product of a creator whose truth is not the cosmic principle that the world must rise to its peak in human freedom and reason but rather that the world will end in blessings for those who live in obedience and faith. Understandably abjuring the support of revelation, and barred by its rationalism for invoking mysteries it cannot dispel, the end-of-history thesis is exposed to the suspicion that it stealthily divides nature against itself and then conveniently assigns contrary roles to the mutilated parts in order to accommodate overwhelming ignorance to the absolute knowledge that rules over it. So doing, the thesis can only lose its authority to proclaim the millennium.

What critique of western civilization would contribute to a judgment on the apotheosis of the liberal state? What weight should be given to the growth in liberal societies of masses of residents, citizens in only the most technical sense, for whom the common standards of civil life have lost their meaning: for whom imprisonment is no disgrace, matrimony no prerequisite to procreation, usefulness no qualification for support; for whom positions of trust and power are passports to plunder and oppression, as they were in the most benighted of times; of hypocrites, fanatics, and swindlers in what remains of religion, just as in all the ages since the first false prophet was exposed? What are we to make of the inner harmony of a society in which the overwhelmingly prevalent religion teaches a love so high as to take precedence of faith itself, while the supreme rule of private and public affairs is the friction of selfish interests? Are these influences indispensable mutual antidotes or are they contradictions that reveal weakness in the framework? Are the arts controlled by mediocrities in whom the insufficiency of genius is compensated by twitchings of solipsism accompanied by stale political ruminations, whinings of neglect, mumblings against philistinism, and perhaps outpourings of tedious smut? In a spasm of fairmindedness we might wonder whether the arts are a stronghold of resistance against the bourgeoisification of everything, a protest against the rule of greed in affairs and banality in leisure, and an expression of the will to be more than the epigoni of dead masters. Let us rather persevere in comfortable self-mortification in the company of Nietzsche, who has done much of the work for us, believing himself to have confounded Hegel. But Nietzsche has not disposed of the issue of the Ultimate Man. Why not find repose in the analgesia of the sheep who may safely graze, and why shake little fists against the eternal return that spares us the absolute sunset? The evocation of the will to power rings indeed of the dignity of man, but it smacks also of theater, of *Menschenmorgendammerung*, part of a transparent myth, *jeu d'esprit* of a hyperthermic spirit. Do Nietzsche's and our own disparagements of liberal life, or discovery of what is problematic within it, suffice to discredit the theory of history which brings everything important to a culmination in us? Not any more than the events in eastern Europe suffice to confirm it. In plain language, we do not know whether our discontent with our civilization has the force of the jeer that sends the actor from the stage or is the admission of flaws that become insignificant when measured by the blessings they accompany. Nor do we know whether the collapsed regimes of the East and any others of their kind which may admit their bankruptcy will become examples of reason and freedom or of some squalid compromise between repression and grumbling.

Whichever way we turn, we find the critique of the end-of-history thesis troubled by the difficulty of determining whether the decisive test of it is empirical or theoretical. If merely empirical, then history must have the unpretentious meaning it has always had and the oceanic character it has been thought to have, exhibiting long ground swells like the many-centuried movement toward democracy pronounced by Tocqueville, the tidal accessions and recessions in the lives of dynasties and nations, and the transient undulations that agitate the decades. It is true that something better than confusion may grow from these perplexities, as becomes clear to us when we consider that the difficulties of the critic of the thesis shed a light on the thesis itself, for the difficulties of the critic are identically the same as those of the proponent: the difficulty of corroborating a hypothesis belongs precisely and in the same degree to the propounder of it and to its critic, for its propounder is its first and most urgent critic. But all of this has as its premise that the decisive test of the end-of-history thesis is empirical. What if the test is speculative?

With some regret, we are pushed to the level of metaphilosophy, of some reflection on the history of speculations. The philosophy of history out of which the end-of-history thesis has grown could be depreciated without malice as an episode of nineteenth-century reaction to political and intellectual currents of the day. This by itself would not deprive that philosophy of history of its right to claim that the circumstances that prepared it were exactly those preclimactic conditions that were foreordained to usher in the climax. But there has been philosophy in the meantime which has changed the terms of speculation about history to such an extent that the transitions of states from socialist to liberal would have anything but the character of a testimony to some great cosmic intervention, and assuredly would not mark an ascent to the peak of social possibility for mankind. Were Heidegger to be believed, the liberal democratic constitutionalism of the West and the socialist communitarianism of the East do not differ sufficiently to make any transitions between them in either direction important enough to excite a deep thinker. And this is not because they do undeniably have a common genealogy in the tradition of thought that runs from Hobbes, Locke, Spinoza, and Hume to Adam Smith on one side but to Rousseau, Kant, and Hegel on the other. Rather, Heidegger's philosophizing comes to a point in some reflections on technology and the dehumanizing of man's relation to the natural ground of his existence. It is safe to assume that Heidegger is not covertly repeating the Marxist thesis that the conditions of production govern everything human. Without going further into his larger purposes, we cannot doubt that he had receded so far from merely empirical or political considerations and advanced so far into abstraction from them – let us say for the present purpose emancipated himself from them – as to illustrate for us the problem that would be faced by an end-of-history theorist who wished to transcend the plane of merely phenomenal history. Heidegger's contemplations enabled him or perhaps compelled him to dismiss as irrelevant the difference between the daily misery of entire peoples and their sufficient satisfaction. That he looked for light as if there were no truth in the visible is of interest to us now only because it helps us to think about the relation between the status of the speculative in a context that is unavoidably political and empirical. How should we choose between the ascent into the heights and subsequent return with the ultimate political order as performed by Hegel on the one hand and by Heidegger on the other, to say nothing of Plato? There is no way to know them by their works, for they have none except their very own intellectual selves.

After having asked ourselves what an end of history might be, we have had to ask how human beings could recognize one – whether through living it or through being persuaded by the force of the argument that announces it. If the former, then we are to count our blessings, which are in truth very many but also mixed enough to make us pause. If the latter, then the philosophy of history must be unique and preeminent in the relevant respects. Let us see if the case can be made for its uniqueness and preeminence.

The end-of-history thesis finds the materialization of the truth of the Whole in the final reality of reason and freedom in a political order. Reason rules in that the will of all is directed to purposes that are free from contradictions or from contradictions that are not themselves fruitful, according to a logic that is fertilized by contradiction rather than offended by it. In some sense, reason rules. But on showing this, end-of-history philosophy is not purely unique. Plato too demonstrates that reason rules by right. To speak briefly, Hegel argues that reason must rule, must rule through institutions of popular freedom, must rule because of the power of flawless and therefore irresistible cosmic reason that enlists itself as the cause of human good and reveals itself as well in politics as in philosophy. Plato argues that if reason ruled in men's affairs, in political life, it would rule through the monarchy of philosophy, but that far from ruling inevitably, it can scarcely ever rule, for the active hegemony of reason, as distinguished from its title to rule, is hindered by the irremovable presence of reason's antithesis in the construction of the Whole. Philosophy of history cannot claim to be unique in the decisive respect, which is an affirmation of reason's title to rule. In every other particular, philosophy of history, and therewith the end-of-history thesis, is no more than one among a number of conceptions about reason, the standing of reason in the universe and the bearing of it on human life. But the end-of-history thesis has no special authority if it does not have preeminent standing, for its claim is to be climactic and absolute. To this date it remains an unconfirmed and probably unconfirmable speculation.

We return to the political realities of the late twentieth century, which gave new life and unaccustomed plausibility to the end-of-history thesis through the collapse, as was said before, of the socialist regimes descended from the philosophic source of that thesis. Before we pronounce the Western democracies to be the true inheritors of the earth, we should be aware of certain facts about their character which would bear on their eligibility for the role. Those facts emerge when we look within and ask ourselves what we truly are, or what is found by one who looks for Western constitutional liberalism. Is it free-enterprise economy? Freely elected responsible government? Equality before the law? The organization of social existence under the natural right to life, liberty, and the pursuit of happiness? It is all of these and more of the same kind. But these conditions have prevailed, say, to take an example, in the United States for two centuries, a period during which the lives of Americans have undergone great changes that have been paralleled in the other Western liberal countries. The American who fought and did not fight in the Civil War is hardly recognizable as the ancestor of the one who, a hundred years later, went either to Vietnam or to Canada. Or to take another example, the Oxford of 1850 must seem like an object of paleontology to an undergraduate of our time. In both cases, one sign of the encompassing change is the altered presence of religion in the two eras. The documents of the Civil War and the impossibility of imagining John Henry Newman in present-day Oxford help us to see this change, but they do not explain it to us. Can it be attributed to the progress of reason through the world, somehow if not exactly as philosophy of history declares? The Western liberal societies have certainly not become godless, but they have just as certainly become secular. Is there not enough of the Enlightenment in our composition, in a moderate mode, to establish a common ground with the communist scheme of dogmatic atheism which grew out of participation in the same Enlightenment? Every consideration of common sense and decency would have to be subverted in order to accommodate these facts to the conclusion that the one system is the moral equivalent of the other. One need not adopt that wrong-minded view in order to perceive the latent or partial pacifism, the automatic anti-imperialism, the welfare elements of social democracy, the gender and family reformations inspired vaguely by the revolt against bourgeois institutions, all these and more that are part of our existence for better and worse and that have modern roots in the ideology of class war. Enough of Marxism is present in our constitutional regimes, through either shared ancestry or hybridization, so that the termination of history in us would have an element in it of perpetuation of what we are to bury.

And what are we to make of the inclusion within the end-of-history thesis of the continued presence of warfare among men in the posthistoric period? Whatever else it signifies, it inevitably draws attention to the fact that the envisioned consummation of the human experience would be an affair of a minority of the human kind. The rejection of this prospect as "elitist" would be as inane as it is inevitable, but there is a weighty reason for giving it some thought. By what principle of selection would the reason of the universe elect these rather than those communities for promotion to the ultimate state? And for that matter, what causes it to be true that the end for man is not also the end for most men? The end-of-history thesis serves us well by reminding us of this question in all of its antiquity, a question answered in one way and on a very different plane in the theology of a chosen people and in another way in the theology of grace and predestination. Those answers are not available to the Enlightenment theory of the end of history, which seems to be pushed toward conceding that reason strikes the earth like lightning – illuminating and energizing but entirely by chance, unless recourse be had to an infinite regression of causes which explains everything in principle by mechanizing the whole. Can the freedom of the Ultimate State of man be understood as an irony of the absolute necessity that we slaves to that necessity call the ground of our freedom? If the saying that we cannot escape history means that we cannot escape necessity, the mind finds itself in doubt. It would seem that the end-of-history thesis has to share the weight of this difficulty, or at least to consider whether humanity's being forced into freedom poses a problem that is more than a quibble based on play of words. Resolved in a certain way, this question would point toward the answer to another question, namely, What might God be? God might be that thrusting power in the universe which expresses itself in the irresistible progress of man toward and into his ultimate-highest condition. God so understood would have the ineffably philanthropic disposition to bring humanity to fulfillment not in spite of man's errant nature but precisely through and because of it. That is to say, the providence of the scriptural God would be replaced by the cunning of nature. That the end-of-history thesis is an implicit theology is neither news nor bad news, and that it might be, from the scriptural point of view, a blasphemy that replaces God with a nature that no longer acts as God's instrument is a thought that must be faced. My purpose is not to blame the end-of-history thesis for being a theology or for being a blasphemous one, if such it were, but only to suggest the heavy burden of clarification which it bears in making good its claim to draw its very attractive conclusions from the current state of world events.

It must be said that the politics, both domestic and international, of the late twentieth century quite properly encourages us to think in terms of the end of history. At a time when the culture of the West gives cause for concern and the centers of its civilization are in disorder, thinkers could be excused for wondering what lies ahead, and especially whether liberal society has resources within itself to remedy what is in disrepair. If it has, then we *might* be the end of history. If it has not, we cannot possibly be the end of history in any but the most melancholy sense. If the present constitutional regime is to look within for the means of cleansing itself, it must look first of all into the Constitution that defines it, in order to discover those means. In plain language, can the Constitution be read in ways that are conducive to confronting the influences that threaten liberal life? It goes without saying that there is so much disagreement about what is threatening liberal life that that issue must be faced before any other can be reached. Is it criminality and the militant decay of traditional standards or is it brutal contempt for rights and prejudiced adherence to traditional standards? There is no assurance that all such problems will be disposed of in ways conducive to the perpetuation of the regime. This is not to cast into doubt the goodness of the liberal society but rather to suggest that its difficulties are considerable enough so that its friends can scarcely avoid thinking about what might follow it if it proved incapable of curing itself by means that lie within itself. What would it turn into? What is available for it to turn into?

In the middle of the seventeenth century, England turned itself briefly from a monarchy into a parliamentary republic, as a preparation for the conversion of its monarchy into a constitutional regime. In the eighteenth century, France transformed itself under the influence of ideas that were actively critical of monarchy. Our own founding was accomplished in the same atmosphere of hostility to monarchy, the affirmative side of which was the assertion of the natural rights of all human beings equally. It is not necessary to recur to the oscillations of Greek cities between democracy and monarchy, the Roman conversions to and from republican forms, and the European drifts into and out of feudal institutions, in order to be reminded that history is the history of constitutional forms, which are the expressions of the urgencies and thoughts of the times. What are the urgencies and thoughts of our time? The convulsion of eastern Europe, which gives rise to the immediate version of the end-of-history thesis, lets us know that in the West our problem is not the repression of individual liberty, for we embody the social arrangements being adopted in the places where the failures are traced to the reality of that repression. Eastern Europe had us to contemplate as a model. What do we have that could serve us in the same way? Although thinkers have spoken about the decline of the West and particularly of the United States, to what place or idea have they drawn attention as an inspiration for reform? National socialism proposed itself for the role and was dismissed in loathing and blood. International socialism has dismissed itself. Perhaps we must look beyond any empirical paradigms, which means looking into the realm of pure speculation on the best regime, abstracting from the questionable argument that we are it. The most fully elaborated philosophy of our time, on behalf of which one might claim that it could form the basis of a new political dispensation, is Heidegger's temporalized metaphysics. To what political form does it attach itself if not to that of the Third Reich? To the regime of the ongoing self-disclosure of *physis*, under the auspices of "another god"? The seer has not yet appeared who could look into that formula and describe, to say nothing of recommend, what it betokens politically. Have we strengthened the end-of-history thesis by arguing that nothing reveals itself to us as replacement for our regime? We have, unless we can satisfy ourselves that it is merely our blindness or complacency that obscures a future without us. Otherwise, we must accept the great truth that we are the future because the truth is us. We denizens of the liberal West are in the curious position of cherishing our institutions, of not being able to see beyond them to anything more true or beneficent, of resigning ourselves to an uncomfortable life within them, and of being loath to believe that the progress that has brought us our rich estate can do anything but march on forever.

Can we believe that we are the children of progress, that part of our endowment from progress is the conviction that ethnocentrism and anthropocentrism, like geocentrism, are the mistakes of people who cannot distinguish a mirror from a telescope, and believe at the same time that the whole progress of progress can come to a halt anywhere, even in the political society that enshrines government of, by, and for the people under the self-evident truth that all men are created equal and are endowed by nature with the right to life, liberty, and the pursuit of happiness? Perhaps it is impossible for us to believe with perfect faith both in progress and in ourselves. As theorists we might incline to believe in progress, as citizens to believe in the self-evident truths that support our liberal constitutional regime in freedom and official rationalism. The end-of-history thesis can claim to have the power to reconcile the theoretical and the civic understandings if it understood itself to maintain that there is indeed a prospect of indefinite progress in the sciences other than political, a progress that will be fostered by, or to the extent of, the perpetuation of the free society beyond which there is no civil progress. If there is an objection to this reconciliation of progress and completion, it might lie in the demonstrated fact that repressive and even wicked regimes are not as such incapacitated for high technology, which they are more likely to use for violent purposes than are the liberal countries as such. Must this depressing empirical truth be included in the truth of the whole as an ingredient of it which recalls as it accuses the grand optimism of the end-of-history thesis?

There remains one resource that might save both the end-of-history thesis and the constitutional regimes of freedom and reason. The end-of-history thesis proclaims the superiority of liberal political life, its status as end, certainly in speech, less certainly in deed. An age-old question arises: is the goodness of the regime impeached if durability is missing among its excellences? If not, then why did Socrates, who knew about the best regime, characterize conflict as the doing of the good city in its typical act? (See *Timaeus*.) We follow Socrates in this, and suggest that the liberal countries adopt the end-of-history thesis as their ruling theoretical dogma alongside their belief in their self-evident truths, never mind any of the apparent contradictions suggested earlier. But it should be understood that the end-of-history thesis is to be made an article of patriotic faith when put in the following hypothetical formulation: liberal constitutional society has the responsibility of proving the truth of the end-of-history thesis; and that thesis would be falsified if empirical history disclosed an opening rupture between the goodness of free society in speech and its goodness in deed, which is its durability. It therefore behooves us to vindicate the goodness of the truth of the whole by securing the prosperity of the political society in which that truth is manifest. If this be thought to imply that the end-of-history thesis can be made useful even if it cannot be made demonstrable, and if it be thought further that this suggestion seems like an Erastian conversion of old theology to new purposes, the propounder of it might take refuge in a privilege sacred to liberal constitutionalism and decline to incriminate himself.

12

Nature, God, and the Enlightenment: What Is at Work in the Whole

The course of the history of philosophy to our time gives reason to suspect that the human effort to understand the whole that we inhabit, our place within it, and thus finally to understand ourselves, is an interminable project. If we had to propose a ground for that judgment, it might run along the following lines. In order to "understand the whole," one cannot be participatory in it, for he who inspects a whole of which he is a part must know himself perfectly, or his limited knowledge of himself would compromise his understanding of the whole of which he is a part – and especially so if he is the uniquely comprehending or "rational" part of the whole. Further, were man to "know" that he cannot know the things as they are in themselves, would he not doubly demonstrate that the whole is beyond him forever, not only because of his confessed limitation but because the whole is such as to have placed at its rational cusp a being incapable of comprehending the whole. Should one add that his knowledge of himself, notwithstanding his insight into the limit of his grasp of the things as they are in themselves, must be imperfect precisely as his knowledge of the whole to which he belongs is imperfect? In what imaginable way – and I use the term "imaginable" wittingly – might the relation, between the human part and the cosmic whole be formed so that our existence within the whole not frustrate our effort to grasp the truth of the whole? The answer has appeared to be ready to hand for millennia: while we cannot stand outside the whole in order to experience its absolute truth, the one who does stand in that position and is correspondingly omniscient can, may and does communicate with us, to share with us from beyond what we could never in all of time discover for ourselves because, to repeat, we are within it and are part of the *explicandum*, that which is to be explained.

The history of philosophy teaches us that the foregoing can be rejected as inconclusive and in fact may be dismissed as either misleading or untrue. By some lights, our strenuous incorporation in our natural habitat is exactly what opens us to its relevant truth. It almost goes without saying that if the relevant truth about the (natural) whole and man's place in it is accessible to the mind of him who is utterly ingested within it, the need for and perhaps the possibility of enlightenment from beyond nature fades.

If we are to move forward from this condition of speculative stalemate, we should perhaps begin by seeking a meaning for the concept of "understanding the whole." For the purpose at hand, let me suggest that mankind might presume to approach the understanding of the whole if humanity could confidently identify the absolute, ultimate agency which is at work, or in act, in the universe – to identify primordial happening or to exhaust the understanding of irreducible occurrence. As the record of man's engagement with this tremendous task shows, more is implicit therein than simply to name the efficient cause or first mover in the whole but rather to confront the question whether the chain of efficacy is itself infinite, thus to put in question the very premise of a beginning and a purpose, perhaps to replace will with necessity as the essence of the Whole. Our immediate purpose is to glance at certain signal episodes in philosophy's effort to identify ultimate agency. We will confine our project to events of the modern time, and in so doing will be pointing to a window that is also a mirror; for we of this epoch are what we are not only by virtue of the cosmic reality, whatever that maybe, but also as creatures of the prevalent human constructions of that reality, including in those constructions everything from technology to ideology.

Continuing on the theme of the involvement of concrete existence with the prevalent opinion of the cosmic, it may be asked whether the modern reconsideration of the whole was not inspired by a conviction that the life of man had been oppressed and deformed by the weight upon it of the received view of the whole. Thus it happens, for example, that Machiavelli, in stating the unadorned truths of political life, emasculates orthodoxy when he attributes to mere chance what piety would ascribe to supernal Providence. Then Hobbes, in a work intended to reconstruct political life, devotes half of the *Leviathan* to the rationalization of Christian theology. The large thesis of his enterprise may be stated briefly as follows. As long as mankind lives without a scientific knowledge of causes, life will be lived in the condition of conflict that accompanies and must accompany irreconcilable because false opinions about the most fundamental and absolute aspects of the whole. Human wellbeing depends upon the rational identification of the absolute in the whole, and that identification is inseparable from knowledge of causation. We begin our brief and highly selective overview of modernity's engagement with the primordial by resorting to the work of Hobbes, who presents the matter with exemplary candor.

In the Epistle Dedicatory of *De Corpore*, Hobbes writes that Galileo "was the first that opened to us the gate of natural philosophy universal, which is the knowledge of the nature of *motion*" (original emphasis). What is to be understood by the nature of motion? To begin with, change. Is all motion change? Yes. Is all change motion? There might perhaps be no question closer to the heart of the ultimate conundrum of the whole. If all change is motion, and motion pertains to body, then all that is and that is subject to change is corporeal. Is anything insusceptible to change? By definition, the eternal is that which is insusceptible to change. Is anything eternal? We do not know whether the universe is eternal, but we do "know" that God is eternal. To the extent that we know God and that he is eternal, we know also that God is that which created the universe. But precisely the attribution to God of the act of creation implicates God in change – from before to after the act of creation. Does it not necessarily also implicate God in the manner of change which is indistinguishable from motion?

Whatever may be in doubt and whatever might necessarily remain forever in doubt, of one thing there can be no doubt: the innermost determinable fact or most certainly primordial condition of the whole is motion. If the certain truth about motion were ever to be obtained by man, the certain truth about the whole would be at hand. Hobbes writes, in *De Corpore*, (Part IV, ch. 26, Molesworth vol.1, p. 412) ". . . though from this, that nothing can move itself, it may rightly be inferred that there was some first eternal movent; yet it can never be inferred, though some used to make such inference, that that movent was eternally immoveable, but rather eternally moved. For as it is true, that nothing is moved by itself; so it is true also that nothing is moved but by that which is already moved. The questions therefore about the magnitude and beginning of the world, are not to be determined by philosophers, but by those who are lawfully authorized to order the worship of God." This brief passage integrates Hobbes's physics, cosmology, and political philosophy with stunning concision. Motion is cosmic agency, but we cannot identify the agent. In their ignorance and presumption, men will trumpet their opinions about the Highest, which they will dishonor by the animus and cruelty, to say nothing of gross ambition, with which they seek to impose their credulities. To bring peace and indeed civilization properly understood, let orthodoxy be established as a feature of the realm, to be defined by the secular authority as a piece of legislation. How does this comport with religious freedom? Hobbes is transparently clear: the sovereign may compel obedience in external observance, but the thinking human being retains, because no power can deprive him of it, the convictions of his secret mind – wherein he is obliged to restrain them. Whatever else civil society might accomplish, it does, when rightly understood, envelope man in an enclave of rational security, protecting him within a whole afflicted with insurmountable uncertainty precisely as it, namely civil society, defends him against the dangers of the condition of mere nature. I wish to emphasize that Hobbes's project for bringing peace to human community never for a moment loses sight of the impact of the cosmic agency and the attached law of inertia on all of human life. Our hopes, our thoughts, our sensations and our memory, our imaginations and our passions, all are explained as phenomena of the motion of our bodily selves. They must all be taken into account in designing the civil authority that is to socialize the motivated human animal.

At the end of the day, what Hobbes cannot explain is the transformation of a motion in the optic nerve into an experience of vision.

As Hobbes implicates the universe and its irreducible agency in prescribing for our political life, so Spinoza invokes the whole and its ultimacy in formulating our ethics. The opening, and one might well say the decisive section, of Spinoza's *Ethics* is "Concerning God." What is made obvious on the first page is that the ultimate is to be approached and indeed defined through ratiocination in the mode of geometry, not by a hearkening to a revelation. As will appear, the reason for this is that there is no transcendent. There is nothing outside nature. God is not transcendent of nature for, as Spinoza is famous for asserting, God and nature are one and the same. Both are infinite and eternal, inclusive of everything that is or can be. Everything that is is in God and God is in everything that is. Because there is no transcendent, the totality, undivided between nature and an other, is One. Only one is, as Parmenides was wont to say. Without necessarily having this as his first intention, Spinoza has closed the awesome gap between divinity and humanity that scriptural religion addressed through Revelation in its various forms. With this behind us by way of introduction, we are prepared to consider Spinoza's conception of ultimate agency.

Spinoza discloses his understanding of the matter clearly and concisely in the Third Proof and the Scholium to Proposition 11, Part I of the the Ethics. He writes, "To be able to exist is power, as is self-evident." And further: "For since the ability to exist is power, it follows that the greater the degree of reality that belongs to the nature of a thing, the greater the amount of energy it has for existence. So an absolutely infinite Entity, or God, will have from himself absolute power to exist, and therefore exists absolutely." Everything to be said about agency in Spinoza's thought is a gloss on that passage.

The power or energy inherent in or possessed by a thing must be in proportion to its persistence in being. If there were something that is infinite in its persistence in being, as indeed there is, namely God or nature, that entity is infinite in power. Does that mean that the infinitely powerful is infinitely productive? Is its power to remain in existence the same power that would enable it to create, for example, all that is in heaven and on earth? Apparently not, since the entity of infinite power and existence is exactly the all that is in heaven and on earth. This conclusion is confirmed, so it seems, by Spinoza's flat declaration that God is without will, and there is only efficient causality, not final causality or intention oriented on a good, in the whole that is God or nature. Let me quote from the Preface to Part IV: "We have demonstrated . . . that Nature does not act with an end in view; that the eternal and infinite being, whom we call God or Nature, acts by the same necessity whereby it exists.

That the necessity of his nature whereby he acts is the same as that whereby he exists has been demonstrated. So the reason or cause why God, or Nature, acts, and the reason or cause why he exists, are one and the same. Therefore, just as he does not exist for an end, so he does not act for an end; just as there is no beginning or end to his existing, so there is no beginning or end to his acting. What is termed a 'final cause' is nothing but human appetite . . ."

It would appear therefore that there is no absolute agent in the whole; there is only the infinite chain of causes - agency without agent. In the truly infinite chain of causes, each part, how small or large soever, is both effect and cause, objective and transmitter of energy. If the primordial must be identified, it is the immanent mathematical truth of the infinity of the chain of causation. In Spinoza's language, God is the immanent cause, not the transitive cause, of the whole (I.18). We might for our own purposes say that God is the intelligible, not the intelligent, cause or truth of the whole. God does not speak or listen.

Is mankind abandoned to an order that is the apotheosis of necessity, thus apparently the venue of moral chaos (what room is there for virtue if all is by necessity?); of man's helpless vulnerability to the overwhelming (there is no God but nature); and thus endemic despair? Spinoza maintains to the contrary that his enlightenment is the way to the perfection of man's virtue, power and tranquil happiness. His formula may be stated briefly. When man once truly understands himself as an entity whose power is the very measure of his being, he will resist by all means every encroachment on his power. But what is an encroachment on his power? Whenever man is a passive object before a force, that he cannot, or worse, will not though he might deflect or repel, he is weakened - his being is diminished. His power is indistinguishable from his freedom. When is he as free as he may be? When by the power of reason he knows himself so well as to realize that when he allows himself to be moved by rage, envy, lust, malice, greed, bigotry, and more, he is doing an act of gratuitous submission or surrender. He need not submit. If he submits, he abdicates a degree of the power that defines his very being. And moreover, if he submits he defies reason and defies morality. Reason is the resource that locates and defines man's being. Man's agency, freedom and virtue are the precipitate of the process that redefined divinity. We might note in passing that the kind, considerate, benevolent and forbearing conduct of one man toward another, and even love, is not in obedience to a dictate from above but is in the service of the acting human being's own tranquility, rationality, and happiness. It proves in the end to be true that man's salvation lies indeed in the love of God and the union with God, knowledge of the absolutely necessary and blessed resignation before it. But God neither speaks nor listens.

In the matter of ultimate agency, it proves to be the case that infinite power lies in the God or nature that embodies intellect without the capacity to deploy it, while man alone in the whole is endowed with agency joined with active intellect, called reason. It would seem that the perfection of agency in the universe depends on the union of God with man. One may wonder if this implication of Spinoza is an anticipation of the thought that the completion of agency in the universe depends on the union of Being with Dasein. But of this, later on.

If one knew of Kant's thought on the theme of cosmic agency only what Kant had written in his "Idea for a Universal History with a Cosmopolitan Intent," one might easily infer that the author belonged among the physiodicists, those who find not only the beginning and end of all things within the order of sensory nature but who find in nature the definition of good and the active if cunning benevolence that gives its direction to the course of human events. One quotation from the first paragraph of the "Idea for a Universal History" tells a remarkable story: "individual men and even entire peoples give little thought to the fact that while each according to his own ways pursues his own end - often at cross purposes with each other - they unconsciously proceed toward an unknown natural end, as if following a guiding thread; and they work to promote an end they would set little store by, even if they were aware of it." The resonance with the language of the most famous sentence in Adam Smith's Wealth of Nations is unmistakable: ". . . man is [often] led as by an invisible hand to promote an end which was no part of his intention." For all of Kant's personification of nature and attribution to it of an agency that we can never in life dispense with or escape from, his last word will, as the world well knows, always reflect the disjunction between "the guardianship of nature [and] the state of freedom" (Remark, "Beginning of Human History"). In brief, for all the potency at nature's disposal, it cannot be averred that the ultimate agency in the whole is that of nature. What, that comports with the freedom which is nature's alternative, stands higher in the order of agency? It might be said that the Critique of Pure Reason is the large answer to that question. .

That the infinite chain of causes that is nature and that envelops the empirical world can, as infinite, have had no first cause or primordial agent is self-evident. Does this preclude the intervention of free agency into the empirical world? It is Kant's overriding purpose to demonstrate that it does not. He, like Spinoza, is supremely aware that the philosopher who concedes potency to cosmic necessity must somehow make provision for human freedom. Kant's efficacy in this regard is monumental, and is of interest to us in itself but also and most urgently for its bearing on our leading theme, the modern search for ultimate agency. I turn briefly to the Critique of Pure Reason.

Nature, the realm of necessity, as such knows no "ought," only "is." Necessity may determine my will, but it can never prescribe the "ought" which, "pronounced by reason confronts such willing with a limit and an end"

(A548 B576). Let me quote: "Reason does not here follow the order of things as they present themselves in appearance, but frames for itself with perfect spontaneity an order of its own . . . according to which it declares actions to be necessary, even although they have never taken place, and perhaps never will take place" (A548 B576). This is one of innumerable intimations that something called Reason wields - in principle and thus in truth - an ultimate power that extends into the realm of necessity. That mankind participates in authoritative reason will prove crucial for the definition of universal agency.

On the way to that consummation, we observe that Kant extends the activity of reason far beyond the insertion of the Ought into the realm of the Is when he authorizes reason to perfect the order of nature by representing it "in idea" as an absolute unity (A674 B702). Let me save time by quoting a crucial passage from the Critique of Pure Reason (A675 B70J): "Thus the transcendental, and the only determinate, concept which the purely speculative reason gives us of God is, in the strictest sense, deistic; that is, reason does not determine the objective validity of such a concept, but yields only the idea of something which is the ground of the highest and necessary unity of all empirical reality. This something we cannot think otherwise than on the analogy of a real substance that, in conformity with laws of reason, is the cause of all things." We approach the end of our reference to Kant's great contribution to modernity's vision of agency. Near the close of the first Critique, Kant completes his thought on the necessity of the concept of intelligent, purposive God as the postulated condition for the idea of the unity of all that is. Kant projects finally the necessity, recognized or conceived by our reason, of the concept of God as the condition for the unity of all the ends demanded by the moral law. In brief, if all the conditions of the realm of necessity and all the conditions of the realm of freedom are to be respected and also be themselves conceived in a shared unity, God and a future life must be affirmed, not as doctrine or orthodoxy but as a matter of each individual's active faith (A828 B856).

Kant not only admits but insists that the existence of the supreme being or ultimate agent in the universe is not an element of certainty. It is, arguably, a demand of our reason when the latter is applied to the Is and the Ought, each in its own form of necessity. Are we compelled to infer that Reason is prior to God in the order of agency; thus that Man and God, once more, exist in modernity in a condition of mutual dependence? Must one add that man and God, equally members of the class of Rational Being, virtually share in the highest agency? Kant leaves us with the question.

On that theme of agency, one must in due order turn to the thought of Hegel, as we now do. One gains a notable insight into the tendency of his entire philosophy if one reflects on the title of his Phenomenology of Spirit. Returning to the title after one has experienced the text - that is, returning to the beginning after realizing the completion - one may conclude that Hegel intends to rationalize the process by which spirit becomes phenomenon. Such indeed is his intention. In the course of his account, it becomes apparent that, in the service of freedom properly understood, he has relocated universal agency out of nature and Deity and in Spirit - whatever spirit may prove to be and wherein soever it may reside. We may consider a few of the innumerable clues that he provides; but first some general considerations.

Hegel on man is a psychologist, perhaps a psychoanalyst. He sees in the human being first an absolutely empty, undetermined mere potentiality which, as mere potentiality, is nothing. Then the ego is in touch with something other than itself of which it takes cognizance. Then it takes notice of the fact that it has taken notice, and when it absorbs this consciousness and makes the awareness of it its own, it has overcome its original nullity and transformed itself into the contradiction of its original mere potentiality, what it is as merely natural. It has so to speak phenomenalized itself. Spirit has been at work in the realm of the ego and set it free, that is, put it in possession of itself and in so doing, brought it to completion. But it could not have done so if the self had not set its process in motion by the action of its will. Spirit and will seem to be inseparably implicated in each other.

Is it possible that the individual's psychology is the paradigm of universal agency? To address the question, we need more light on the subject of spirit. In a single passage in the Philosophy of Right, (Addition H,G to sec.4) Hegel adverts to the conjunction of spirit, thought and will. "Spirit is thought in general," he says; and adds, "will is a particular way of thinking - thinking translating itself into existence, thinking as the drive to give itself existence." And Hegel speaks of "thought asserting itself in the will," (sec 21) repeatedly representing thought in its character as contributory to self-affirmation. But if spirit is thought so understood, may we not conclude that spirit itself is indistinguishable from the drive to give itself existence. Hegel is explicit, as follows: "The free spirit consists precisely in not having its being as mere concept or in itself, but in overcoming this formal phase of its being and hence also its immediate natural existence, and in giving itself an existence which is purely its own and free" (sec.57).

We are not here to set out Hegel's political philosophy but to gain some sense of what he means by spirit, and one cannot do justice to his understanding of that supreme agent without attending to the import of spirit for political life. Hegel writes, "The state consists in the march of God in the world, and its basis is the power of reason actualizing itself as will." And then he refers to the state in general as "the Idea, this actual God" (sec. 258). His innovative exegesis becomes even clearer when he writes, contrasting his own sense with that of religion, "the state is the divine will as present spirit, unfolding as the actual shape and organization of a world" (sec.270). Hegel is a virtuoso of Revelation, but Revelation in a manner unfamiliar to Scripture, for he, like

Hobbes and Spinoza, seems to be asking himself what deserves to be thought divine and is therefore fit to be called God. He, like his predecessors, responds to his own question to the effect that God is what conforms perfectly to reason and assuredly does not challenge it. In Hegel's case one should add, reason as bonded with spirit, and thus with the freedom of the self-conscious human self. For the present purpose it might be in order to describe the human being as spirited, to suggest the inclination of Hegel's vocabulary of spirit in the direction of a certain element of assertiveness, what one might call a will to power. Rightly understood, that will to power would be the gift of the philanthropic God whose concern was to bring to salutary, free, and dignified fulfillment the human being hitherto supposed most properly configured when on his knees.

If there were reason to believe that the ultimately and absolutely intelligible is in the locus of divinity and therefore of ultimate agency, there would be reason to believe that Heidegger has for once and all disposed of the question of agency in the universe. For Heidegger claimed, although respectfully of the Greeks, to have addressed conclusively for the very first time in all of human experience the question of Being; and only with knowledge of the meaning of Being can one answer the famous question with which he begins the Introduction to Metaphysics: Why is there anything rather than nothing? One could not make a more egregious mistake than to suppose that any eventual definition of Being will be also the identification of the Creator, whatever "made" all things. It will prove to be the case that Being is indeed the ultimate agency without in any way producing anything or even being the genus or class to which the existent things belong, certainly without itself being a thing (as even Aristotle thought he knew.) In what sense, then, can Being be represented as ultimate agency, or indeed as "agency" at all? That the question of the relation between being and agency so put is not merely fanciful, and is very far from being without critical influence on man's life, may be understood from the following. In the Introduction to Metaphysics, Heidegger exhorts his nation to resist and reverse the "spiritual decline of the earth [already] so far advanced that the nations are in danger of losing the, last bit of spiritual energy that makes it possible to see the decline (taken in relation to the history of 'being'), and to appraise it as such." In brief, the nation that harbors the definitive truth of Being and incorporates that truth comprehendingly and actively in its own definition will be in a position to be transposed "into the primordial realm of the powers of being.[1] It appears that humanity, or a part of it, that is invested with an understanding of Being - an understanding never hitherto possessed because the profound question of Being has never hitherto been raised - such humanity will be unprecedentedly empowered. What in or about

1 Heidegger, *An Introduction to Metaphysics*, trans. Ralph Manheim (Yale University Press, 1959), p.38.

Being and knowledge related to it conveys power, or "energizes?" And what is the meaning or character of such power?

A convenient way to approach the question is through Heidegger's famous opening of the Introduction to Metaphysics: Why are there things rather than nothing? It will prove to be the case that there are things because of Being and man, that which discloses itself and that which is constituted to receive the disclosure, each possessing a power that is complemented by the power of the other. It is our task to glance, however selectively, at the elaboration of this famous thesis, to discern its intention, not to pronounce on its validity.

One might say that Heidegger's largest purpose is to change the course of history, which he might hope to do by inspiriting the human being, or the decisive human beings, by awakening them to the truth about being. How a consciousness of being in its authentic truth might have so historic an effect is not our immediate concern. More relevant to the issue of agency in the world is Heidegger's repeated judgment that humanity is in a state of spiritual decay. Let me quote from the Introduction to Metaphysics: "The lives of men began to slide into a world which lacked that depth from out of which the essential always comes to man and comes back to man, so compelling him to become superior and making him act in conformity to a rank. All things sank to the same level, a surface resembling a blind mirror that no longer reflects, that casts nothing back. The prevailing dimension becomes that of extension and number. Intelligence no longer meant a wealth of talent, lavishly spent, and the command of energies. . . ." (emphasis mine, p. 46). And further, "One of these signs [of the plight of Europe] is the emasculation of the spirit through [its] misinterpretation." The crucial misinterpretation "is the reinterpretation of the spirit as intelligence, or mere cleverness in examining and calculating given things [i.e., not letting them reflect their being] and the possibility of changing them and complementing them to make new things" (p. 46). This passage indicates sufficiently for our purpose Heidegger's famous animadversion on modernity as the epoch dominated by the science of matter in motion and by the aspiration to conquer nature, as if nature were the ultimate in motility, and the conquest of it were to rescue man from the condition in which his life is solitary, poor, nasty, brutish and short. Distracted from the inquiry into being its very self, man has accepted an enlightenment that replaced God as ultimate by an emancipation within a moving nature deprived of volition. This regimen expressed itself, if we may speak so, in the despised technology, the fruit of science that is blind to being, and egalitarian polity, both Russian and American. Again and again, Heidegger refers repeatedly to the emasculation of the spirit in the world as it has become, and he quotes himself (from the Rektoratsrede) as defining spirit as "neither empty cleverness nor the irresponsible play of the wit, nor the boundless work of dismemberment carried on by the practical intelligence; much less is it world-reason [i.e., Hegel] no, spirit is a fundamental knowing resolve toward the essence of being" (p. 49).

Of Heidegger's conception of the whole it might be said that, in the end, every serious aspect of our environment and ourselves proves to be a power or force, of course beginning with Being and extending to Dasein. Does the attribution of agency to Being imply a personification of Being and thus a personification of the Absolute, as if God were to appear among men in person? One is reminded, whether fairly or not, of the headline to the famous interview of Heidegger in Der Spiegel, September 23, 1966: "Nur noch ein Gott kann uns retten."

My purpose has been to pose the question "What is Modernity?" in the context of certain leading, and perhaps decisive answers to the question "What is the ultimate agency at work or in act in the whole?" A plausible way to address the question is by identifying that which in the mind of each philosopher was the deficiency in the prevalent opinion as to ultimate agency. Recurring first to Hobbes and Spinoza, it comes readily to mind that they perceived a need to demonstrate, not merely to assert but to demonstrate, that the ultimate does not violate the criteria of human experience nor does it challenge the authority of reason as we know it. If it did so, it disqualified itself as absolute. This affirmation of the world as we experience it and as we can penetrate to its corporeal foundation could be interpreted as a manifesto of human spiritedness, the reclamation by mankind of its humanity. So construed, it implies its other, that state of man to which it relates as negation, namely, a bondage spiritual and quotidian imposed in the name of transcendent agency. The scientific revolution as relocation of agency was a crucial episode in modernity's self-definition as the age of freedom and reason. There is no distortion in the perception of modernity as founded on the transmutation of the natural or cosmic principle of inertia into the human principle of energy. I wish to put the matter in this light in order to suggest that the apotheosis of physics, mathematics and logic and of matter in motion may properly be regarded as the original modern effort to reverse mankind's emasculation rather than as the ground of that emasculation as would be averred in a later period of modernity.

And what should one say of Kant's great project if not that it aimed to protect man's intellectual, moral and political agency in a world wherein the hegemony of nature could not be denied. The categorical imperative is man's resolute affirmation of his irrepressible spirit, call it will, but never lose sight of its character as energy. What can exceed in magistracy the power of the self to impose its discipline on itself, and to do so in the name of empowered mankind? God himself is a projection of humanity in the act of convincing itself that, whatever might be the case with the whole as it is in itself, it is as if God almighty is in his heaven because he must be. This is not philosophy infecting modernity with emasculation, rather the opposite, to the point of installing God in thought.

We have seen how Hegel may well appear to locate primordial energy in an abstraction called Geist, which discloses itself in agathistic history. A consummation of Geist's agency in the human world is the state which Hegel admonishes some of his fellow moderns not to confuse with civil society, the latter being the venue of the subjective and potentially perverse will. When Hegel conflates the agency of Geist or world spirit and the will of the individual in his being as citizen of the state, Hegel is making man the participant in absolute agency and elevating him as far as may be out of nature's grip and releasing him to freedom. I suggest this image of Hegel's purpose in order to advance the argument that modernity as such is not fairly, certainly not incontrovertibly, represented as the age of emasculation.

As has appeared, of those who have contributed to the constitution and to the introspective self-judgment of modernity, some have seen our age as a testimony to progress toward freedom and reason, and even toward the practical unification of mankind hitherto united only in the abstract as "rational being." Others have decried the age as a scene of the squalid confinement of man within a horizon that stretches only to the fingertips, an epoch of moral solipsism in which nothing of the force of the cosmos enters the being of the individual. How can one deny the coeval presence of the evidence for both judgments, arrived at by the collective philosophic genius of the age? If the one evaluation is correct, must not the other be rejected, conflicting as they are? May I propose for consideration a way to acknowledge the force of both judgments that hints at their tolerant coexistence? Think for a moment of so-called free enterprise. Is it driven simply by mundane greed oriented on survival or does it live on the spirit of ambition and rivalry? With the instruments of technology in hand, does it not aspire to, and increasingly achieve, a global power that can claim not only empire but, if only collaterally, a gift of human convenience. Is it to be held to the account of this symptom of modernity that its spiritedness does not, in itself or in its concept, eventuate in bloodshed or dominion? Or, in the context of constitutional politics, a critical phenomenon of the age of freedom and reason, is not partisanship the manifestation of spirited ambition, deployed in contention over conflicting conceptions of the good?

My purpose is not to apologize for modernity by any denial of the obvious presence in it of a squalid vulgarity that may be described as the detritus of uninstructed freedom, or as a mortification of animus. Self-indulgent subjectivity and ruthless aggressiveness are known among us. Nevertheless, I might suggest that what we know as modernity, shaped in the laboratory of philosophy experimenting with cosmic agency, is, like every other regime that we know of, a conglomerate of discordant elements that can cohere with benefit as long as they remain in an equilibrium. Spiritedness indeed, but with respect for its various kinds and matrices.

One last consideration. The point has been made that the foundations of modernity were laid in doctrine regarding motion and agency, and specifically such doctrine as, to be brief, tended to replace theology with physics and to invade the definition of deity. What and where then is God in the life of modern man? I would suggest that the answer to this question is in the image of the answer to the previous one. Inherent in the constitution of modernity is an equilibrium between concession to the immanent agency of nature and to the transcendent agency of divinity. It may be acknowledged that modern man lives a natural life from day to day, but is not deterred thereby from affirming his faith in the transcendent agent in the course of the weekly cycle of life. Thus it might appear that profound, fatal confusion or tornness has been introduced into modern man's life by philosophy's influence on everymans view of his world. A more temperate judgment might be that, in the face of the likelihood that man's place in the whole will always and necessarily remain problematic, those who can subscribe, however innocently, to both parts of the fractured alternative enjoy the plausibility of each. They live in unconscious confirmation of the wisdom of the poet who declared that, when ignorance is bliss, 'tis folly to be wise. It may be objected that philosophy may or must never abandon its effort to invest man's existence with the ultimate truth of absolute agency, and to do so in such a way as to infuse all of consciousness and practice with that truth. Until that effort consummates itself, mankind in general will do well to do what it must do and what modern man seems to do so well, which is to exist in the weird condition of resignation to uncertainty and benign unconsciousness of its pragmatic accession to both horns of a cosmic dilemma.

It might be appropriate to add to this brief account of modernity's past and present an even more brief speculation on its future. Supposing it true that everything that comes into being is fated to pass away, and recognizing that modernity is surely among the things that have come into being, what in our existence might be the source of our evanescence? I would for this purpose recur to an ancient wisdom, proposed by Aristotle, namely, that the exaggeration of a merit is a defect, and the more gross the exaggeration, the more fatal the defect. To deploy this wisdom, one must begin by identifying the defining merit. What is the signal virtue of modernity? Let us accept the formula, Freedom and Reason. No great insight or originality are needed to recognize that the collapse of' freedom into perversity, into sociopathic rebellion against the received and the prescribed as being intrusions on the ego, for example, is in its essence fatal. But what of reason? How can it possibly have any consequence that is not salutary? I will mention only one possibility. Reason, in its manifestation as genetic science, claims to have perfected the map of the entire genetic structure of a human being. Widespread is the apprehension that, alongside its vast promise for the cure of disease, the new knowledge will make possible such unprecedented human intervention in the human condition, and perhaps such uncontrollable intervention, that the very premises of man's life will be compromised. I mention only this one example of the nightmare of science, that is, reason, consuming itself and with it what we call modernity - and all of this the illustration of the glory exploding as its own negation.

May I close by saying that this is a speculation and not a presumptuous prediction? What makes it less than authoritative as a "prediction" is the degree to which modernity seems to have learned its own lesson of moderation, perhaps from Montesquieu, who admonished that even the law of nature should be applied with moderation. As one sign of that saving virtue, may I point to the fact that modernity has effectively suppressed that oxymoron of piety that leads to prideful zealotry in the cause of submissive humility? And too, for it deserves repetition, the results of the triumph of science, what was once called the conquest of nature, are looked upon with an apprehensive eye, as if humanity must intervene through the agency of political power to secure the application of knowledge to human life within the boundaries of moderation. One can only say, so be it.